TRADING NATIONS

BRILL'S SERIES
IN JEWISH STUDIES

VOL. XIV

TRADING NATIONS

*Jews and Venetians
in the Early Modern Eastern Mediterranean*

BY

BENJAMIN ARBEL

E.J. BRILL
LEIDEN · NEW YORK · KÖLN
1995

The paper in this book meets the guidelines for permanence and durability of the Committee on Production Guidelines for Book Longevity of the Council on Library Resources.

Library of Congress Cataloging-in-Publication Data

Arbel, Benjamin.
    Trading Nations : Jews and Venetians in the early-modern eastern Mediterranean / by Benjamin Arbel.
        p.   cm. — (Brill's series in Jewish studies, ISSN 0928-2261 ; vol. 14)
    Includes bibliographical references and index.
    ISBN 9004100571 (cloth   :   alk. paper)
    1. Jews—Mediterranean Region—History—16th century. 2. Jews- -Italy—Venice—History—16th century. 3. Jewish businessmen- -Mediterranean Region—History—16th century. 4. Jewish businessmen—Italy—Venice—History—16th century. 5. Venice (Italy)—Ethnic relations. I. Title. II. Series.
    DS135.M43A73   1995
    305.892'404531—dc20   95-303394
                                                                                                                    CIP

Die Deutsche Bibliothek - CIP-Einheitsaufnahme

Arbel, Benjamin:
Trading nations : Jews and Venetians in the early modern Eastern mediterranean / by Benjamin Arbel. – Leiden ; New York ; Köln : Brill, 1995
    (Brill's series in Jewish studies ; Vol. 14)
    ISBN 90–04–10057–1
NE: GT

                    ISSN   0926-2261
                    ISBN   90 04 10057 1

PRINTED IN THE NETHERLANDS

DS
135
.M43
A73
1995

In memory of my father - Dr. Joseph Ambach

(Czernowitz, 1901 - Tel Aviv, 1989)

CONTENTS

PREFACE

Venice's rise to power and opulence has always been associated with its leading role in the international trade of the Mediterranean world. The involvement of Jews in this field is more problematic. Despite being engaged in international commerce at various stages of their history, particularly in the Mediterranean world, Jews were largely excluded from this field during the last centuries of the Middle Ages. It was in the sixteenth century eastern Mediterranean that Jewish involvement in international commerce became again an important phenomenon. Even if a relatively small number of Jews were involved in this activity, their impact on the Mediterranean economy was sufficiently marked to create an association between Jews, as an ethnic and cultural group—or in sixteenth-century terminology, a "nation"—with the world of international trade and finance. In the course of this change, the Jewish traders had to confront the powers, which had been tradition-ally involved in this field. Venice, in particular, at this last phase of its prominence in Mediterranean trade, did not view with favour the penetration of Jews into this sphere, even if she was forced to put up with it. This book attempts to deal with various aspects of this new relationship which developed between Venice and the Jewish merchants during the sixteenth century.

The present book was originally conceived as a collection of articles, some of which had already appeared in various English, Italian and Hebrew publications. An earlier version of Chapter One and part of the Introduction appeared in *The Mediterranean and the Jews: Banking, Finance and International Trade (XVI-XVIII Centuries)*, A. Toaff, S. Schwarzfuchs (eds.), Bar-Ilan University Press, Ramat Gan, 1989, pp. 39-56. An original Hebrew version of Chapter Two is about to appear in *Chapters in the History of the Jews in the Ottoman Empire*, ed. M. Rozen, Tel Aviv University, 1995. Chapters Three, Four and Five are based partly on the following two papers, originally published in Italian: "Venezia, gli ebrei e l'attività di Salomone Ashkenasi nella guerra di Cipro", in *Gli ebrei e Venezia, secoli XIV-XVIII*, ed. G. Cozzi, Edizioni Comunità, Milan, 1987, pp. 163-190; "Salomone Ashkenazi:

mercante e armatore", in *Il mondo ebraico. Gli ebrei tra Italia nord-orientale e Impero asburgico dal Medioevo all'Età contemporanea*, eds. G. Todeschini and P.C. Ioly Zorattini, Pordenone, Edizioni Studio Tesi, 1991, pp. 109-128. I am grateful to these editors and publishers for kindly enabling the inclusion of these papers in this book.

It should be noted, however, that while translating and re-editing these papers I have considerably modified the original texts. Since they are closely inter-related and deal, in one way or another, with a common theme, I have not only brought them up to date, but also attempted to knit them into a more coherent whole by breaking down some existing texts and welding them together in a somewhat different structure. Moreover, three totally new chapters, constituting more than half the present volume, have been added to the text. The final product is a collection of monographic chapters which present different aspects of what I believe to be an important historical development within a common thematic framework. It should be emphasized that the re-edited chapters and the new ones are all based to a great extent on archival research, presenting and analyzing material which has not yet been exploited by other scholars. A small sample of these archival documents, illustrating some of the themes treated in this book, are presented in the Appendix.

Maintaining a rigorous system of transliteration in a book containing names and technical terms in Hebrew, the Venetian dialect and Ottoman Turkish, to mention only the main languages concerned, is hardly possible. For Hebrew names and expressions I have basically adopted the system of the Encyclopaedia Judaica. However, I chose to distinguish between א and ע by using the signs ' and ', and between כ and ק, by the letters k and q, as in Arabic transliteration. I have also preferred the form Nassí, in conformity with the Hebrew pronunciation. Biblical Hebrew names appear in their traditional anglicized form. For Ottoman Turkish names and expressions I have generally adopted the modern Turkish form, except for terms such as Kadi, Vizier or Pasha, which have become part of the English vocabulary. With regard to the name of the Ottoman capital, I have used both Constantinople, the term which normally appears in the Venetian documents, and Istanbul, the 'Turkish' term. I believe that consistency is not imperative in this case, at least not in works such as the present one. Readers unfamiliar with sixteenth-century sources should note that the orthography of names and other terms is often inconsistent in those documents. In Venetian texts, for

example, the letters g, x and z are often interchangeable. I made no
attempt to unify the various forms appearing in the original documentation. On several occasions, not least in order to convey to the reader
the way in which names and terms, especially foreign ones, appear
in the sources, I preserved the orthography of the original documents.
Unless otherwise specified, all dates appearing in the book follow the
modern style, *i.e.*, with the year starting on the first of January. Dates
marked with the letters m.v. *(more veneto)* indicate that the original
Venetian style, with the year starting on the first of March, has been
preserved. In references to archival material, only the *verso* pages have
been indicated; when no indication appears, the page referred to is
the *recto* one.

This book too is a product of many visits to Venice during a period
of over twenty years. My long acquaintance with the Venetian world
has produced many friendships, which, I am convinced, are also an
integral part of my scholarly activity, even if not always directly related
to it. Among the staff members of the Venetian State Archives, all
of whom have been of great help, I am especially indebted to the former
director, Maria Francesca Tiepolo, to Giustiniana Migliardi O'Riordan
Colasanti, the present deputy director of this institution, and to Maria
Pia Pedani-Fabris. Many good friends in Venice and the Veneto, have
been very helpful and supportive, and deserve my deepest gratitude.
Among them, I am particularly obliged to Gigi Corazzol, for completing
some archival research which I was unable to do during my short visits
to Venice as well as for reading and commenting on the manuscript.
I am also deeply grateful to Pallina Pavanini and Nubar Gianighian,
my Venetian companions and regular hosts during recent years, who
have been an integral part (and a very important one) of my Venetian
endeavours.

In Israel too, several friends and colleagues have been helpful in
bringing this book to its final form. Minna Rozen read the manuscript
and offered valuable comments; Tamar Erez, Ruth Vitale and Michalis
Firillas have been of great help in proof-reading, the preparation of
the Index and the Bibliography; Yael Lotan translated Chapter Two
and polished my English in the rest of the book; Alisa Meyuhas Ginio
was helpful in deciphering a Ladino document. I am also thankful to
Anita Shapira, Dean of the Faculty of Humanities of Tel Aviv University, for according financial support to this publication.

ILLUSTRATIONS

The illustrations were provided by the Photographic Department of
the Venetian State Archives in Venice. They are published by courtesy
of the Ministero per i Beni Culturali ed Ambientali (Atto di concessione
No 28, 3 Oct. 1994).

ABBREVIATIONS AND ARCHIVAL TERMS

AN	Atti notarili: Notarial acts
ASV	Archivio di Stato, Venice
c.	carta: pagination of archival material according to the original enumeration
Capi X	Capi del Consiglio dei Dieci: Heads of the Council of Ten
Cons. X	Consiglio dei Dieci: Council of Ten
CP	Costantinopoli [Istanbul]
Delib.	Deliberazioni: decisions of Venetian governing councils
Disp.	Dispacci: dispatches of Venetian representatives abroad to governing bodies in Venice
f., ff.	folio[s]: pagination of archival material according to the new enumeration
filza	File
IB	Indice Bombaci: Bombaci's abstracts of Turkish documents of the ASV
Lett.	lettere: letters of Venetian officials
LST	Lettere e scritture turchesche: Turkish letters and writings
m.v.	*more veneto*: date according to the Venetian style, with the year starting on 1 March
reg.	register
Sen.	Senato

INTRODUCTION

> The entire Hebrew nation feels itself
> highly obliged to this most excellent
> Republic, for indeed, in no other part
> of the world was it better treated than
> there.
> [Solomon Ashkenazi to the
> Venetian *Bailo*, May, 1573][1]

> Nobody is more adverse to the Jews...
> than this Illustrious Republic.
> [Doge Alvise Mocenigo to
> the Papal nuncio, June, 1573][2]

From the earliest years of her existence Venice developed as a city of seamen and merchants. The main foundation of Venice's prosperity consisted in its function as an intermediary in the international trade between the eastern Mediterranean and the West. Before the end of the Middle Ages Venice had become the leading commercial power of the Mediterranean in general, and of the eastern Mediterranean in particular. Its position was weakened, but by no means shattered, following the advance of the Ottomans in the area, and even the wars between Venice and the Ottoman Empire during the second half of the fifteenth century did not bring about a collapse of Venetian predomi-

---

[1] Biblioteca Nazionale Marciana, Venice, Ms It. VII 390-91 (8872-73) [hereafter: Barbaro's Letter-book], II, f. 439v.

[2] *Nunziature di Venezia*, Istituto Storico italiano per l'Età Moderna e Contemporanea, Fonti per la Storia d'Italia, 11 vols, Rome, 1958, vol. 11, ed. A. Buffardi, Rome, 1972, pp. 140-41.

nance in this field.[3]

Venice's commercial ascendancy was the result of long efforts, alike on the individual and on the public level. The experience and expertise of the Venetian traders were enhanced by the protection and incentives provided by the government, by an elaborate legislation intended to sustain and develop Venetian commerce, and by diplomatic and military action, when needed. International maritime trade became the privilege of a limited group of Venetian patricians and citizens. Trade with the eastern Mediterranean always received special attention in Venetian commercial policy and practice, and the Republic was vigilant in its exclusion of foreigners from participation in the trade with this area.[4]

Among the groups of foreigners excluded in Venice from the Eastern trade were the Jews, who were explicitly referred to in the Venetian legislation on this subject during the fourteenth and fifteenth centuries. In the case of the Jews, this specific prohibition can be considered not only in the framework of Venetian commercial policy, but also as part of a more general anti-Jewish policy. With the exception of a short interval of fifteen years at the end of the fourteenth century, Venetian authorities refused for centuries to admit the stable and continuous presence of Jews in the city of the lagoons. While consenting to the presence of Jews in many centres throughout the Venetian empire, Venice's leaders took special care to prevent Jews from establishing themselves in the capital.[5] The institution of the first Venetian ghetto in 1516 (the Ghetto Novo, or the 'New Ghetto') was a significant turning-point in this tradition, even more so since it occurred in a period

---

[3] G. Luzzatto, *Storia economica di Venezia,* Venice, 1961, pp. 185-188; E. Ashtor, "Venetian Supremacy in the Levantine Trade: Monopoly or Pre-Colonialism?", *Journal of European Economic History*, 3 (1974), 5-53.

[4] F.C. Lane, *Venice, A Maritime Republic*, Baltimore and London, 1973, pp. 67-81, 119-152.

[5] R.C. Mueller, "Les prêteurs juifs de Venise au Moyen Age", *Annales ESC,* 30 (1975), pp. 1277-1302; D. Jacoby, "Les Juifs à Venise du XIVᵉ au milieu du XVIᵉ siècle", in *Venezia, centro di mediazione tra Oriente e Occidente (secoli XV-XVI), aspetti e problemi*, Atti del II Convegno internazionale di storia della civiltà veneziana (Venezia, 1973), Florence, 1977, I, pp. 163-216; B. Ravid, "The Jewish Mercantile Settlement of Twelfth and Thirteenth-Century Venice: Reality or Conjecture?", *Association for Jewish Studies Review*, 2 (1977), pp. 210-25; E. Ashtor, "Gli inizi della comunità ebraica a Venezia", in *Venezia ebraica*, ed. U. Fortis, Rome, 1982, pp. 17-39.

025

22 INTRODUCTION 3

of growing religious fanaticism characterized by anti-Jewish persecutions.

During the first half of the sixteenth century, Venetian trade with the Levant, once the principal source of Venice's wealth and power, experienced some difficult moments. The structural changes which took place in the field of international trade dealt heavy blows to Venetian maritime commerce. The Ottoman occupation of the entire coastline of the eastern Mediterranean was accompanied by a series of military conflicts with Venice, whose eastern colonial dominions were on the front line of Ottoman advance. These periods of wars were exploited by Venice's commercial rivals to penetrate areas which had previously been almost a Venetian commercial monopoly.

The involvement of Jews in Mediterranean trade, which had been an important phenomenon before the rise of the Italian maritime communes, was rather marginal by the fourteenth and fifteenth century. Various testimonies from that period prove that Jews participated in the maritime trade between Venice and the East, but on the whole, despite the periodical renewal of the prohibitions against their involvement in this sector,[6] they do not seem to have constituted any serious threat to Venetian commercial hegemony.[7]

A significant increase in the involvement of Jewish merchants in eastern Mediterranean trade occurred during the sixteenth century. It seems to have resulted from the Jewish migration to the East before, and especially after, the expulsions from Spain, Portugal and Sicily, and from the protection granted to them by the Ottoman Empire. In particular, Jews became prominent in the Balkan peninsula trade and its commercial intercourse with Italy. As a result, several Italian states endeavoured to attract Jewish merchants in order to stimulate their respective economies.[8] Already in 1493 the Dukes of Ferrara invited

---

[6] E. Ashtor, "The Jews in Mediterranean Trade in the Fifteenth Century", in *Wirtschaftskräfte und Wirtschaftswege, I: Mittelmeer und Kontinent* (Festschrift fur Hermann Kellenbenz), ed. J. Schneider, Nuremberg, 1978, pp. 449-450.

[7] D. Jacoby, "Les Juifs à Venise", pp. 185, 200-202.

[8] A. Milano, *Storia degli ebrei in Italia*, Turin, 1963, pp. 267-68 (the Dukes of Ferrara), 242, 250 (the Popes Paul III and Julius III), 251 (the Duke of Urbino); B.D. Cooperman, "Venetian Policy Towards Levantine Jews and Its Broader Italian Context", in *Gli ebrei e Venezia*, ed. G. Cozzi, Milan, 1987, pp. 65-84; R. Segre, "Sephardic Settlements in Sixteenth-Century Italy: A Historical and Geographical Survey", *Mediterranean Historical Review*, 6 (1991), pp. 112-137; For later attempts, see also B. Ravid, *Economics and Toleration in Seventeenth-Century Venice: the Background*

Jewish refugees from Spain to their duchy, and they pursued the same policy during the sixteenth century with regard to Milanese and Neapolitan Jewish refugees.[9] In 1514, and again in 1518, Ancona accorded special privileges to several groups of Ottoman merchants; on the latter occasion, the charter was arranged by a Jewish merchant from Valona.[10] In the first year of his pontificate, Pope Paul III (1534-49) issued a safe conduct for "all merchants of whatever nation, profession or sect, even if Turks, Jews or other infidels", to stay and trade at Ancona and other centres in the area under special privileges, including exemptions from wearing distinctive marks.[11] In 1544 the same Pope granted a residence charter, apparently the first of its kind on Italian territory, to Levantine Jews.[12] These charters and their ensuing utilization reflected the rather lenient policy of Pope Paul III towards former *Marranos,* linked to the projects of settling them at Ancona so as to promote the role of this port in the trade with the Ottoman Empire.[13] Florence followed suit in 1551 with a similar invitation, addressed to all merchants, but explicitly mentioning "Greeks, Turks, Moors,

---

and Context of the "Discorso" of Simone Luzzatto, Jerusalem, 1978, p. 34, n. 29. For a general survey of Jewish economy in the Mediterranean following 1492, see M. Rozen, "La vie économique des Juifs du bassin méditerranéen de l'expulsion d'Espagne (1492) à la fin du XVIIIe siècle", in *La société juive à travers l'histoire, t. III: Le passage d'Israel,* ed. S. Trigano, Paris, 1993, pp. 296-570; on trade and finance, *ibid.,* pp. 324-49.

[9] Milano, *Storia degli ebrei in Italia,* pp. 267-268. In 1538, The Ferrarese Duke invited Spanish and Portuguese merchants, and equally "all and each who speak Spanish or Portuguese", see Cooperman, "Venetian Policy", p. 72.

[10] Cooperman, "Venetian Policy", p. 71.

[11] S. Simonsohn, "Marranos in Ancona under Papal Protection", *Michael,* 9 (1985), pp.235, 243; B. Ravid, "A Tale of Three Cities and their *Raison d'Etat*: Ancona, Venice, Livorno, and the Competition for Jewish Merchants in the Sixteenth Century", *Mediterranean Historical Review,* 6 (1991), p. 141.

[12] Cooperman, "Venetian Policy", p. 73; Simonsohn, "Marranos in Ancona", pp. 249-58; Ravid, "A Tale of Three Cities", p. 143.

[13] Simonsohn, "Marranos in Ancona", pp. 234-266; P. Earle, "The Commercial Development of Ancona, 1479-1551", *The Economic History Review,* ser. 2, 22 (1969), p. 43; J. Delumeau, "Ancône, trait d'union entre l'Orient et l'Occident à l'époque de la Renaissance", *Sociétés et compagnies de commerce en Orient* (Huitième colloque international d'histoire maritime, Beyrouth, 1966), Paris, 1970, pp. 419-433; R. Paci, *La 'scala' di Spalato e il commercio veneziano nei Balcani fra Cinque e Seicento,* Venice, 1971, pp. 71-96; Cooperman, "Venetian Policy", p. 72; Ravid, "A Tale of Three Cities", pp. 138-162.

Jews, Armenians and Persians".[14]

The development of Jewish and *Marrano* centres in Italy, in conjunction with the settlement of their brethren in the East, gradually developed into a challenge to Venetian supremacy in the Levant trade, and became a real threat to Venetian interests in the East during the war with the Ottomans in the late 1530s. The war disrupted Venice's trade in the Mediterranean and enabled some of her rivals, particularly the Jewish merchants of the Mediterranean world, who were by then established both in Ottoman and in Italian centres, to replace the Venetians in the role of intermediaries between East and West.[15] At the conclusion of this war the Venetians were apparently unable to regain their former positions in the trade with Istanbul and the Balkans as they had done in the wake of former wars. Indeed, this time the Republic was in danger of losing the important market of the Ottoman capital, and perhaps also other markets in different parts of the Ottoman Empire. Moreover, the position of Venice itself, as a leading emporium of trade with the eastern Mediterranean, and particularly of the trade with the Balkans, was threatened by the growing prosperity of Ancona, Ferrara, Ragusa, and other centres in the Italian peninsula and the Adriatic.[16]

On 2 June 1541, in the wake of the Ottoman war, the Venetian Senate declared that Venice's international trade was in a state of grave crisis, since high customs tariffs, and various imposts caused merchants to transfer their activities to rival trading centres. In order to attract the trade to Venice once again, a number of administrative measures were decided upon, notably an outright abolition of customs-duties on goods originating from the Balkans and the Aegean (Romania alta e bassa),

---

[14] Ravid, "A Tale of Three Cities", p. 144.

[15] Cooperman, "Venetian Policy", pp. 65-84; Ravid, "A Tale of Three Cities", pp. 138-162. On the penetration of other rivals into Venetian markets during the 1537-40 war, see N. Mirkovich, "Ragusa and the Portuguese Spice Trade", *The Slavonic and East European Review*, 21 (1943), pp. 175, 181, 185; Earle, "The Commercial Development of Ancona", pp. 37-38; F.C. Lane, "The Mediterranean Spice Trade: Its Revival in the Sixteenth Century", *The American Historical Review*, 45 (1940), p. 587, reprinted in *Venice and History The Collected Papers of F.C.Lane*, Baltimore, 1966, p. 32; S. Anselmi, "Motivazioni economiche della neutralità di Ragusa nel Cinquecento", in *Il Mediterraneo nella seconda metà del '500 alla luce di Lepanto*, ed. G. Benzoni, Florence, 1974, pp. 37-38; Inalcık, *The Ottoman Empire*, p. 136.

[16] F.C. Lane, "The Mediterranean Spice Trade", p. 587, reprinted in *Venice and History*, p. 32.

and goods which had normally been sent to these regions from Venice. A special clause of this lengthy enactment referred in particular to Jewish merchants who, in wording of the act, held in their hands the greater part of the commerce between Venice and those regions.[17] The concern of the ruling circles in Venice with the danger that the Venetian trade would fall into foreign hands led them to adopt a new policy, encouraging Jewish merchants to settle in the city. However, the Jews, though mentioned as a principal element of the reform, were not meant to be the only group of foreign merchants who would benefit from the reform. The enactment of June 1541 envisaged a much wider change, of which the Jews were an important, but not the only element. Subsequently, the customs exemptions were periodically renewed until the fiscal reform of 1578.[18] The Jewish merchants who were Ottoman subjects, described as *Levantini*, were offered the possibility of residing in Venice for a limited period in a new segregated section of the city, the Ghetto Vecchio, or 'Old Ghetto', which was adjacent to, but separate from, the first, or 'New Ghetto', the city quarter allotted to the Jewish moneylenders and the community which had grown around them.[19] But the so-called Levantines who established themselves in Venice, though defined as transient residents (*viandanti*), tended to disregard

---

[17] For the full text of this enactment, see the Appendix. *Cf.* B.Ravid, "The Establishment of the *Ghetto Vecchio* of Venice, 1541: Background and Reappraisal", *Proceedings of the Sixth World Congress of Jewish Studies* (Jerusalem, 1973), Jerusalem, 1975, p. 162. The short passage of the above-mentioned enactment which refers to the Jews has been published by Ravid in his "The Religious, Economic and Social Background and Context of the Establishment of the Ghetti of Venice", in *Gli ebrei e Venezia*, ed. G. Cozzi, Milan, 1987, pp. 250-251.

[18] Archivio di Stato, Venice [hereafter: ASV], Cinque savi alla mercanzia, reg. 137 (the *Savi's* report of Dec. 1584); ASV, Senato, Mar, reg. 43, ff. 179-181 (7 Feb. 1577 *m.v.*); B.Ravid, "The Third Charter of the Jewish Merchants of Venice: a Case Study in Complex Multifaceted Negotiations", *Jewish Political Studies Review*, 6 (1994), p. 110 (the *Savi's* report of 1609).

[19] Ravid, "The Establishment of the *Ghetto Vecchio*", pp. 162-63. For a presentation of these developments from a somewhat different perspective, see M. Rozen, "Strangers in a Strange Land: The Extraterritorial Status of Jews in Italy and the Ottoman Empire in the Sixteenth to the Eighteenth Centuries", in *Ottoman and Turkish Jewry: Community and Leadership*, ed. A. Rodrigue, Bloomington, IN, 1992, pp. 128-134.

the legal restrictions on their period of residence.[20] Consequently, their continuous stay in Venice, often accompanied by their families, made them into an integral part of the city's social fabric.

The institution of the two first Ghetti in 1516 and 1541 was followed in 1589 by the charter inviting Jewish merchants of various origins, including the *Ponentini*, whose religious affiliation sometimes tended to be secondary to their business interests, to settle in the city and enjoy considerable privileges, including protection against harassment on religious grounds. In the charter of 1589 Jewish merchants, *Levantini* or *Ponentini*, were officially permitted to establish themselves with their families in Venice under favourable conditions, though they had to pay "the usual customs-duties".[21] This decision was actually part of a larger project, initiated by the Jewish merchant Daniel Rodriga, which instituted the Venetian port of Spalato (Split) in Dalmatia, as a principal way station in the trade between Venice and the East, with special fiscal arrangements aimed at encouraging Jewish and non-Jewish merchants to use this route.[22] Alongside their Ashkenazi and Italian brethren, whose *condotte*, or charters, were periodically renewed, the Jewish merchants remained part of the Venetian social system with hardly any break until the downfall of the Republic. Moreover, these

---

[20] B. Pullan, *Rich and Poor in Renaissance Venice: the Social Institutions of a Catholic State, to 1620*, Oxford and Cambridge, Mass., 1971, p. 512; *idem, The Jews of Europe and the Inquisition of Venice, 1550-1670*, Oxford, 1983, pp. 169-170; Ravid, "The Establishment of the *Ghetto Vecchio*", pp. 166-67; idem, "The First Charter of the Jewish Merchants of Venice, 1589", *Association of Jewish Studies Review*, I (1976), pp. 190-91. See, for instance, the case of Jacob Naḥmias, a "Levantine" Jew, who declared in 1576 having been living in Venice for 15 years, ASV, Senato, Dispacci da Costantinopoli [hereafter: Sen. Disp. CP], filza 1, f. 336v.

[21] For the change in 1578, see above, n. 18; for the 1589 *condotta*, see Ravid, "The First Charter", pp. 219-222.

[22] R. Maestro, *L'attività economica degli ebrei levantini e ponentini a Venezia dal 1550 al 1700*, unpublished doctoral dissertation, University of Venice, 1935, pp. 6-52; L. Morpurgo, "Daniel Rodriguez i osnivanje splitske skele u XVI stoljeću", *Starine*, 52-53 (1962), pp. 185-248, 363-415; Paci, *La 'scala' di Spalato, op. cit.*; Ravid, "The First Charter", *op. cit.; idem*, "An Autobiographical memorandum by Daniel Rodriga, *Inventore* of the *Scala* of Spalato", *The Mediterranean and the Jews. Banking, Finance and International Trade, XVI-XVIII*, eds. S. Schwarzfuchs and A. Toaff, Ramat Gan, 1989, pp. 189-212; *idem*, "Daniel Rodriga and the First Decade of the Jewish Merchants of Venice", in *Exile and Diaspora. Studies in the History of the Jewish People Presented to Professor Haim Beinart*, Jerusalem, 1991, pp. 203-223.

merchants enjoyed commercial privileges which many of Venice's inhabitants and subjects did not enjoy.[23] No wonder, therefore, that Jewish experience in Venice has generally been presented in the historical literature in rather positive terms.[24] Indeed, on various occasions, the Venetian Jews themselves expressed their gratitude to a government which accepted and tolerated them, at a time when other states persecuted and expelled them from their territories.[25]

But the reality behind this ostensibly positive façade was much more complex. Before becoming a de facto integral part of Venetian society, where they could find a relatively safe and peaceful haven, Jewish traders experienced some difficult moments in their relations with the maritime republic. Venice and its rulers had to accept a new and somewhat painful situation, in which a group of foreigners, belonging to a traditionally despised race, penetrated to the very heart of Venetian existence. It took about fifty years or so for this relationship to stabilize on a more peaceful level. This difficult transitory phase, roughly between 1530 and 1580, is at the focus of the present book. During those years the relations between Venice and the Jewish merchants were strongly influenced, on the one hand, by the general trend of Christian attitudes to Jews, and, on the other hand, by various Venetian difficulties in the Mediterranean scene. The latter aspect will be at the focus of our discussion in the eight chapters of this book. The former aspect, the Christian attitude to Jews in the Venetian state, will only be briefly recapitulated in the following paragraphs.

Parallel with the establishment of Jewish merchants in Venice, various factors led to an increasingly hostile atmosphere vis à vis the Jews in various parts of the Venetian state. The century preceding 1570 has recently been characterized as a most difficult period in the history of Western and Central European Jews, who were progressively pushed

---

[23] G. Cozzi, "Politica, società, istituzioni", in *La Repubblica di Venezia nell'età moderna, vol. 1: Dalla guerra di Chioggia al 1517*, eds. G. Cozzi and M. Knapton, Turin, 1986, pp. 133-40.

[24] *E.g.* L.A. Schiavi, "Gli Ebrei in Venezia e nelle sue colonie", *Nuova Antologia*, 3rd ser., 47 (1893), pp. 313, 316; C. Roth, *Venice*, Jewish Communities Series, Philadelphia, 1930, pp. 116, 119-20, 369.

[25] *E.g.* S. Luzzatto, *Discorso circa il stato de gl'hebrei et in particular dimoranti nell'inclita città di Venezia*, Venice, 1638, ff. 35-35v, 91v; see also Solomon Ashkenazi's dictum, cited at the head of the introduction.

to the margins of economic life.[26] Venice, it is true, witnessed the institution of its first ghetto in 1516, after a long period in which a continuous presence of Jews in the city had been officially denied. Yet, during the two-and-a-half decades preceding the war over Cyprus, which broke out in 1570, the hardening of the Republic's official attitude, the anti-Jewish policy of the Roman Church and the increased hostility of Christian society as a whole, made life harsher for Jews in the Venetian dominions. To illustrate the intensity and the dynamics of the anti-Jewish sentiments which were developing during that period, it would be useful to note some of the highlights of that process. From 1547 on, several towns of the Venetian mainland officially asked Venice to abolish Jewish moneylending and replace it with the Christian credit institutions of *Monti di Pietà*. Consequently, Jewish moneylending was abolished at Crema and Padua in 1547, at Verona, Conegliano and Asolo in 1548, at Rovigo in 1551, at Udine in 1556, at Bergamo in 1557, to name only the more important centres.[27] This process was sometimes accompanied by manifestations of anti-Jewish violence (at Asolo and the Trevigiano in 1544 and 1547, at Udine in 1556), attempts to restrict Jewish economic activities (in Padua in 1545), enclosing Jews in separate quarters (at Udine in 1543, in Padua in 1547), or expelling them altogether (Udine, 1556).[28] At the same time, the condition of Jews in the city of Venice also deteriorated. The growing difficulties in renewing the *condotta* of the Jews in the Ghetto Novo reflected the worsening of their social and economic status.[29] During those years the restrictions on professional and economic occupations of the Jews in Venice were renewed, and probably also more rigorously

---

[26] J. Israel, *European Jewry in the Age of Mercantilism, 1550-1750*, Oxford, 1985, pp. 23-31.

[27] Pullan, *Rich and Poor in Renaissance Venice*, pp. 518-20, 522-23, 526.

[28] *Ibid.*, pp. 519-20, 527-28; P.C.Ioly Zorattini, "Note e documenti per la storia degli Ebrei a Udine nel Cinquecento", *Ufficina dello storico*, 1 (1979), pp. 157-59; *idem*, "Gli Ebrei a Udine dal Trecento ai giorni nostri", *Atti dell'Accademia di Scienze, ed Arti di Udine*, 74 (1981), pp. 50-51.

[29] Pullan, *Rich and Poor*, pp. 529-34; R.C. Mueller, "Charitable Institutions, The Jewish Community and Venetian Society. A Discussion of the Recent Volume by Brian Pullan", *Studi Veneziani*, 14 (1972), p. 82; B. Ravid, "The Socioeconomic Background of the Expulsion and Readmission of the Venetian Jews, 1571-1573", *Essays in Modern Jewish History. A Tribute to Ben Halpern*, eds. F. Malino and P. Cohen Albert, London and Toronto, 1982, pp. 34-40.

applied.[30]

This policy of encroachment has rightly been related to the anti-Jewish policy of the Counter Reformation papacy.[31] From the beginning of his pontificate, Pope Paul IV declared his intention to force the Jews to admit their inferiority through a series of measures aimed at their humiliation and at their segregation from Christian society. The stake lighted under the 25 or more *Marrani* at Ancona in 1556, though technically not against professing Jews, demonstrated how determined the Pope was to carry out his intentions. Pius V renewed this policy after his election in 1566. Three years later, the Jews were expelled from the Papal States, with the exception of Ancona and Rome.[32] The activity of the Holy Office of the Inquisition in Venice, in collaboration with the Venetian state, served as a link between this papal policy and the line followed by the Venetian rulers. In this context one should note the decision, decreed in 1550, to expel the *Marrani* from Venice, and the destruction of Hebrew books in 1553 and 1568.[33]

How far did these developments affect the fate of the Jewish merchants of the Ghetto Vecchio, who, as we have seen, had been formally invited to settle in Venice from pragmatic interests? In other words, could the famous Venetian pragmatism withstand the growing pressures of intolerance which were triumphing in so many places around Venice, and occasionally in Venice itself? Without denying the influence of

---

[30] See the prohibition on trade in and production of cloths (1554-58), Pullan, *Rich and Poor*, pp. 527, 529; the prohibition to function as brokers at Rialto: M. Ferro, *Dizionario del diritto comune e veneto etc.*, vol. 9, Venice, 1781, under the voice "sensale", p. 10 (1551?); the exclusion of Jews from the College of Physicians (1555, repeated in 1567): N.E. Vanzan Marchini, "Medici ebrei a Venezia nel Cinquecento", in *Venezia ebraica*, ed. U. Fortis, Rome, 1979, pp. 79-80.

[31] Pullan, *Rich and Poor*, pp. 528-9; *idem*, "A Ship with Two Rudders: Righetto Marrano and the Inquisition in Venice", *The Historical Journal*, 20 (1977), pp. 33-40, 58.

[32] Milano, *Storia degli ebrei in Italia*, pp. 247-51; R. Segre, "Nuovi documenti sui Marrani d'Ancona (1555-1559)" *Michael*, 11 (1985), pp. 130-232.

[33] D. Kaufmann, "Die Vertreibung der Marranen aus Venedig im Jahre 1550", *Jewish Quarterly Review*, 13 (1900), pp. 520-32; A. Ya'ari, *On the Burning of the Talmud in Italy*, Tel Aviv, 1954 [Hebrew]; Milano, *Storia degli ebrei*, p. 249; P.F. Grendler, "The Destruction of Hebrew Books in Venice, 1568", *Proceedings of the American Academy for Jewish Research*, 45 (1978), pp. 103-130; B. Arbel, "The Jews in Cyprus: New Evidence from the Venetian Period", *Jewish Social Studies*, 41 (1979), p. 28; Pullan, *The Jews of Europe, op. cit.*

these developments on Venetian attitudes towards the Jewish Levantine merchants, it is suggested that a similar influence worked in the opposite direction, namely, that the fate of the Jews in the various Venetian Ghetti was greatly affected by the changing relations between Venice and the Ottoman Empire, in which the Levantine Jewish merchants had a very sensitive position. Venice's compulsion to deal repeatedly with Jewish merchants and entrepreneurs had a negative impact on the official attitude towards Jews in general. The relationship between Venice and the Jewish Levantine merchants, characterized by considerations of expediency, on the one hand, and by growing hostility, on the other, constitutes the core of the present study. The Jews of the Ghetto Novo, who were not allowed to engage in international trade, are therefore in the margin of our analysis, although their fate, as we shall see, was strongly influenced by the issues treated in this book.

The eight chapters of this book deal, in one way or another, with various aspects of the re-emergence of large-scale Jewish trade in the Mediterranean during the sixteenth century, and its intricate relationship with the Venetian Republic. Most of the subjects treated refer to the first 50 years or so, which saw the massive Jewish entrance into Venice's eastern trade. The later phase, largely connected with the activities of Daniel Rodriga and the development of the Dalmatian port of Spalato as Venice's main gateway to the East, which has already been studied by several historians in great detail, will not be treated here.[34] Since the rise of Jewish traders in the early modern Mediterranean was greatly dependent upon Ottoman protection, the system of relations between the big Muslim empire and Venice, and particularly those aspects of this relationship affecting Jews and international trade, will also be at the centre of the following discussions. Some chapters of this book focus around Jewish figures, who for various reasons left many footprints in the Venetian sources. Beyond the individual stories of these men, which may seem exceptional (as they sometimes are), the issues which arise from the reconstruction of their activities transcend the particular history of each one of them. The last chapter reveals the emergence of Jewish shipowners in the early modern Mediterranean, and the continuation of this phenomenon in other areas, and attempts to explain this development in a larger chronological perspective.

Though an effort has been made to integrate sources of different

---

[34] For the main studies regarding this issue, see above, n. 22.

provenance and studies based on other sources, this book is based primarily on Venetian archival sources, and therefore dwells broadly on Venetian policies and attitudes. The richness and the variety of Venetian documentation is unmatched by the source material of Jewish or Ottoman provenance pertaining to the same subjects. This does not, of course, exclude the possibility that additional relevant evidence, certainly Venetian, but probably also of other origins, may yet be discovered. The subject of Jewish involvement in international trade in the early modern Mediterranean seems vast, and is certainly worthy of continuous research on a wider scope.

CHAPTER ONE

VENICE AND THE JEWISH MERCHANTS OF ISTANBUL IN THE SIXTEENTH CENTURY

A Venetian merchant colony had been established in Constantinople long before the Ottoman takeover, and during the greater part of the late Middle Ages, Constantinople was a most important base of Venetian Levantine trade. The citizens of the Republic who lived on the Bosporus enjoyed a privileged position under the administration of their *Bailo*, who presided over them and took care of Venetian interests in the entire Levant.[1]

The Ottoman conquest of Constantinople did not substantially change this long-established connection. It is true that during the sixteenth century, the ports of Syria and Egypt attracted a greater share of Venetian commercial shipping and that several Venetian representatives in the Ottoman capital in the 1550s and 1560s explicitly referred in their reports to the decline of Venetian trade there.[2] But we should keep in mind that the importance of trade between Venice and Istanbul cannot be measured exclusively by the direct participation of the Venetians, or by the number of Venetian ships visiting the Ottoman capital, considering that other groups were also involved in this activity and that some of this trade was conducted over land. Moreover,

---

[1] H. Brown, "The Venetians and the Venetian Quarter in Constantinople to the Close of the Twelfth Century", *Journal of Hellenic Studies*, 40 (1920), pp. 68-88; M. Roberti, "Ricerche intorno alla colonia veneziana in Costantinopoli nel secolo XII", in *Scritti in onore di Camillo Manfroni nel XL˙ anno dell'insegnamento*, Padua, 1925, pp. 136-147; C. Diehl, "La colonie vénitienne à Constantinople à la fin du XIVᵉ siècle", in his *Etudes byzantines*, Paris, 1905, pp. 241-275; T. Bertelè, *Il palazzo degli ambasciatori di Venezia a Costantinopoli e le sue antiche memorie*, Bologna, 1932; Χ.Α. Μαλτέζου, Ο Θεσμόσ του εν Κωσταντινουπόλει Βενετού Βαΐλου (1268-1453), Athens, 1970.

[2] On the decline of Venice's trade with Istanbul, see the testimonies of the *Baili* Navagero (1553), Trevisan (1554) and Barbarigo (1565) in *Relazioni degli ambasciatori veneti al Senato durante il secolo decimosesto*, ed. E. Albèri, ser. III, vol. 1, Florence, 1840, pp. 101, 183-85; *ibid.*, vol. 2, Florence, 1844, pp. 53-54.

according to the figures published by Lane, it seems that in spite of
the structural changes in international trade following the great discoveries, and the growing importance of the trans-Balkan land routes, linking
the ports of Dalmatia and Albania with Salonica, Edirne and Istanbul,
there is no clear indication of a decline in the volume of Venetian
shipping to the Bosporus during the first half of the sixteenth century,
and probably not until 1570.[3] Even if it was not the most important
centre of Venetian trade in the eastern Mediterranean, Ottoman Istanbul
certainly continued to be one of the main foci of Venetian shipping
and trade in the Levant.[4] According to Mantran, the Venetians were
the still largest group of Western merchants in the Ottoman capital
as late as the early seventeenth century.[5]

During the sixteenth century, Istanbul was the greatest city of Europe
and the Mediterranean, and represented a huge market.[6] The presence
of the Ottoman court, a great consumer of luxury goods of all kinds,
was a substantial source of income for Western merchants, particularly
the Venetians. Moreover, the picture of Istanbul drawn by Braudel,

---

[3] F.C. Lane, "Venetian Shipping during the Commercial Revolution", *American Historical Review*, 38 (1933), pp. 219-239, reprinted in his *Venice and History*, Baltimore, 1966, pp. 3-24, esp. pp. 238-239; R. Romano, "La marine marchande vénitienne au XVIe siècle", in *Les sources de l'histoire maritime en Europe du Moyen Age au XVIIe siècle*, ed. M. Mollat, Paris, 1962, pp. 33-68. For a different view, see B. Simon, "Contribution à l'étude du commerce vénitien dans l'Empire Ottoman au milieu du seizième siècle (1558-1560)", *Mélanges d'Archéologie et d'Histoire de l'Ecole Française de Rome. Moyen Age-Temps Modernes*, 96 (1984), pp. 977-78. However, Simon, who based his evaluation on *Bailo* Cavalli's information on Ottoman customs revenues derived from Venetian trading activities, did not take into account the possibility that a large part of the goods paying customs dues in Ottoman centres in the Balkans was also directed to Istanbul.

[4] H. Inalcik, "An Outline of Ottoman-Venetian Relations", in *Venezia, centro di mediazione tra Oriente e Occidente (secoli XV-XVI), aspetti e problemi*, Atti del II Convegno internazionale di storia della civiltà veneziana (Venezia, 1973), Florence, 1977, col. 1, pp. 83-90.

[5] R. Mantran, *Istanbul dans la seconde moitié du XVIIe siècle*, Paris, 1962, pp. 162-163.

[6] For different estimates of the population of Istanbul in the sixteenth century, see Mantran, *Istanbul*, pp. 44-47; B. Lewis, *Istanbul and the Civilization of the Ottoman Empire*, Norman, Okl., 1963, pp. 102-103; O.L. Barkan, "Research on the Ottoman Fiscal Surveys", in *Studies in the Economic History of the Middle East from the Rise of Islam to the Present Day*, ed. M.A. Cook, London, 1970, pp. 168, 170; H. Inalcik, *The Ottoman Empire. The Classical Age, 1300-1600*, London, 1973, pp. 140-146.

according to which the city was a great consumer but had little to offer for export[7], though seemingly justified, deserves further elaboration. In fact, the importance of Istanbul in the Mediterranean economy was related to other functions in the commercial, financial, political and administrative spheres. The Ottoman capital seems to have served as an emporium for different wares originating in various parts of the Empire, and probably countries beyond its borders.[8] It also served as an entrepreneurial centre for the international commercial transactions of exports from, and probably also imports to, other parts of the Empire.[9] Finally, this great city must also have offered some of its own products to the West.[10]

A great variety of merchandise was exchanged between Venice and the Ottoman capital during the sixteenth century. Among the goods most frequently imported by Venetian merchants to Istanbul were different kinds of cloths originating in the textile industries in the West, in particular Venetian woollen and silk industry, whose spectacular rise during that century depended greatly upon the Ottoman markets, especially that of Istanbul.[11] Other Venetian imports to the city on the Bosporus included Venetian glass products, tin, paper, and a great variety of luxury goods: clocks, diamonds, pearls, jewels, ornamented boxes, and even food, such as Italian cheese for the refined cuisine

---

[7] F. Braudel, *The Mediterranean and the Mediterranean World in the Age of Philip II*, London, 1973, vol. I, pp. 347-351.

[8] *E.g.* H. Inalcik, "The Ottoman Economic Mind and Aspects of the Ottoman Economy", in *Studies in the Economic History of the Middle East from the Rise of Islam to the Present Day*, ed. M.A. Cook, London, 1970, p. 212; *idem, The Ottoman Empire*, pp. 130, 145-146; U. Tucci, "Un ciclo di affari commerciali in Siria ((1579-1581)", in his *Mercanti, navi monete nel Cinquecento veneziano*, Bologna, 1981, pp. 98, 111.

[9] On the exports of grains and alum, see below, pp. 19-20, 104-108.

[10] *E.g.* R. Collier and J. Billioud, *Histoire du commerce de Marseille, Tome III: de 1480 à 1599*, Paris, 1951, pp. 255-256; S. Faroqhi, "Textile production in Rumeli and the Arab Provinces. Geographical Distribution and Internal Trade (1560-1650)", *The Journal of Ottoman Studies*, 1 (1980), pp. 75-76.

[11] P. Sardella, "L'épanouissement industriel de Venise au XVIᵉ siècle", *Annales E.S.C.*, 2 (1947), pp. 195-196; D. Sella, "The Rise and Fall of the Venetian Woollen Industry", in *Crisis and Change in the Venetian Economy in the Sixteenth and Seventeenth Centuries*, ed. B. Pullan, London, 1968, pp. 106-126.

of the various pashas.[12] The products exported during the sixteenth century to Venice from Istanbul, including the larger area of which it was the main trading centre, included mainly wool, raw silk, camlets, various kinds of cloth, hides, dyes, Turkish tapestry and sometimes spices.[13] Caviar and salted sturgeon, which were also imported by Venetian merchants from Istanbul, were an important component in the diet of well-to-do Italians in the sixteenth century, especially on Fridays and during Lent.[14] Until the 1550s at least, Venetian merchants also concluded important transactions in Istanbul for the export of grain from other parts of the Empire, especially from the northern shores of the Aegean, as well as for the export of alum from western Anatolia and other regions.[15]

It was principally for the supply of those products from Istanbul that the Venetians had to rely on Jewish merchants, whose growing involvement in the internal trade of the Ottoman Empire rendered them

[12] *E.g.* ASV, Senato, Deliberazioni Costantinopoli (hereafter: Sen. Delib. CP), reg.3, f. 103; *ibid.*, reg. 4, f. 22v (exports of glass products to Istanbul, 1567, 1569); Marino Sanuto, *I diarii*, 58 vols, Venice, 1879-1903, vol. 58, cols. 305-306, 380, 623, 625, 634 (luxury cloths, Piacentine cheese, ornamented boxes, precious stones exported in 1533); *Relazioni*, ed. Albèri, ser. III, vol. I, p. 183 (woollen and silk cloths, tin and other wares, 1554); Jean Le Carlier, Sʳ de Pinon, *Voyage en Orient [1579]*, ed. E. Blochet, Paris, 1920, p. 93 (a list of a great variety of products imported by Venetians to Istanbul). *Cf.* also A. Galanté, *Histoire des Juifs d'Istanbul depuis la prise de cette ville en 1453 par Fatih Mehmed II jusqu'à nos jours*, vol. II, Istanbul, 1942, p. 24 (Galanté seems to confuse exports with imports of certain articles); H. Kellenbenz, "Venedig als internationales Zentrum und die Expansions [sic] des Handels im 15. und 16. Jahrhundert", in *Venezia, centro di mediazione, op. cit.*, vol. 1, pp. 298-299; Simon, "Contribution", pp. 982, 1000.

[13] *E.g.*, *Relazioni*, ed. Albèri, ser. III, vol. I, p. 183 (camlets as the main export article previous to 1554); Le Carlier, *Voyage*, p. 93 (leather, wool, tapestry, camlets, etc.); Kellenbenz, "Venedig als internazionales Zentrum", pp. 298-299; J.C. Hocquet, *Le sel et la fortune de Venise, vol. 2: Voiliers et commerce en Méditerranée, 1200-1650*, Lille, 1979, p. 484, n. 13 (pepper exported from Istanbul, 1555); Maestro, *L'attività economica*, p. 11 (importation of dyes, 1568).

[14] Le Carlier, *Voyage*, pp. 71, 93; L. Messadaglia, "Schienale e morona: storia di due vocaboli e contributo allo studio degli usi alimentari e dei traffici veneti con il Levante", in *Atti del R. Istituto Veneto di Scienze, Lettere e Arti, Classe di Scienze Morali e Letterarie*, vol. 101/II (1941), pp. 1-57, esp. pp. 5-6, 13-15, 25-27, 40.

[15] M. Aymard, *Venise, Raguse et le commerce du blé pendant la seconde moitié du seizième siècle*, Paris, 1966, pp. 50-51, 56-57, 60, 127-140. For the alum exports, see below, pp. 19-20, 104-108.

indispensable as middlemen for foreign exporters. This collaboration served the interests of the Venetian merchants as long as they could maintain their quasi-hegemonic position in the international trade between Istanbul and the West, and as long as they were able to choose from the different supply sources for their wares, and bargain on an equal footing, or even as superiors, with their local suppliers. It was precisely this position which began to change in the early sixteenth century.

Among the Jewish immigrants to the different countries under Ottoman rule, and in particular to Istanbul, there were businessmen with capital, financial expertise and connections with important centres of European and Mediterranean economy. Their dispersal between East and West, their command of languages, their adherence to the same legal and socio-religious traditions (in spite of the differences between the various schools and ethnic groups), the disposition of their rabbis to recognize the legality of commercial practices even when not strictly in accordance with traditional law, the use of Hebrew, and sometimes Ladino, as an international language of commercial correspondence, their ability to use letters of exchange for transfer of capital between the two worlds of Islam and Christendom, and last, but not least, the protection and support granted them by the Ottoman authorities—all these were important assets in their participation in the Levant trade.[16] Foreign travellers who passed through Istanbul in the mid-sixteenth century were impressed by the important role of the Jews in the economic life of the Ottoman capital, as well as in the international trade centred around it.[17]

---

[16] Paci, *La 'scala' di Spalato*, esp. pp. 31-43; E. Bashan, "The Freedom of Trade and the Imposition of Taxes and Customs Duties on Foreign Jewish Traders in the Ottoman Empire", in *East and Maghreb*, eds. H.Z. Hirshberg and E. Bashan, Ramat Gan, 1974, pp. 105-166 [Hebrew]; H. Gerber, "Enterprise and International Commerce in the Economic Activity of the Jews of the Ottoman Empire in the 16th-17th Centuries", *Zion*, 43 (1978), pp. 38-67 [Hebrew]; M. Rozen, "The *fattoria*: A Chapter in the History of Mediterranean Commerce in the 16th and 17th Centuries", in *Miqqedem Umiyyam. Studies in the Jewry of Islamic Countries*, Haifa, 1981, pp. 101-132 [Hebrew]; H. Gerber, *Economic and Social Life of the Jews in the Ottoman Empire in the 16th and 17th Centuries*, Jerusalem, 1982, pp. 66-69 [Hebrew]; S.W. Baron, *A Social and Religious History of the Jews*, vol. 18, Philadelphia, 1983, pp. 233-252.

[17] E.g. Pierre Belon, *Les observations de plusieures singularités et choses memorables trouvées en Grèce, Asie, Iudée, Egypte, Arabie et autres pays étrangers* etc., Paris, 1588, p. 400 [travelled in 1546-49]; Nicolas de Nicolay, *Discours et histoire véritable des navigations, pérégrinations et voyages faites en la Turquie* etc., Antwerp, 1586,

***

Following the establishment of the Ghetto Vecchio in 1541, the new privileged position of Jewish merchants in the international trade of Venice was offensive to many Venetians. What had constituted the main source of Venetian prosperity was now in great part controlled by a despised and lowly people. The anti-Jewish atmosphere of the Italian Counter-Reformation also contributed to Venetian animosity towards Jewish merchants. Thus the necessity of attracting them to Venice, combined with the fear of their competition and anger at their success, were to characterize Venetian policy towards the Jewish merchants for many years after 1541. The animosity towards the Jewish Levantine merchants was aggravated by several factors, mostly, though not exclusively, connected with the activities of the Jewish merchants of Istanbul.

The main threat to the prosperity of Venetian traders in Istanbul and in other centres of the Ottoman Empire during those years seems to have been the success of Jewish businessmen in monopolizing the wholesale trade of certain products which were of particular interest to the Venetian merchants. The official representatives of the Republic in the Turkish capital reiterated time and again during the 1550s and 1560s that Jewish merchants completely dominated the supply of wool,

---

p. 168 [with ref. to 1551]; *Hans Dernschwann's Tagebuch einer Reise nach Konstantinopel und Kleinasien (1553-55)*, ed. F. Babinger, Munich, 1923, cited in *The Jews in the Medieval World*, ed. J.R. Marcus, Cleveland, New York and Philadelphia, , 1961, pp. 412-417. Recently several scholars cited different demographic data on the Jews of Istanbul during the sixteenth century. Yet, beside the general impression of a spectacular demographic expansion during the first half of the century, the attempts at a systematic analysis of this data still leaves many questions unanswered; see B. Lewis, *The Jews of Islam*, Princeton, 1984, pp. 118, 122 (containing two markedly inconsistent data for the 1520s-1530s); H. Inalcik, "Jews in the Ottoman Economy and Finances, 1450-1500", in *The Islamic World from Classical to Modern Times: Essays in Honor of B. Lewis*, eds. C.E. Bosworth *et. al.*, Princeton, 1989, p. 514; S. Shaw, *The Jews of the Ottoman Empire and the Turkish Republic*, New York, 1991, pp. 37-38 (where one gets an impression of a spectacular rise during the sixteenth century); A. Levy, *The Sephardim in the Ottoman Empire*, Princeton, 1992, pp. 7-11 (who does not refer at all to the higher data cited by Lewis and Shaw, and suggests that Sephardi immigration to Istanbul was relatively small in the course of the sixteenth century); M.A.Epstein, *The Ottoman Jewish Communities and their Role in the Fifteenth and Sixteenth centuries*, Freiburg, 1980, pp. 102-122, 133-35, 138, 141, 143.

cloth and camlets, and that the Venetian merchants in Istanbul were unable to acquire these products and export them unless they were willing to comply with the conditions imposed on them by the Jewish businessmen.[18] "Those Jews", wrote the Venetian *Bailo* Navagero in 1553, "have totally destroyed this route, because, among other things, they concentrate in their hands all the wool and sell it as they please; they have also monopolized the trade in fine camlets, all of which they either order or acquire, thus gaining the profit previously enjoyed by the [Venetian] merchants who used to be active on that route".[19] During the 1560s, the *Baili* Cavalli and Barbarigo described in similar terms how the entire trade between Istanbul and Venice, including the wool and cloths trade, passed through the hands of Jews, who forced the Venetians to comply with their conditions, collecting the profits which had formerly belonged to Venetian traders.[20] The supply of alum from mines in the Ottoman Empire was also in the hands of Jewish entrepreneurs of Istanbul, who, during the 1560s, shipped this important mineral directly to Venice.[21] It should be noted that alum was an essential material for various Venetian industries, particularly the textile industry, which was rapidly expanding during those years.[22] The Republic itself had tried in 1546 to gain a monopoly of the alum production in Turkey, and was willing to pay the Sultan's treasury 25,000 ducats for this purpose.[23] This attempt either failed or was short-lived, and the Jewish businessmen from Istanbul were more successful in acquiring the lease

---

[18] *Relazioni*, ed. Albèri, vol. 1, pp. 102 (1553), 274-275 (1560); *ibid.*, vol. 2, Florence, 1844, pp. 53-54 (1564).

[19] *Ibid.*, vol. 1, p. 102.

[20] *Ibid.*, vol. 2, pp. 274-75 (Cavalli's report, 1560), pp. 53-54 (Barbarigo's report, 1564).

[21] According to Simon, the rich alum mines of Phocaea, in western Anatolia, were leased in 1560 to Joseph Nassí and Aaron Segura: Simon, "Contribution", p. 990, n. 59. For later years, see for instance, ASV, Senato, Dispacci da Costantinopoli (hereafter: Sen., Disp. CP), filza 1, ff. 338, 341 (1566); *ibid.*, filza 2, f. 118 (July 1567); ASV, Capi del Consiglio dei Dieci, Lettere da Costantinopoli (hereafter: Capi X, Lett. CP), busta 3, No 63 (20 July 1566). See also B. Pullan, *The Jews of Europe and the Inquisition of Venice, 1550-1670*, Oxford, 1983, p. 169.

[22] Sella, "The Rise and Fall", pp. 108-115. On the uses of alum, see C. Singer, *The Earliest Chemical Industry*, London, 1948, pp. xvii-xviii.

[23] Inalcik, *The Ottoman Empire*, p. 137. For earlier Venetian attempts to get hold of Turkish alum production, see Singer, *The Earliest Chemical Industry*, p. 100 and n. 137.

and imposing themselves as alum suppliers for Venice.[24] In a similar manner Jewish merchants in Cairo in the 1550s succeeded in buying up most of the pepper which had reached Egypt from the Far East, forcing the Venetians to buy this costly product from them. Consequently Venice was obliged, in the 1550s, to transfer its consulate from Alexandria to Cairo.[25] In 1557 it was even claimed in Venice that Jews were dominating the grain trade with the Levant.[26]

A similar source of friction was the growing dependence of Venetian merchants in Istanbul on Jewish merchants for the retail sale of goods imported by the Venetians to the Ottoman capital. In the late 1550s a dispute on this issue resulted in a mutual boycott lasting two months, and was solved only by the intervention of the Ottoman authorities. Consequently, the Venetians even succeeded in retaining the shops which they had opened in the course of the dispute to dispense with the need to sell their merchandise (mainly woollens and silk cloth) through the Jewish intermediaries.[27]

Another factor which favoured the Jewish merchants of Istanbul, to the detriment of the Venetians, was the involvement of high Ottoman officials in the Jewish foreign trade, or rather the use of Jews by these officials in the conduct of their own business affairs. This association sometimes impaired the delicate relations between Venice and the Porte.[28] In 1563, for instance, Venetian officials confiscated as contraband the merchandise of a Jewish Levantine merchant. Later it was discovered that the wares actually belonged to the Grand Vizier, Mehmed Sokollu, and Venice had to cope with a good deal of unpleasantness, and finally had to compensate the pasha for his losses.[29]

The influence of certain prominent Jews in the highest echelons of the Ottoman polity, and the relative ease of access of Jewish merchants to the supreme Ottoman authorities in Istanbul, also contributed

---

[24] On the importation of alum, see also below, pp. 104-108.

[25] Lane, *Venice, A Maritime Republic*, p. 302 (were this event, dated to 1555, is related to Jewish involvement in the pepper trade); Simon, "Contribution", p. 990 (where the same event, dated to 1552, is related to the hegemony of Cairene Jews in the spice trade, as well as the silk and copper trade).

[26] Pullan, *The Jews of Europe*, p. 169.

[27] Simon, "Contribution", pp. 991-92.

[28] *Ibid.*, p. 1007.

[29] See below, pp. 101-104.

to the growing animosity between Venice and the Jewish merchants, subjects of the Sultan. It is significant that the most prominent Jewish figures in Istanbul during the sixteenth century, like Doña Gracia Nassí, Don Joseph Nassí or Solomon Ashkenazi, were also engaged in international trade.[30] Less known are the frequent intercessions of other Jewish merchants of the Ottoman capital in the *Divan*, with different Pashas and with influential women of the harem, often in direct conflict with Venetian merchants or the Venetian authorities.[31] The Sultan and his advisers must have grasped how easily the Jewish merchants of their capital could be manipulated to exert pressure on Venice for various purposes.

Jewish businessmen were also very successful in obtaining the positions of customs collectors in important commercial centres throughout the Ottoman Empire. Though not limited to Istanbul, but also noticeable in other commercial centres, such as Beirut, Alexandria or Bursa, this phenomenon certainly contributed to the impact of the encounter between Venetians and Jews in the Ottoman capital.[32] Evidently, the control of key positions in the customs administration, combined with commercial enterprise, offered Jewish entrepreneurs

---

[30] On Doña Gracia's and Don Joseph Nassí's trading activities, see C. Roth, *Dona Gracia of the House of Nasi*, Philadelphia, 1977, pp. 85-86, 111-116; *idem*, *The House of Nasi: The Duke of Naxos*, Philadelphia, 1948, pp. 157-158, 163. On Ashkenazi, see below, pp. 82-86. *Cf.* also Epstein, *The Ottoman Jewish Communities*, p. 155.

[31] *E.g.* ASV, Sen., Disp. CP, filza 1, f. 50 (Mar. 1566); ASV, Capi Cons. X, Lett. CP, busta 3, Nos 59-61 (1566); ASV, Sen., Disp. CP, filza 2, f. 199 (Sept. 1567); ASV, Consiglio dei Dieci, Secreti [hereafter: Cons. X, Secreti], reg. 11, ff. 140v-141v (1577). See also H. Brown, "Venetian Diplomacy at the Sublime Porte during the Sixteenth Century", in his *Studies in the History of Venice*, vol. II, London, 1907, pp. 25-26. One particular group of Jewish entrepreneurs based in Istanbul, originally lead by Aaron di Segura, was at the origin of many harassments suffered by Venetians during the 1560s and 1570s. On this issue, and on the use of *Sultane* by Jewish entrepreneurs, see below, Chapters Six and Seven.

[32] Roth, *The House of Nasi: The Duke of Naxos*, pp. 46-47; P. Grunebaum-Ballin, *Joseph Naci, duc de Naxos*, Paris, 1968, p. 163; A. David, "The Economic Status of Egyptian Jewry in the Sixteenth Century According to the Responsa of RADBAZ", in *Miqqedem Umiyyam*, *op. cit.*, pp. 92-93 [Hebrew]; Gerber, *Economic and Social Life*, pp. 54-60; M. Winter, "The Jews of Egypt in the Ottoman Period According to Turkish and Arabic Sources", *Pe'amim*, 16 (1983), pp. 11-13 [Hebrew]. A. Levy, *The Sephardim of the Ottoman Empire*, p. 23 (citing Epstein, *The Ottoman Jewish Communities*, pp. 101, 112). See also below, Chapter Two.

another advantage over their competitors, including the Venetians. Venice was sometimes obliged to intervene officially at the Porte against the Jewish customs officials who treated her merchants unfavourably.[33]

Another factor which added to the animosity was the activity of Christian pirates in the Adriatic and the eastern Mediterranean against unbelievers, Muslims and Jews, their ships and their goods. Venice, it is known, considered the Adriatic sea as its own "gulf", and the Ottomans, therefore, understandably considered Venice responsible for the security of shipping there. Furthermore, Venetian colonies in the eastern Mediterranean were sometimes used by Western corsairs as victualling bases, which could hardly be concealed from the Ottomans. Whenever Ottoman Jews were captured and their merchandise confiscated by those pirates, a mechanism of combined Jewish and Ottoman pressure was set off in Istanbul, to the great embarrassment of the Venetians, who were often unable to prevent such piratical activities.[34]

Last, but not least, the Venetian attitude towards the Jewish Levantine merchants was strongly influenced by the nature of Venetian-Ottoman relations in general. The delicate relationship between the commercial Republic, which dominated a colonial empire in the eastern Mediterranean, and the Ottoman Empire, which sought to strengthen its hold in the same area, were influenced by political, military, ideological and economic considerations. It is not surprising that the contacts between Venetians and Ottoman subjects which took place in Istanbul had a special effect on this relationship. The imperial metropolis was probably not the most important centre of Venetian trade in the Levant in this period, considering the amount of capital invested, the frequency of shipping, or the number of Venetian merchants established there, as compared to other centres, such as Aleppo, Alexandria or Tripoli. But the combination of the still relatively busy trade between Istanbul and Venice with the special importance of the Ottoman capital in the

---

[33] See below, Chapter Two.

[34] *E.g.* ASV, Sen., Delib. CP, reg. 3, f. 20 (May 1565); ASV, Sen., Disp. CP, filza 1, f. 49 (Mar. 1566), f. 422 (Dec. 1566), f. 475 (Feb. 1567). See also G.E. Rothenberg, "Venice and the Uskoks of Senj, 1537-1618", *Journal of Modern History*, 33 (1961), pp. 148-156; A. Tenenti, *Piracy and the Decline of Venice*, London, 1967, pp. 1-15; A. Shmuelevitz, *The Jews of the Ottoman Empire in the Late Fifteenth and the Sixteenth Centuries. Administrative, Economic, Legal and Social Relations as Reflected in the Responsa*, Leiden, 1984, p. 165; B. Simon, "Venise et les corsaires (1558-1560)", *Byzantinische Forschungen*, 12 (1987), pp. 701-702.

larger framework of Venetian interests, transformed any issue connected with the commercial relations between the two cities into a major problem of Venetian foreign policy, and could also have repercussions on Venetian social organization. We have already noted that the success of Jewish businessmen, from the 1530s on, in gaining a firm hold on the international trade with *Romania* resulted in Venice being forced to integrate the Levantine Jewish merchants into its own system of international trade, and finally also to accept them, willy-nilly, as part of the Venetian social reality. But when the clouds of war approached the Venetian lagoons in the late 1560s, the Levantine Jews found themselves drawn into the confrontation between the two powers. Jewish merchants of the Ghetto Vecchio were arrested during the war of Cyprus (1570-73), and their merchandise was confiscated by the Republic.[35] The religious and patriotic fervour which characterized the war period finally led to the Senate's decision to expel all the Jews from Venice. Though later abrogated, this move was directly related to the process described above, in which Jews were increasingly viewed as rivals and enemies, an image which was easily extended, aided by traditional Christian attitudes, from the Levantine Jewish merchants to Jews in general.[36]

It is significant that the revocation of the decree of expulsion, following the conclusion of the war in 1573, also stemmed from the activities of Jews in Istanbul. Solomon Ashkenazi, a key figure in the peace negotiations between the two powers, approached the Venetian authorities, asking them to reconsider their treatment of his Venetian brethren. The diplomatic services of this extraordinary Jewish physician were still indispensable to Venice, and his intercession in favour of the Venetian Jews must have carried some weight. Moreover, at the same time, Jewish merchants of Istanbul proposed to transfer their commercial activities from Ancona to Venice, or to the nearby Venetian port of Chioggia. Another Levantine Jew, Daniel Rodriga, may also have been active on the same occasion in trying to change Venice's

---

[35] See below, pp. 64-65, and the Appendix, No V. It should be stressed that Ottoman subjects of Christian faith were excluded from these measures. Merchandise belonging to Ottoman subjects had also been sequestrated at the beginning of the earlier war between the two states in 1537, see Ravid, "The First Charter", pp. 189-190.

[36] See below, Chapter Three.

anti-Jewish policy by offering tempting commercial proposals.[37]

                                    ***

Until recently, the growing participation of Jews in the international
trade of the Ottoman Empire during the sixteenth century has been
known mainly from the testimonies of foreign travellers and diplomatic
agents, who generally reported their impressions in verbal descriptions
rather than in figures.[38] Consequently, it has been impossible to reach
a quantitative evaluation of the scope of the Jewish involvement in
this field. Even the rich archives of the Venetian Republic do not seem
to have preserved a lot of quantitative material which could help us
to draw a clearer picture of this chapter in the economic history of
the Jews. However, the Venetian archives do contain bits of evidence
which may elucidate, at least partially, the nebulous picture of Jewish
participation in the trade between Venice and Istanbul after the establishment of the Ghetto Vecchio. The 1541 enactment, including the statement
that Jewish merchants held the greater part of trading transactions
between Venice and 'Upper and lower Romania' is, of course, of great
significance. Quantitative data related to the activities of individual
merchants have barely come to light until now. The case of Ḥayyim
Saruq, a Jewish businessman from among the *Levantini*, who was active
in the trade between these two cities, is particularly interesting in this
respect, and will be discussed in greater detail in two of the following
chapters. In the present context it is enough to note that when Saruq
went bankrupt in 1566, his debts, according to his own estimate,
amounted to the considerable sum of 112,000 ducats, including interest
payments at the rate of 40% per annum. Attempting to get rid of his
debts, Saruq agreed to transfer merchandise which he had imported
from the East, including alum, camlets, wool and hides, to his creditors.
The value of these goods was estimated at 77,000 ducats. Saruq's
property at that moment also included three small vessels (*bregantini*)
worth 1,000 ducats each.[39] By way of comparison, in 1560 the Venetian *Bailo* evaluated the entire capital invested by Venetians in import

---

[37] See below, Chapter Five.

[38] See, for instance, the testimonies cited in Baron, *A Social and Religious History*,
vol. 18, pp. 236-37.

[39] On Saruq and his bankruptcy, see below, Chapter Six.

to and export from Istanbul at about 280,000 ducats.[40] The capital invested by Saruq and his associates in Venice and Istanbul seems impressive, all the more since they were certainly not the only Jewish merchants in this trade.

A memorandum by the Venetian Board of Trade (*Cinque savi alla mercanzia*) from 1584 also includes some quantitative data regarding the trading activities of the Levantine merchants of the Ghetto Vecchio.[41] According to this document, merchandise imported by these Jews to Venice brought an annual income of 14,000 ducats to the Venetian customs, while the customs dues deriving from merchandise exported by them came to 24,000 ducats. The same memorandum evaluates the capital invested annually by these merchants in exports from Venice at 460,000 ducats; it attributes great importance to Jewish imports from the Levant and their contribution to Venetian economy, although it states that it would be difficult to measure their overall value. These figures can be juxtaposed with the ones cited by Braudel, referring to 1583-5, according to which Venice's overall maritime export to destinations within the Adriatic sea (*dentro del golfo fin a Corfù*) was worth 1,600,000 ducats, and to destinations outside the Adriatic—600,000 ducats.[42]

Venetian sources from the late sixteenth and early seventeenth century still point to the important role played by Jewish merchants in the trade between Venice and the Ottoman capital. The Venetian *Bailo* Matteo Zane noted in 1594 that Jews were in control of Istanbul's trade and customs administration (*le mercanzie, il traffico e li dazi sono in loro mani*).[43] A similar statement may be found in the report of the *Bailo* Contarini of 1612.[44] It should be noted that the Venetian *Baili*'s observations are much more reliable than those of other foreign observers,

---

[40] *Relazioni*, ed. Albèri, III, vol. 1, pp. 274-275; Simon, "Contribution", p. 977.

[41] ASV, Cinque savi alla mercanzia, reg. 137, ff. 135v-136 (18 Dec. 1584).

[42] Braudel, *The Mediterranean*, vol. 1, p. 128, n. 91.

[43] Relazioni, Albèri, ser. III, vol. 3, Florence, 1855, pp. 389-443 (rel. Matteo Zane, 1594).

[44] Baron, *A Social and Religious History*, vol. 18, p. 237. *Bailo* Contarini actually referred to the greater part of the commercial transactions (and not to "commission houses", as Baron translated the word *facende*) as being in the hands of Jews. Contarini demanded that the Jews should also pay the tax imposed by the Venetian *Bailo* in Istanbul on wares shipped to Venice or brought thence (and not "the land tax", as Baron translated the term *cottimo di terra*).

considering their long stay in the Ottoman capital and their constant occupation with matters of international trade. We may also quote two memorials presented in the first decade of the seventeenth century to the Venetian Senate. The first was presented by Alvise Sanuto, one of the *Cinque savi alla mercanzia*, in 1603. In this document, in which he sought to curtail the privileges of Jewish merchants in Venice, Sanuto stated that whereas in former times, of the merchants in Constantinople who were engaged in trade with Venice three quarters were Venetian subjects and one quarter were Jews and Turks, at his times (1603) the proportion was reversed in favour of the Ottoman subjects.[45] Even if exaggerated, this statement by a senior magistrate in a memorandum to the Senate deserves serious consideration. The second memorial was presented in 1609 by the *Cinque savi* as a collective body, in the course of their dispute with another magistracy, the *Cattaver*, regarding the jurisdiction over the Ghetto Vecchio. In this memorandum the Savi declared that in addition to the trade through Spalato, the Republic was benefitting from the trade of "that nation" (*i.e.*, the Jewish traders) "with Constantinople and other Eastern countries", the greater part of which was in the hands of these merchants.[46] Finally, in 1625, the *Cinque savi* noted that Venice gained about 100,000 ducats every year from customs dues levied on merchandise imported and exported by the Jewish merchants.[47]

The importance of the Jewish share in Venice's maritime trade with these regions was questioned a few years ago by Bernard Blumenkranz. Availing himself only of data regarding maritime insurance drawn from the registers of two Venetian notaries, which had been published by Alberto Tenenti, Blumenkranz suggested that the relative importance of Jewish merchants and their merchandise in the maritime trade between Venice and certain Ottoman provinces, during the years covered by Tenenti's study (1592-1609), was not as great as had been claimed by Tenenti and Cecil Roth.[48] The attempt to draw general conclusions

---

[45] Maestro, *L'attività economica*, p. 54.

[46] *Ibid.*, pp. 57-58. In January 1610, the *Cinque savi* again declared that the Jewish merchants controlled the trade "with Spalato and Constantinople", *ibid.*, p. 63.

[47] Maestro, *L'attività economica*, p. 71.

[48] B. Blumenkranz, "Les Juifs dans le commerce maritime de Venise (1592-1609), à propos d'un livre recent", *Revue des Etudes Juives*, 3rd ser., 2 (1961), pp. 143-151, reviewing A. Tenenti, *Naufrages, corsaires et assurance maritime à Venise, 1592-1609,*

about the extent of Jewish participation in Venice's maritime trade, merely on the basis of the said notarial registers, seems rather questionable. In the first place, it should be noted that all the insurance contracts referred to in those documents, which are actually cessions of rights by the insured in favour of the insurers, were signed in Venice. However, it is most likely that some of the merchandise and ships which sailed between Venice and the East, especially those belonging to Ottoman Jews and heading westward, were insured in the Ottoman Empire, and may have left no traces in the registers of the two Venetian notaries.[49] Secondly, even assuming that most of the insurance contracts covering trade between Venice and the East were drawn up and executed in Venice, there is no basis for the assumption that practically all the affairs of maritime insurance in that city were concentrated in the hands of those two notaries, whose registers served Tenenti for his book. Thirdly, the attacks by Christian pirates against Jewish merchants and their merchandise could have induced some of these traders to send their goods under Christian names, a device already encountered in different circumstances.[50] In this context we should also note the presence of *Marranos* in Venice, some of whom were rather prosperous and, as we shall see, were also involved, directly or indirectly, in Venice's trade with the eastern Mediterranean. Obviously, in the documents discussed by Blumenkranz they do not figure as Jews, though, as their contemporaries believed and modern scholarship has confirmed, their religious identity was often rather ambivalent. Fourthly, limiting our discussion to the route between Venice and Istanbul, it should be noted that the ports of Valona and Corfu, where Jewish trade with Venice was prominent even according to Blumenkranz, as well as Spalato, Ragusa and other ports, could serve as entrepôts on the long route between the Venetian lagoon and the Bosporus, combining land routes across the Balkans with shorter maritime passages across the Adriatic.[51] To these remarks we may add the illuminating information

---

Paris, 1959.

[49] On maritime insurance as practiced among Ottoman Jewish merchants in the sixteenth century, see Shmuelevitz, *The Jews of the Ottoman Empire*, pp. 149-153.

[50] *Cf.* Jacoby, "Les Juifs à Venise", pp. 201-202; Ashtor, "The Jews in the Mediterranean Trade", p. 449.

[51] *Cf.* Braudel, *The Mediterranean*, pp. 285-289; Paci, *La 'scala' di Spalato, passim*, esp. pp. 16, 51 and n. 27, 62-64, 94.

included in Alberto and Branislava Tenenti's book on maritime insurance
in Ragusa during the second half of the sixteenth century. Merchants
who shipped their goods from this important Adriatic port did not always
have recourse to maritime insurance, and even when they did, they
often did not cover the full value of the merchandise involved. Of special
relevance to the present discussion is the impression drawn from this
material, that Jewish merchants tended to undervalue their insured goods
to a greater extent than did the Christians.[52] It is likely that similar
patterns could be traced among Jewish merchants in Venice during
the same period. The use of evidence from the Venetian insurance market
as a measure of Jewish participation in Venice's maritime trade is
therefore problematic. Indeed, the listed considerations reinforce my
impression that the share of Jewish merchants in the international trade
between Venice and Istanbul was considerably larger than the mere
ten percent attributed to this route by Blumenkranz.

The cited patchy, quantitative, or quasi-quantitative evidence does
not allow us to trace the ups and downs of Jewish participation in
Venice's trade with the Ottoman Balkans and Istanbul. But all these
documents point in the same direction, namely, that between 1540 and
1625, and probably also earlier and later, Jewish traders occupied a
central position, and at certain times even a hegemonic position, in
Venice's trade with these regions. This general statement will be
elucidated in greater detail in some of the following chapters.

[52] A. and B. Tenenti, *Il prezzo del rischio. L'assicurazione mediterranea vista
da Ragusa (1563-1591)*, Rome, 1985, pp. 130-131, 160-166.

CHAPTER TWO

ABRAHAM CASTRO MULTIPLIED: VENETIAN TRADERS AND JEWISH CUSTOMS FARMERS IN THE LEVANT, c. 1530 - c. 1540

Before the establishment of the *Levantini* in the Ghetto Vecchio in Venice, most of the contacts between Venetian merchants and Jewish entrepreneurs seem to have taken place in the Levant. One particular phenomenon, which preceded the massive penetration of Jews into the international trade itself, was the appearance of a relatively large number of Jewish customs-farmers in key positions of the Levant trade. The present chapter deals with this phenomenon as it arose in the ports of Egypt and Syria, particularly during the fourth decade of the sixteenth century. Beside a discussion of the growing dependence of Venetian maritime trade on Jewish customs-farmers in the Levant, this chapter also points to the great potential of Venetian sources for the study of Jews in the Ottoman Empire, especially in reference to trade and navigation.

Abraham Castro, one of the heroes of 'The Book of Egypt's Purim'—which describes, from a Jewish viewpoint, the revolt of Ahmet Pasha against the central government in Istanbul (1523-24)[1]—has again attracted interest, this time among Israeli scholars. Six articles have been published in the past ten years of which he is the main subject, most of them offering new source evidence and raising new questions, which remained largely unanswered. The subject of Abraham Castro is particularly interesting, not only because of the historical problems involved, but also because it can be observed from a variety of sources: Hebrew ones (chronicles, letters, dedications, *responsa*), Arabic,

---

[1] Y.Y. Yehuda, "The Egyptian Scroll", *Reshumot*, Vol. 5 (1927), pp. 385-403 [Hebrew]. See A. David, "The Termination of the Office of *Nagid* in Egypt and Biographical Data Concerning the Life of Abraham Castro", *Tarbiz*, 41 (1972), pp. 332, n. 42 [Hebrew]. On the revolt of Ahmet Pasha, see P.M. Holt, Egypt and the Fertile Crescent, 1516-1922, London, 1966, pp. 48-51 and M. Winter, *Egyptian Society under Ottoman Rule, 1517-1798*, London, 1992, pp. 14-16.

Ottoman, and, as we shall see, Western sources too.

To recapitulate briefly the development of the historiographic discussion of the subject. To the best of my knowledge, the first serious study concerning Castro was written by Abraham Pollack in 1936.[2] Pollack's study, which was based mainly on the Arabic chronicle of Ibn Iyās, focused on two issues: Abraham Castro's position as the head of the Egyptian mint in the early days of Ottoman rule in Egypt, and the fate of the presidency (*Negidut*) of Egypt's Jewish community in the transition from Mamlūk to Ottoman rule. In contrast to Graetz and Rozanes, Pollack maintained that Castro was not the first Jew to head the mint in Egypt. He linked the active role of Jews in the money market of Egypt with the management of the mint, against the background of the general trend to speculative investment at the end of the Mamlūk period, and noted that at that time, and perhaps even in the early days of the Ottoman rule, the mint was managed by a Jew by name of *mu'alim* Ya'qūb. On the basis of certain testimonies, Pollack concluded that Castro was appointed to the post some time between late 1519 and 1520/21. In the same chronicle Pollack also found the curious story of Castro's Ethiopian maidservant, who had a daughter by him and later declared herself to be a Muslim, thereby depriving him of the child. This story was recorded in 1521, when Castro was still described as the head of the mint. The second issue on which Pollack focused was, as we have noted, that of the presidency of the Jewish community. We know that there is some obscurity in the Jewish sources regarding the end of the Jewish *Negidut* in Egypt at the end of the Mamlūk period, and one source even attributed the position to Abraham Castro. Pollack found no reference in Ibn Iyās to Castro as *Ra'īs al-yahūd* ('Head of the Jews'), which is the Arabic equivalent to *Nagid*. He speculates that among the Jews the title continued as an honorary epithet, without any official standing.

The second article on the subject of Abraham Castro was published about twenty years ago by Abraham David, and reawakened the interest in this figure.[3] David dealt with the two issues that Pollack had raised, but expanded the discussion by analyzing the Hebrew sources, some of which had not been previously examined in this connection. David

---

[2] A.N. Pollack, "The Jews and the Egyptian Mint in the Times of the Mamluks and the beginning of the Turkish Rule," *Zion*, 1 (1935), pp. 24-36 [Hebrew].

[3] David, "The Termination", pp. 325-337.

rejected Pollack's hypothesis that the title *Nagid* had lapsed from an official designation into an honorary epithet. He lended credence to the testimony of Rabbi David ben Zimra, who was a contemporary and lived in the same region, namely that the position of *Nagid* ceased to exist following the Ottoman conquest, in contrast to the statement of Joseph Sambari, who lived in the seventeenth century, that the *Negidut* survived until the late sixteenth century. David noted, moreover, that Joseph Sambari, who referred to Abraham Castro as one of the last *Negidim*, also wrote that Sultan Süleyman "built the walls of Jerusalem with the help of the late *Nagid* Rabbi Abraham Castro, who was the governor of the mint of Egypt" (We know that the city walls of Jerusalem were built between 1536 and 1540). Another testimony, a dedication to Abraham Castro in the book *Even Hashoham*, written in Jerusalem in 1537 by the kabbalist Joseph Ibn Ziyyaḥ, led David to conclude that Castro must have left Egypt at some point and settled in Jerusalem no later than 1537, where he was "the moving spirit" in the building of the new city walls. David even speculated that Castro served as the head of the Jewish community in Jerusalem at that time.

In addition to these interesting testimonies, David's article includes a number of complementary elements from the Hebrew sources. References in the writings of David Hareuveni and Elijah Capsali reveal that Castro headed the Egyptian mint at least until 1524. This is an important date, for in that year ended the revolt of Ahmet Pasha, the governor of Egypt, in the course of which Castro proved his loyalty to the central government in Istanbul. As a result, he was held in high regard by the authorities, as well as by the Jewish community which benefitted from his status. This affair was described, as noted above, in 'The Book of Egypt's *Purim*', which saw several editions.[4] Another testimony, quoted by David in the same article, is by the traveller Moses Basola. Passing through Beirut in 1522, Basola noted that in that city there was "a great man serving the governor, by name of Abraham Castro, who stands at the gate of the customs-house, in full charge and authority thereof". David rejected the possibility that this might be a reference to another man by the same name, suggesting that Abraham Castro, while running the Egyptian mint, could also have been responsible for the customs-house in Beirut. As he put it, "It is difficult to imagine that these are two senior entrepreneurs with identical

---

[4] *Ibid.*, Note 1.

given names and family-names, active at the same time, one in Egypt
and the other in Syria".

A brief article by David Tamar in 1972 took issue with some of
David's conclusions.[5] As Tamar saw it, Sambari's testimony combined
with the dedication in Ibn Ẕiyyah's book do not add up to sufficient
proof that Castro moved to Jerusalem in his later years. He suggested
that we consider the possibility that there were indeed two men of
identical given and family names, since, in his view, it is difficult to
reconcile the position of Castro, the public figure and financier, with
the titles with which he is lauded in the Hebrew literature of the period
- "the divine sage", "saintly man of God", "a great teacher of God's
Law to His people".

An interesting development in the study of this personage took place
in 1980, when Ḥayyim Gerber published a testimony concerning
"*mu'alim* Ibrāhīm", from an incomplete and undated Ottoman document
that was found in the binding of an old volume in a private collection.[6]
Gerber sought to conflate the fragments of information in the Ottoman
document—which looks like a copy of an official paper—with the
biographical data of Abraham Castro, as reconstructed by David. From
the title of the same "*mu'alim* Ibrāhīm", who is mentioned in the
document ([*Amīr*] '*umarā*' *al-millah al-yahūdiyah*), Gerber concludes
that a form of "*de facto* presidency" continued to exist among the Jews
of Egypt in the early Ottoman period, and that this might have been
the embryonic precursor of the *millet* system, which would be institution-
alized in the Ottoman empire in the nineteenth century.

Castro's important position in the financial world of one of the chief
provinces of the Ottoman Empire, and the various testimonies which
link him to significant events in that Empire, left room for hope that
additional Ottoman documents might be found which would fill gaps
in the biography of this personage. This hope was fulfilled in 1982,
with the publication of Amnon Cohen's article concerning the building

---

[5] D. Tamar, "Three Comments to the Article 'The Termination of the Office of
Nagid in Egypt and Biographical Data Concerning the Life of Abraham Castro'",
Tarbiẓ, 43 (1974), pp. 325-337 [Hebrew].

[6] H. Gerber, "An Unknown Turkish Document on Abraham Castro", *Zion*, 45
(1980), pp. 158-163 [Hebrew].

of the city walls of Jerusalem.[7] Cohen had discovered in the archives of the *Sharī'ah* court in Jerusalem some new and even startling testimonies concerning our protagonist.

Cohen did not find in the archives any confirmation of Abraham Castro's direct connection with the building of Jerusalem's city walls. On the contrary, he produced explicit and unequivocal testimonies showing that the person in charge of the construction was one Mehmed Çelebi al-Naqqāsh, who was sent for the purpose from the Ottoman capital to Jerusalem. However, while there is no evidence in the Muslim court's archives to support Joseph Sambari's seventeenth-century statement on the subject, other material clearly links Castro to Jerusalem in the years when the walls were being built. Cohen produced several testimonies showing that Abraham Castro supplied the governor of Cairo with credit amounting to over 10,000 *'uthmānī*, which were destined for the construction of the walls of Jerusalem. Moreover, the sources discovered by Cohen indicate that Castro had property in Jerusalem and invested money in purchasing additional land, for the purpose of building residences within the walls and perhaps without. These testimonies, which date from the years 1538 and 1558, as well as another document from 1540, suggest that Abraham Castro held an important position in the Jewish community in Jerusalem, in addition to his official position as "head collector of taxes for the Sultan", though they do not state where and when he held this position.

Cohen suggested that the Ottoman authorities made use of Castro's capabilities and experience when he stayed in Jerusalem when the city walls were being built, supposedly as an assistant to Mehmed Çelebi al-Naqqāsh. What these documents do reveal, he said, is the economic status of some of the Jews of Jerusalem, the fact that they could purchase real-estate and develop it, and were able to participate in the administration of this province of the Empire. But in addition to all these, Cohen introduced a piece of evidence which could be described as sensational. In a document dating from 1540, the epithet after Castro's name is not 'the Jew', as in the documents from 1538 and 1558, but "Ibrāhīm

---

[7] A. Cohen, "Were the Walls of Jerusalem Built by Abraham Castro?", *Zion*, 47 (1982), pp. 407-418 [Hebrew]. See also *idem*, "The Walls of Jerusalem", in C.E. Bosworth et alii, eds., *The Islamic World from Classical to Modern Times: Essays in Honour of Bernard Lewis*, Princeton, 1989, pp. 467-477, where Cohen supplemented his Hebrew article with a few additional points.

Castro *al-muhtadī*, official tax-collector [*'āmil*] for the Sultan". The adjective *muhtadī*, which signifies 'one who returns to the true path', was applied to converts to Islam, from which Cohen concluded that Abraham Castro had indeed become a Muslim.

If Castro converted, how is it possible that later Jewish documents still referred to him as a Jew, and indeed praised him highly? Cohen's article proposed no solution to the puzzle. One might also ask why the epithet 'the Jew' continued to appear after Castro's name in the records of the Muslim court from 1558, eighteen years after he was described as a Muslim convert?

Cohen's discovery prompted Eliav Shochetman to publish an article on the subject of Abraham Castro, whose main purpose was the rejection of the theory that he converted to Islam.[8] According to Shochetman, the term *muhtadī* could be interpreted simply as 'one who follows the true path', and might also have been a copying error or misunderstanding. As he put it, it is inconceivable that a man who converted to Islam would be described in later Jewish sources in such glowing terms. Shochetman's article emphasized the spiritual aspects of Abraham Castro's personality, describing him as associating with the kabbalists, encouraging scholars and aiding them. Like Abraham David, he discounted the possibility that there were two Abraham Castro: "there is little likelihood that two men by the same name engaged in the same occupation at the same time". However, he added: "this is not entirely impossible".

In 1985 David published another article about Abraham Castro, summing up the known facts and adding further testimonies, this time from the Cairo *Geniza*.[9] The main evidence comes from an undated letter written by Abraham Castro, which shows that our protagonist was head of the customs administration in Alexandria. In the letter, which was sent from Alexandria to a group of Jewish merchants, Castro informs them that he had sent the 'tower men' to capture a ship which tried to escape from the harbour, and promises them that the affair would cause them no real harm. The article also dealt with Castro's estate and his heirs, but that subject falls outside the present discussion.

---

[8] E. Shochetman, "Additional Information on the Life of Abraham Castro", *Zion*, 48 (1983), pp. 387-405 [Hebrew].

[9] A. David, "New Data about Abraham Castro in Some Cairo Geniza Documents", *Michael*, 9 (1985), pp. 147-162 [Hebrew].

We see, then, that some questions about the personality of Abraham Castro remained unanswered. Was he or was he not the *Nagid* of Egypt's Jewry? Did he or did he not supervise the construction of the walls of Jerusalem? Did he convert to Islam, or was he the Jewish "saintly man of God"? Was he a financier of international stature, who headed the Egyptian mint as well as the customs house in Beirut, and perhaps also in Alexandria? Or were there, after all, two men of the same given and family names?

Some of these questions, though not all, can be answered on the basis of Venetian sources, which had not yet been examined in this connection. During the period under consideration, many Venetians and the Venetian state itself had major interests in the Ottoman Levant. The principal routes of international trade, one of the main sources of the Republic's wealth and power, passed through the Ottoman Empire, and most of Venice's overseas territories lay within the sphere of that Empire's expansion. In addition to the Republic's permanent representative (*Bailo*) at the Sublime Porte in Istanbul, Venice maintained a regular network of consuls at the main loci of international trade, such as Alexandria, or at the provincial capitals of the Turkish empire, such as Damascus. All these representatives maintained continuous contact with the central government in Venice. To these must be added the commanders of the fleets of merchant galleys, which sailed annually along regular routes, the captains of private merchant vessels,[10] and the various Venetian merchants, all of whom reported back about events and problems they encountered in the course of their business activities in the Eastern Mediterranean. These reports, official and unofficial alike, were closely studied by the Venetians authorities, which discussed them rather frequently. The following analysis is based on these sources, only some of which have been published. Of all the sources which had so far been mined on the subject of Abraham Castro, the material offered here is, for sheer quantity, the richest.

The first reference to Abraham Castro (giving his full name), which I have found in the Venetians sources, appears in a report to the Venetian authorities by Giovanni Alvise Bembo, the commander of a fleet of two merchant galleys which sailed to Alexandria in August 1530 and

---

[10] On the distinction between galleys and regular merchant ships, see Lane, "Venetian Shipping During the Commercial Revolution", pp. 219-239, reprinted in *Venice and History*, pp. 3-24.

returned in February 1531. This is an unusually brief document, but about one half of it is devoted to our protagonist, as follows:

> ... There is in Alexandria a Jew by name of Abraham Castro, a *mu'alim*. He is a deadly enemy of our nation, and I have been told that he has contracted to collect all the customs duty at Alexandria on behalf of the Sultan, in return for 85,000 ducats a year, that is to say, a year which includes visiting galleys loading goods. When there are no loading galleys, he pays only 55,000 ducats. As soon as the galleys arrive, the said Jew, seeing that the quantity of spices is small, meaning that he would have but little profit, intercedes with the Pasha, with the aid of lavish payment, for the latter to ban all such trade and prevent the export of what little spices there be while the galleys are in harbour. This is what happened this year - he troubled them greatly, which caused great loss to the Sultan and brought ruin to the galleys. His Highness [the Doge] will be sure to know what steps to take...[11]

Here Abraham Castro is described in the Venetian sources as head of the customs house at Alexandria in October 1530, when the said Venetian galleys arrived, matching the position attributed to him by David on the basis of the undated *Geniza* document.[12] In addition, this short report reveals the Porte's income from the Alexandria customs duty and the important share of the Venetian trade in this income, as well as Castro's position, his influence with the governor and his bad relations with the Venetian merchants. Of course, the Venetian merchants who traded in the Levant ports, particularly those engaged in the spice trade, had other, no less difficult, problems to contend with, above

---

[11] For the full Italian text of this report, see the Appendix. The sailing of the fleet of galleys to Alexandria and its return were documented in the diary of Marino Sanuto. See principally Sanuto, *I diarii*, vol. 53, cols. 265, 389, 482; *Ibid.*, vol. 54, col. 297.

[12] According to the letter of the Venetian consul in Alexandria, the fleet of galleys commanded by Giovanni Alvise Bembo arrived on 6 October 1530. See Sanuto, *I diarii*, vol. 54, col. 184. It should be noted that farming the customs in Alexandria was apparently linked with other governmental functions. Official Venetian documents from the early 1550s show that the Jewish customs farmer of Alexandria—who is described in Venetian documents as *malem* or *malen* [*mu'alim*], *scaliero* (port-master) or *nadar* [*nāzir*]—was authorized to sell wheat for export to the Venetian merchants; see *Ibid.*, cols. 295, 305.

all the competition of the Portuguese route around Africa. But the document shows that at this time the Venetians ascribed a central role to Abraham Castro where their commercial activity in Egypt was concerned. One might add that the galleys mentioned did indeed return to Venice without spices, and the merchants who had invested their capital in this voyage suffered heavy losses.[13]

Giovanni Alvise Bembo was not alone in attributing the difficulties of Venetian commerce in Egypt to the Jewish customs-farmer. Venetian sources of the early 1530s contain numerous complaints about the activities of Abraham Castro, the customs-farmer of Alexandria. A letter from the Venetian consul in Alexandria, Nadalin Contarini, sent to Venice in January 1532, includes the following paragraph:

> This scoundrel, the Jewish customs-farmer Abraham Castro, is the source of all our troubles... A ship of 400 barrels (*botte*), owned by the Pasha of Cairo, laden with wheat and rice, bound for North Africa (Barbaria), foundered on that night [23 January] because of that villainous Jew customs man, who daily does his best to harm us. All the consuls have complained about him to the Sublime Porte, but to no avail. The Pasha does nothing without his advice. Ser Zuan Francesco Venier, son of Ser Nicolo, concluded

---

[13] For the farming of customs duties in Egypt and the role of the Jews in it, see S. Shtober, "On the Issue of Customs Collectors in Egypt", *Pe'amim*, 38 (1989), pp. 68-94 [Hebrew]. For the title *mu'alim* and its application to tax and customs collectors in the rabbinical literature, see E. Bashan, "Economic Life from the 16th to the 18th Century", in *The Jews in Ottoman Egypt (1515-1917)*, ed. J.M. Landau, Jerusalem, 1988, p. 99, n. 181 [Hebrew]. For more on this title and its use in this context, see A. Cohen, *Jewish Life Under Islam. Jerusalem in the Sixteenth Century*, Cambridge, Mass. and London, 1984, pp. 141, 145-46, 170; As we have seen, "*m'ualim* Ibrāhīm" is mentioned in the document published by Gerber, quoted above, and likewise in the chronicle of Ibn Iyās, as quoted in Pollack,"The Jews and the Egyptian Mint", pp. 29-31 (*mu'alim Dār al-Darb*), and in the judicial document quoted in Cohen, "Were the Walls of Jerusalem Built by Abraham Castro?", p. 409 (*mu'alim* Ibrāhīm, son of Joseph, known as Castro). For the use of the term *mu'alim* (as *malen* or *malem*) in the Venetian sources, see Sanuto, *I diarii*, vol. 57, col. 268 (13 Oct. 1532); ASV, Senato, Mar, reg. 32, f. 58 (22 Sept. 1555); Lorenzo Tiepolo, *Relazioni dei Consolati di Alessandria e di Siria per la Repubblica Veneta negli anni 1552-1560*, ed. E. Cicogna, Venezia, 1857, p. 16 (1555), and above, p. 36 and n. 12. For the term *scalliero*, see C. Poma, "Il consolato Veneto in Egitto con le relazioni dei consoli Daniele Barbarigo (1554) e Marco Zen (1664)", *Bollettino del Ministerio degli Affari Esteri*, 109 (1897), p. 32. For the title *nadar* [*nāzir*] in the Venetian sources: Sanuto, *I diarii*, vol. 56, col. 314, (June 1532); *ibid.* vol. 58, cols. 716-717 (June 1533).

with a Muslim to purchase five *qintars* of long pepper, and hoped for the
best. But the Jew intervened and prevented the sale, as he himself was
interested in the goods, and indeed obtained his consent for this purpose.[14]

Other letters sent from Alexandria to Venice in 1532 shed additional
light on the continuous conflict between Castro and the Venetian
merchants. A letter written on the 12th of May by Hieronimo Contarini,
the commander of the Venetian fleet of merchant galleys in Alexandria,
states:

> The Jew Abraham Castro, the customs-farmer, who is the misfortune of
> this port city and of our nation, has caused the Pasha to issue three orders,
> in [one of] which he orders to bring to shore the consul Polo Bembo, at
> the demand of one Jew. Another [order] concerned one of the merchants
> and the third, my sailing master (*armiraio*). The last matter was arranged
> by means of a bribe (si conzo in manzarie), and likewise the matter of
> the merchant.[15]

Evidently Abraham Castro detained the Venetian ships in port because
of claims made by local persons, including one Jew, against the Venetian
merchants and captains, and he made use of his influence with the
governor to stop the Venetian consul from leaving Egypt at the end
of his tour of office, and perhaps to arrest him. It is tempting to link
this information with the *Geniza* letter published by David, which deals
with a similar affair, though it does not explicitly mention the Venetians.
However, we cannot be certain that the two sources refer to same event,
as such incidents were probably fairly common in those days.

Additional details about this and other events appear in the later
letters of the Venetian consul in Alexandria. An undated letter written
by Consul Contarini, which was received in Venice on 1 June of that
year, says: "A special messenger (*Çavuş*) has arrived from Cairo,
bearing letters from the Pasha concerning the same Francesco de Vigo,
son of Ser Domenico, who had fled from there burdened with debts
to the Arabs (*Mori*), the Turks and the Jews, as well as the Sultan and
the *nadar*, the Jew Abraham Castro." The consul asks the Signory

---

[14] The consuls' letters are quoted in Sanuto's diaries. For Consul Contarini's letter,
see Sanuto, *I diarii*, vol. 56, col. 85.

[15] *Ibid.*, vol. 56, col. 298.

to take the appropriate steps. Further on in the same letter the consul writes about two vessels, one owned by Piero Lucasolta and the other by Zorzi Vagolin of Corfu, which had been loaded with wheat by a Genoese and were about to sail with the said cargo under a Venetian flag from Alexandria to Djerba, part of the shipping fee having already been paid. The vessels were seized by a caravel with a crew of 24, on the pretext that they were pirate ships. They were forced to pay the full shipping fees in Alexandria and even to share the cargo (with the caravel) - which the consul described as intolerable. Contarini goes on to say that the same Jew Castro had sent a petition ('*arḍ*) in this matter to the Pasha, wherein he claimed that the sailing master (*armiraio*) of the galleys, one Saba, was a business partner of the said Lucasolta. As a result, the Pasha issued the order to detain the galleys, since it concerned the Sultan's finances.[16]

On 9 June 1532 letters from the consul in Alexandria were read out before the Venetian Senate, which described the arrest of the former consul, Polo Bembo, as a result of Abraham Castro's connivance. The consul had complained about him before the Kadi and the *Amīn*, and even threatened to appeal to the Sublime Porte.[17] On 7 August that year the Senate received a report from the commander of the fleet of merchant galleys which had returned from Egypt, also complaining about the Jewish customs-farmer, Abraham Castro, who had grievously harmed the Venetian merchants. The report recommended that the galleys avoid Alexandria, and go instead to the 'old port'.[18] In November another letter arrived from Consul Contarini, which had been sent on 2 August that year, in which he asked to see to it that the Porte issue a decree forbidding the Jew Abraham Castro from detaining the Venetian vessels longer that the period agreed in advance.[19] On 13 October Consul Contarini dispatched another letter to Venice, with another interesting tale about our protagonist. According to the consul, "*Mu'alim* Ibrāhīm Castro the Jew" (*malem Abraim Castro zudeo*) had gone to

---

[16] *Ibid.*, col. 314. For the term 'arḍ, or, as the Venetian called it - *arzo*, see H. Gibb and H. Bowen, *Islamic Society and the West. A Study of the Impact of Western Civilization on Moslem Culture in the Near East*, London-New York-Toronto, 1963, p. 116, n.2.

[17] Sanuto, *I diarii*, vol. 56, col. 373.

[18] *Ibid.*, col. 682.

[19] *Ibid.*, vol. 57, col. 267.

Cairo and there spent 2000 ducats bribing the Pasha, 1000 ducats bribing
the 'mirigiani', and a further 2000 ducats on various other bribes. But
when the accounts were examined, it transpired that he still owed the
Sultan 80,000 Venetian ducats. Having given his written promise to
pay the sum, he obtained the contract for the customs of Alexandria
for another year. In the meantime, on 2 September, as he was about
to leave Cairo, the caravan from Mecca arrived, and with it Scander
[Iskender] Çelebi, the *Defterdār* (Master of the treasury) of Istanbul.
Castro complained to this great personage about the Pasha in Cairo
who, as he claimed, had defrauded him. After Castro left Cairo the
Pasha heard about it and ordered him to return, and even sent orders
to Alexandria to remove him from the management of the customs.
The consul makes no attempt to disguise his satisfaction with these
developments. He writes: "While I am consul we shall live here in
peace, now that the scoundrel has been removed from his post, for
so long as it was in his hands, everything was going to rack and ruin...."
He goes on to report that he expects large consignments of spices, which
it will finally be possible to purchase without hindrance from Abraham
Castro.[20]

On 12 November, about a fortnight before he died, Consul Contarini
sent one more letter from Alexandria to Venice, describing how his
predecessor was released from prison. The consul had received letters
from the Signory addressed to the Pasha in Cairo, and sent them on
at once with Lorenzo Morosini, who was accompanied by the interpreter
of the consulate. Morosini read out the letter before the Pasha, but
the interpreter translated it in a manner which was favourable to
Abraham Castro. The latter heard about it and hurried to the *Divan*,
but the Pasha, who had not forgiven him, dismissed him angrily.
Subsequently, the Pasha sent an order to the Kadi and the *Amīn* of
Alexandria ordering the release of the former consul Bembo. The Pasha
claimed that he was unaware of the measures which had been taken
against Bembo, but Contarini comments in his report that this was a
lie, since his orders were kept at the Kadi's in Alexandria. The former
consul Bembo was meanwhile staying at the house of his successor,
awaiting the letters of the Venetian *Bailo* in Istanbul, which would
confirm his release. The dishonest interpreter was replaced by one

---

[20] *Ibid.*, col. 268. In October 1532 the commander of the Venetian navy still refers
to "the Jew who controls the Sultan's customs in Alexandria"; *Ibid.*, col. 233.

Cristofolo Corso, an Arabic-speaking Venetian.[21]

We see Castro, then, as a man wielding great influence, commanding vast sums of money, hostile to the Venetian merchants, and full of self-confidence. Perhaps he was too self-confident, as his overly free chat with the *Defterdār* from Istanbul might have cost him dear. But, as we shall see further on, this affair apparently did not bring about his immediate downfall.

Alexandria was not the only Ottoman port in the Levant in those days in which Venetian merchants encountered a hostile Jewish customs official. A similar situation existed in Syria, as evidenced by a fragment of testimony from the commander of the fleet of Venetian galleys which returned to Venice from Syria in February 1531. The commander, Lorenzo Da Mulla, reported to the Senate on 18 February that when the ships docked in the harbour of Tripoli "that Jew Ibrāhīm... [the customs collector?]... in the Sultan's ports, objected to the conducting of commerce aboard the galleys." Following the captain's appeal to the Kadi, Ibrahim lifted his objection, but then found another way to trouble the Venetians when the galleys docked in Beirut harbour, where he attempted to charge them excessive customs duty.[22]

Before attempting to answer the obvious question which arises from this testimony, let us see what further evidence may be found in the official correspondence of those years between the Venetian *Bailo* in Istanbul and the central government in Venice. In a letter dispatched from Istanbul to Venice on 14 April 1532, the *Bailo* reported a conversation he had had with Skandar Çelebi, the *Defterdār* who was mentioned above in connection with Abraham Castro's disgrace in Cairo. Evidently at this meeting they discussed other complaints, brought by Venetian merchants in Damascus, against Abraham Castro, whom the *Bailo* describes as the "contractor of those harbours" (*apaltador de quele marine*). The *Defterdār* assured the Venetian representative that Castro would be summoned to the Imperial capital, since there were other complaints against him.[23]

Evidently Abraham the customs man of Beirut and Tripoli was indeed called Abraham Castro, which brings us back to the question raised by David in connection with the testimony of the traveller Moses Basola

---

[21] *Ibid.*, cols. 503-504.

[22] *Ibid.*, vol. 55, col. 511.

[23] *Ibid.*, vol. 56, col. 228.

in 1522. Did the same man manage the customs houses of Beirut and
Alexandria at one and the same time? We must keep in mind that every
year highly valuable cargoes passed through both these ports, and the
duty paid on them reached vast sums, as implied by Consul Contarini
in the letter quoted above. The solution of the mystery lies in the
subsequent correspondence of the representatives of the Venetian
Republic in the Levant.

On 8 June 1532 the Venetian Senate heard a report from Adrianople,
which had been sent by the Secretary Jacomo di la Vedoa on 14 May,
describing his audience with Ibrāhīm Pasha, the Grand Vizier. Vedoa
had asked the Vizier to take steps against Abraham Castro (Sanuto
spells the name Cascio, but there is no doubt about its identity, as we
shall see presently), who was causing the Venetians great harm in the
ports of Tripoli and Beirut, and who enjoyed great support. The
Secretary reports that an order was issued to compel the man to pay
the vast sums he owed the Sultan and to dismiss him from his post.[24]
The reference to the debt to the Sultan, which was also mentioned
in Consul Contarini's letter from Alexandria, might lead us to conclude
that the man Abraham Castro who ran the customs at Alexandria held
the same position in Beirut and Tripoli. On the other hand, if that were
so, surely the representatives of Venice would have emphasized the
damage this man was causing their shipping everywhere, not only in
the Syrian ports. The solution is found in a letter sent from Istanbul
on 26 July 1533 by two Venetian ambassadors, Pietro Zen and Thoma
Contarini, together with the *Bailo* Nicolo Giustinian, containing an
almost verbatim report of their audience with the Grand Vizier, Ibrāhīm
Pasha. The *Bailo* demanded that "that traitorous Jew, Abraham Castro
of Syria" (here the name is spelled correctly) be stopped from interfering
with the Venetians' business. He [the Pasha] replied: "We receive reports
that he is loyal and serves the Sultan well, but nevertheless we shall
remove him, so that he will not hinder your nation, just as if he were
dead." And then the *Bailo* went on: "As for that other Abraham Castro
of Alexandria, I have heard from Zen that he has become our friend,
so I said nothing [about him]."[25]

Here, finally, is the answer to the mystery. There were, indeed,
two men bearing the same name, the one active in Syria and the other

---

[24] *Ibid.*, col. 363.
[25] *Ibid.*, vol. 58, col. 636.

in Egypt. There is no doubt about the reliability of the testimony of the Venetian representatives in the Ottoman Empire. They were in daily contact with the customs officials in the Levant and knew them well. The distinction between Castro in Alexandria and Castro in Beirut is unequivocal. At the same time, this does not mean, as David hypothesized, that there was one Abraham Castro who was a public figure and a financier, and another who was a "true divine sage", a "saintly man of God". Rather there were two entrepreneurs, men of great wealth and power, who took part in the financial running of the Ottoman Empire and its power struggles. The Abraham Castro whom Moses Basola met in Beirut in 1522 must have been the customs contractor who was active in Beirut and Tripoli in 1532-33, and not the Abraham Castro who held the same position in Alexandria in the early 1530s, and who may be identified with reasonable confidence with the head of the mint in Cairo in the 1520s.

At this point let us go back a few months and pick up the Venetian reports concerning the Egyptian Castro. A letter of Pietro Zen, the ambassador who stood in for the *Bailo*, dated 11 February 1533, makes a curious reference to Abraham Castro of Alexandria, whose import is not clear to me. "Concerning that Jew Castro of Alexandria", he writes, and here comes the clause "*meiora li datii del Signor*", which may be read in one of two ways: either "It was said to the Pasha that he has increased the Sultan's income from the customs duty"; or else: "It was said to the Pasha that [in order to] increase the Sultan's income from the customs duty", which may tie in better with what follows: "...I brought him [the Pasha] a Jew, the son of the elder of the Jews [the leader of the community?] (*fiol del prothoiero di iudei*), who will offer securities, and who has here [in Istanbul] both mother and father, and he will accept this post." In the margin of this letter Zen noted that the Pasha had given an order to release Consul Bembo in Alexandria.[26]

---

[26] *Ibid.*, vol. 57, col. 634. The title *prothoiero* is taken from the Graeco-Byzantine terminology, signifying "elder" (προτόγερος). For example, in Corfu in 1415 the peasants called on the authorities to appoint a *prothoierus* from their community to be responsible for the tax collection. See D. Jacoby, "Un aspect de la fiscalité vénitienne dans le Péloponnèse aux XIVᵉ et XVᵉ siècles: le *zovaticum*", *Travaux et Mémoires du Centre de Recherche d'Histoire et Civilisation Byzantines*, 1(1965), p. 414, reprinted in Jacoby's collected essays, *Société et démographie à Byzance et en Romanie latine*, London, 1975 (IV). In sixteenth-century Ottoman terminology the term designated

Is this a reference to a Jewish protégé of the Venetian ambassador, whom he is proposing to the Porte as a replacement for Castro at the Alexandria customs house? It does seem that the Venetians were making every effort to topple their enemy from his position. Pietro Zen writes from the Ottoman capital on 8 March that Iyās Pasha promised to remove Abraham Castro from "those harbours".[27] It is not clear which of the Castros is meant, but in Pietro Zen's letters sent from Istanbul on 18 and 23 of April 1533 he reports his meeting with Ibrāhīm Pasha, in which they discussed the detention of the Venetian galleys in Alexandria. "The Jews are oppressing us and the Muslims do not keep their word," he says in these letters.[28] The instructions to the ambassador in Istanbul in April that year order him explicitly to do his best to cause "the scoundrel Abraham Castro" to be punished for having caused the Venetians so much damage in Alexandria.[29]

The Venetian lobbying at the Porte must have had some effect, as Daniel Diedo, the Venetian vice-consul in Alexandria, wrote on 22 June 1533:

> ...These days the Jew Abraham Castro, *nadar* [*nādir*] of this city, who has caused the inhabitants of this city such depredation, fearing that he would be dismissed from his post following the intercession of our ambassador in Constantinople, has left for Cairo, whence he departed for the Porte, accompanied by Janon Bey, Master of the Cairo Treasury. He carries with him costly gifts, intending to return to an even higher position than he has held heretofore, saying that he would collect the costs later from our people...[30]

---

a middle- or low-ranking official, who generally functioned alongside a more senior one. See, for example, the accounts of the Venetian *Bailo* in 1525, which include payments to various functionaries bearing this title, such as the *prothogero* of the gate-keepers of the Sublime Porte, the *prothogero* of the governor of Gallipoli, the *prothogero* of Ibrāhīm Pasha or the *prothogero* of the Kadi: T.F. Jones, *Venice and the Porte, 1520-1542*, unpublished Ph.D. thesis, Harvard University, 1910, Appendix II, pp. 4, 6. It is possible that the use of this Greek term to designate these functionaries was limited to the central administration in Istanbul, and that it was used chiefly by the Greeks and Venetians in the Ottoman capital.

[27] Sanuto, *I diarii*, vol. 58, col. 41.

[28] *Ibid.*, col. 205.

[29] *Ibid.*, col. 21.

[30] *Ibid.*, cols. 716-717.

Perhaps fear for his skin caused Castro to change his attitude to the Venetians, for already on 26 July, Venice's representatives at the Porte reported that he had become the Venetians' friend.[31] On 15 August the Venetian ambassadors and the *Bailo* wrote that Janon Ağa, the sheikh (*Siech*) Granes and Abraham Castro of Alexandria arrived in Istanbul laden with gifts. Janon Ağa discussed with the *Bailo* the crisis in the spice trade in Egypt, created by Portuguese harassment of Muslim ships, whereas in a conversation with Castro the subject of the dismissal of the interpreter in Alexandria came up. According to the *Bailo*, Castro told him that the *Bailo* had been slow to act, as everything had already been achieved (*ha dito son sta tardi, za è sta fato ogni cosa*).[32] Following this piece of information of August 1533, the Egyptian Abraham Castro disappears for several years from the Venetian sources.[33]

Castro's disappearance from the Venetian documents after the summer of 1533 may be due to his changed attitude towards the Venetian merchants, as noted in the sources quoted above. If that was so, then from the Venetian viewpoint no news was good news. In any case, it is interesting to note the methods adopted by the Venetians to protect their interests from this man, who behaved as their enemy. In addition to applying pressure at the centre of Ottoman government, they proposed a replacement for Castro, also a Jewish dignitary and an Ottoman subject. It would seem that the link between the farming of customs duties and the Jews had become automatic. It is possible that "the Jew Abraham Castro" who is mentioned in the archives of the Kadi's court in Jerusalem from 1538 onwards was indeed the Alexandrian Castro, who preferred to move, if only temporarily, to a place where he did not have so many enemies. But that is mere conjecture.

Though the Egyptian Abraham Castro disappears for a while from the Venetian sources, not so the Syrian Abraham Castro, who was also a thorn in their side. His personality continues to sour the relations between Venice and the Porte for several more years. On 10 February 1537 the Venetian Senate dispatched a letter to the ambassador and

---

[31] *Ibid.*, col. 636.

[32] *Ibid.*, col. 699.

[33] On 9 July the information reached Venice from Corfu that Abraham Castro had managed to obtain the customs duty collection in Alexandria for three further sailing periods (*mude*), (*ibid.*, col. 415), but there is no telling where the information originated and when it left Egypt.

the *Bailo* in Istanbul, as follows:

> ...When our [merchant] galleys returned from Beirut, they brought us letters
> from our consul in Damascus confirming the rumours which had reached
> us from merchants returning from that place. It transpires that the merchants,
> having invested there, as is their wont, substantial sums in commercial
> transactions, trusting wholly in the Sultan's public promises as expressed
> in various decrees, were presented at the end of their stay in harbour (*muda*)
> with an order from the Sublime Porte to pay an impost of 10 percent on
> all the spices that they had purchased. Furthermore, they were ordered
> to pay an impost of five percent on silk and other export goods, and an
> impost of five percent on all imported goods. This order has not only hurt
> our trade and that of the Arabs (*Mori*), but has caused many of the goods
> to be left behind, gravely harming that country and our merchants alike,
> for this is an intolerable and unusual impost in those ports...

The consul added that whenever such imposts had been demanded in
the past they were later repealed by the Sultan, which could be shown
in detail. Stressing that this impost was laid on transactions which had
already been concluded, he stated that it would utterly ruin the sea
trade with Syria, because merchants would refuse to send their capital
there and the Venetian galleys would cease to sail. The only beneficiary
would be the king of Portugal, whose trade routes would flourish once
again, whereas Syria would suffer want. The letter emphasizes that,
for its part, Venice had done all it could to keep the Levant trade
competitive, by cancelling the duty on pepper, thereby reviving the
importation of the spice to Venice, after the merchants had for some
time preferred to send it to Portugal. To enable the galleys to leave,
since they were already loaded and ready to set sail, the consul in
Damascus, Antonio Marcello, decided to deposit a personal security
to cover the payment, and to undertake before the Syrian provincial
administration to see to it than an order repealing the new impost would
arrive from the Porte within five months. The Senate instructed its
representatives in Istanbul to act in all haste to get the impost repealed,
making it clear that the Venetian sea trade with Syria might otherwise
cease, diminishing the Sultan's income. If the process should take too
long, the letter went on, they were to obtain a temporary order to prevent
the calling in of the consul's security, or to extend its period. The Senate
noted that meanwhile the time had come for merchant ships to sail

for the Levant (*muda delle nave per Levante*). Formerly, many of them sailed there with rich cargoes, but this time only two had set out and they carried little capital, because of the said developments. Most of the ships sailed to other destinations.[34]

Abraham Castro's connection with this affair is made clear in another letter of the Senate, sent on the same day to the ambassadors and the *Bailo* in Istanbul: "All that *garbuglio*[35] was caused by the arrival of Abraham Castro at the Sublime Porte, for it was he who caused that order to be issued, having persuaded the Sultan that this would increase his income." The Senate instructs its representatives at the Porte to invite Abraham Castro and warn him to stop troubling the Venetians, and to point out that the Republic's demand was based on its peace treaty with the Sultan. The ambassadors were also instructed to tell Castro that if he complied with their demand he would enjoy the same treatment as did all who behaved well towards the Republic, including its support for his continued position in those ports.[36]

A week after these instructions were dispatched, another letter on the same subject arrived from the *Bailo*, which must have been sent before he received the Senate's instructions of 10 February (The contents of the *Bailo*'s letter can only be deduced indirectly from the Senate's reply). The Senate responded ten days later in the same spirit as its earlier instructions. Its response suggests that negotiations were going forward in Istanbul with the participation of Abraham Castro himself. The Senate instructed the *Bailo* to point out to Castro that he faced utter ruin if he did not comply, as Venetian ships would cease to come to Syria. On the other hand, if he did comply with their demand, he would enjoy special consideration from the Venetians. The Senate added various arguments to help the *Bailo* in the negotiations, and empowered its representatives in the Ottoman capital to spend what monies they saw fit to make their arguments more persuasive.[37] In true Venetian fashion, the Senate promptly ensured that the expenditure would be covered by ordering a special impost on goods imported from Syria.[38]

---

[34] ASV, Senato, Mar, reg. 23, ff. 206-207.

[35] Literally: 'knot'. An expression meaning 'mess', 'annoyance', particularly as suffered by Venetian merchants in the Levant.

[36] *Ibid.*, f. 207.

[37] *Ibid.*, ff. 212-213 (23 Feb. 1537).

[38] *Ibid.*, ff. 213-214v.

Here, then, we find the Syrian Abraham Castro at the centre of one of the less known but significant episodes in the economic relations between Venice and the Levant, and in a broader sense, at the heart of the structural changes in the international spice trade following the Portuguese discoveries. The intense competition between the Mediterranean and Atlantic routes produced some stormy and fascinating chapters, which fall outside the scope of the present study. We merely note that this commerce underwent a severe crisis in the early years of the sixteenth century. Frederic Lane has shown that the Mediterranean spice trade recovered in the mid-sixteenth century, and even reached levels unprecedented in previous centuries, but his data refer mainly to Egypt and not to Syria.[39] Castro, who seems to have been the person responsible for the increased customs duty in the ports of Syria, appears in this wider context as a man who concentrated on the short term and was unaware of, or unwilling, to consider the wider implications of his actions. It is possible that his activities affected the changes in the international trade routes along which the spices flowed through the Ottoman territories on their way from the Far East to Europe. Castro is seen here as a significant figure, with access to the Sultan's *Divan* in Istanbul, much like his namesake in Alexandria, who likewise had good connections at the Imperial centre of power.

This crisis in the commercial relations between Venice and the Levant was to continue for a long time, for in August 1539 a war broke out between the Republic and the Ottomans, which ended only with the signing of the peace treaty between the two states in October 1540, and its final ratification in Venice in April 1541.[40] No sooner did that war end, than the subject of the new customs duty came up again in the official relations between the states. It was, indeed, one of the subjects which came up in the negotiations leading up to the peace treaty. In the instructions to the Venetian ambassador in Istanbul, sent on 11 June 1540, he is told to demand, in the course of the peace negotiations, the cancellation of the 10 percent impost on the Venetian merchants in Syria.[41] The draft agreement, which was delivered to

---

[39] Lane, "The Mediterranean Spice Trade", pp. 581-90, reprinted in his *Venice and History*, pp. 25-34.

[40] W. Lehmann, "Der Friedensvertrag zwischen Venedig und der Türkei vom 2. Oktober 1540", *Bonner Orientalistischen Studien*, 16, (1936), p. 1.

[41] ASV, Sen., Delib. Secrete, reg. 61, ff. 37-38V.

Venice by the ambassador Badoer on 30 August 1540, stated explicitly that the Venetian merchants would not be subject to the 10 percent impost, which had been fixed "in the days of Abraham Castro, contrary to the usual practice."[42] And the peace treaty itself, which was signed in Istanbul on 2 October 1540, stated quite explicitly: "The new taxes upon both capital and merchandise, which were imposed by the islamized Jew Abraham Castro in the ports of Beirut and Tripoli in Arabistan, are to be cancelled. All these, which are contrary to the Sultan's former practice and order, will be undone and no man will dare alter them."[43]

And so, in the end, though the issue remained suspended for a long time due to the war, the Venetians managed to get rid of the impost. And along the way, while discussing the customs duty in the Syrian ports, we find the solution to another Abraham Castro mystery - the question of his conversion to Islam. Amnon Cohen interpreted correctly the document of the Jerusalem judicial record of 1540, dealing with additions to the synagogue in Jerusalem which were carried out in the time of "Ibrāhīm Castro al-muhtadī, the collector of the Sultan's taxes." We may well identify this person with Abraham Castro who flourished in Beirut and Tripoli. By correlating these testimonies we may conclude that he, too, and not only his Egyptian namesake, came to Jerusalem and held a high position there. At some stage about the middle of the sixteenth century, though not necessary at the very same time, there must have been in Jerusalem two dignitaries by name of Abraham Castro, and to distinguish between them the judicial documents referred to one as a Jew and to the other as a muhtadī, i.e., one who became a Muslim.

What befell Abraham Castro the convert? In the Venetian archives there is a series of documents, including some Ottoman ones with

---

[42] Ibid., f. 48v.

[43] ASV, Commemoriali, reg. 22, f. 50: I libri commemoriali della Repubblica di Venezia, Regesti, ed. P. Predelli, vol. 4, Venice, 1904, No. 43, p. 237; Bonelli, "Il trattato turco-veneto del 1540", Centenario della nascita Michele Amari, Vol. 2, Palermo, 1910, p. 13; F. Babinger, "Zum turkisch-venedigischen Friedensvertrag vom Jahre 1540", Rivista degli studi orientali, 8(1919-20), pp. 651-52; Lehmann, "Der Friedensvertrag", text, p. 8; T. Gökbilgin, "Venedik Devlet Arşivindeki vesikalar külliyatında Kanunî Sultan Süleyman devri belgeleri", Belgeler, 1/2 (1964), p. 127. See also later references to this clause in the peace treaty in the Senate resolutions of 8 February, 1541, (ASV, Senato, Delib. Secrete, reg. 61, f. 150), 20 October 1543 (ASV, Senato, Mar, reg. 27, f. 68v), and 4 June 1544 (ibid., f. 111v).

Venetian translations (the latest of which bears the date 30 January 1545), dealing with the final settlement of the customs duty.[44] The clause in the peace treaty which dealt with the matter did not resolve the issue, and it was necessary to obtain a final settlement of Consul Marcello's personal security, which he had given before the war. It seems that the consul remained in the East throughout the war, and even after it ended was barred from returning to Venice, on account of the security he had given in 1537. In 1544 he was still in Istanbul and the *Bailo* had orders to give the matter the highest priority so as to set the man free. It appears from these documents that there was also some Venetian commercial capital in Syria which was tied to that guaranty, and which had been seized by the Ottoman authorities during the war.

One of the sequels of that affair tells us a little more about our protagonist. On 10 August 1543 the Venetian Senate sent a secret letter to Yūnis Bey, the interpreter at the Sublime Porte and the Venetians' contact man. It deals with a certain Venetian merchant by name of Nicolo Mocenigo, who left Syria some six years previously, that is to say, just before the outbreak of war, and returned after it ended. Mocenigo became entangled in a network of local rivalries and plots in connection with Castro and the raised impost, an issue which in 1543 was still inconclusive. The letter refers to Abraham Castro in the past tense, as the person who had been responsible for imposing the new taxes. But at the centre of the current plots was his son-in-law, Solomon, whom the letter describes as "detested by Turks, Arabs (*Mori*) and Jews, on account of the new impost created by Abraham Castro." Solomon's local rivals sought to implicate him by charging that he had received from Nicolo Mocenigo the sum of 4000 ducats in payment for the new impost. When Mocenigo returned to Syria, the *Defterdār* in Aleppo demanded that he pay this sum into the Ottoman treasury, which he was compelled to do, getting deep in debt. Yūnis Bey was asked to help get the charge against Mocenigo—which the Senate's letter claimed was a false one—dropped, and the money restored to him.[45] A day after the letter to Yūnis Bey the Senate also wrote a formal appeal in this matter to the Sultan himself.[46]

---

[44] See below, note 47.

[45] ASV, Sen., Delib. Secrete, reg. 63, ff. 70-70v.

[46] *Ibid.*, ff. 70v-71.

The problems of Consul Marcello's security, and seemingly that of the merchant Mocenigo, too, were finally resolved to the Venetians' satisfaction, though in the meantime the Ottoman authorities had found another pretext for imposing higher tariffs upon the Venetians. In any event, the indications are that Abraham Castro was no longer involved in this new round of the conflict over the customs tariffs in Syria. His name still crops up in documents from the 1540s, but always in connection with the changed tariffs and his role as customs-farmer ('āmil al-muqāṭa'ah) in Beirut and Tripoli before the war. All these references suggest that following the 1537-40 war, and perhaps while it was going on, Abraham Castro the Muslim convert was no longer the customs-farmer of the two cities.[47] Moreover, it is possible that his role in the affair of the raised tariffs, which made him many enemies, among them Jews, drove him to become a Muslim. The conversion of the Syrian Abraham Castro might be interpreted as an act of self-defence in distress.

After the signing of the peace treaty and the restoration of normal relations between Venice and the Ottomans, the Egyptian Castro appears once more in the international diplomatic correspondence. Guillaume Pellicier, the French ambassador at Venice, wrote to the king of France on 31 March 1541 that, according to Venetian reports from Istanbul of the previous February, Abraham Castro the Jew was jailed, being accused of several acts of theft.[48] Since the previous sentence in the ambassador's letter refers to the Sultan's income from Egypt, and Castro is described as a Jew, it is clear to which of the two Castros he is referring. It is significant that not only the Venetians were interested in the fate of this man. The fact that the French ambassador saw fit to report to his king about this matter shows how important this Castro was, and that he was a known personage in the international arena of his time. This is the last reference to the Egyptian Castro that I have

---

[47] ASV, Senato, Mar, reg. 27, f. 59v (3 Sept. 1543); *ibid.*, f. 68v (20 Oct. 1543); *ibid.*, f. 111v (4 June 1544); ASV, Documenti Turchi, 522 (19 Sept. 1544), where the title *'āmil al-muqāṭa'ah* also appears; *ibid.*, 526-27 (28 Sept.- 7 Oct. 1544); *ibid.*, 537-38 *(30 Jan. 1545)* and ASV, Commemoriali, reg. 22 (30 Jan. 1545); Gökbilgin, "Venedik Devlet Arşivindeki Vesikalar", pp. 191-92 (30 Jan. 1545). See also the abstracts of these documents in *I documenti turchi dell'Archivio di Stato di Venezia* [with the *regesti* of A. Bombaci], ed. M.P. Pedani Fabris, Venice, 1994, pp. 80-82.

[48] *Correspondance politique de Guillaume Pellicier, Ambassadeur de France à Venise, 1540-42*, ed. A. Tausserat-Radel, Paris, 1899, vol. 1, p. 261.

found so far in the sources at my disposal, but it is not inconceivable that the Venetian archives and those of other Western nations contain additional testimonies about this affair, or others in which he figured. It should be noted, however, that in the reports submitted to the Venetian Senate by the consuls in Egypt, Daniel Barbarigo and Lorenzo Tiepolo, who spent the years 1550-55 in Egypt, there is no mention of Abraham Castro.[49] It is safe to assume that if the Venetians had to deal with situations like the ones described above, his name would have cropped up in those detailed documents.

The Venetian sources presented above contain rich and unequivocal information about the role of the Jewish customs farmers in the fiscal system of two provinces of the Ottoman empire in the first half of the sixteenth century. Several scholars have already noted the association between Jews and the farming of customs duty and taxes in various regions of the Empire, as early as the fifteenth century.[50] The importance of this association is expressed in the literature of Jewish *responsa* from the sixteenth century on,[51] in the Ottoman documents,[52] and in Western sources[53], where it is repeatedly stated that the Jews had all but taken over this occupation. The identity of several of these Jewish customs farmers is known, some of them being of Spanish origin.[54]

---

[49] Poma, "Il consolato Veneto", pp. 23-35; Lorenzo Tiepolo, *Relazioni dei consolati di Alessandria e di Siria*, pp. 10-27.

[50] Gerber, *Economic and Social Life*, p. 54, and reference there to the fourth chapter in Epstein, *The Jewish Communities*, *sub vocem* "tax farms" in the index.

[51] *Ibid.*, pp. 54-55; Shtober, "On the Issue of Customs Collectors", pp. 68-94; Bashan, "Economic Life", p. 99, n. 181. The name of the collectors are rarely mentioned in the *responsa* literature.

[52] Gerber, *Jews in the Ottoman Empire*, pp. 49-60; Cohen, *Jewish Life Under Islam*, pp. 153-158.

[53] B. Arbel, "Venice and the Jewish Merchants of Istanbul in the Sixteenth Century", in *The Mediterranean and the Jews: Banking, Finance and International Trade (XVI-XVIII Centuries)*, eds. S. Schwarzfuchs and A. Toaff, Ramat Gan, 1989, p. 55, note 51; see also the testimonies of the French traveller and scholar Pierre Belon, who lived in the Levant in the years 1546-1549, and the traveller Regnaud, who passed through the region in 1549: Belon, *Les observations*, p. 400; Antoine Regnaud, *Discours du voyage d'Outre-mer au Sainct-Sépulcre de Ierusalem et autres lieux de la Terre Saincte en 1548*, Lyons, 1573, p. 34.

[54] Winter, "The Jews of Egypt", p. 11; Bashan, "Economic Life", p. 101; Gerber, *Jews in the Ottoman Empire*, p. 55; Cohen, *Jews Under Islam*, pp. 141-45; Grunebaum--Ballin, *Joseph Naci*, p. 163; Arbel, "Venice and the Jewish Merchants", p. 56, note.

It seems that the impression of Western travellers of an extensive involvement of Jews in the fiscal and financial administration of the Ottoman Empire is being gradually borne out by current research.[55] The data about the two figures examined in this chapter blend with this general picture. It should be emphasized, moreover, that these were not minor posts, but the two main gateways of Levantine commerce in the sixteenth century.[56] To obtain control of the customs houses of Alexandria, Beirut and Tripoli, the candidates must have had to pay considerable sums, and in all likelihood to bribe various senior officials. These men must already have had a good deal of experience in finance before they attempted to manipulate such immense sums of money.[57]

The information about these individuals which may be found in the Venetian documents might also help us to understand the patterns of leadership in the Jewish communities in the East in early modern times. Both the Hebrew sources and the judicial documents analyzed by Amnon Cohen show that the two personages we have been discussing were leading figures in the Jewish communities in the Levant. It would seem that this fact was due primarily to their great wealth. Needless to say, the Venetian documents reflect Venetian interests, and present the Jewish customs farmers from a particular viewpoint. Nevertheless, they provide a different aspect of the two personalities. Some scholars have been

---

[55] See H. Gerber, "Jewish Tax-Farmers in the Ottoman Empire in the 16th and 17th Centuries", *Journal of Turkish Studies*, 10 (1986), pp. 143-154. In the Venetian archives I found references to the Jews who ran the mint in Damascus in the 1520s: "Moses the Jew, the lessee of the mint of Damascus" signed the receipt for the tax paid by Venice for Cyprus in December 1521; Moses son of Joseph Milan and Samuel son of Judah, assayers (*sazadori*) of the Damascus mint, were concerned with the receipt of the said tax at the end of January 1523 (*I documenti turchi*, p. 29, No 193). See also the report of the Venetian consul in Damascus in 1525, which refers to "the Jews of the mint" in Damascus, who are doing all they can to compel the Venetians to bring money to Damascus (ASV, Collegio, Relazioni, busta 61, f. 21).

[56] In 1560, the *Bailo* Cavalli evaluated the income collected as customs dues on Venetian trade in Alexandria at 220,000 ducats a year, and 120,000 in Syria: Simon, "Contribution", p. 976.

[57] According to Gerber, "tax farming was the highest administrative position in the Ottoman Empire which was open to Jews": Gerber, *Jews in the Ottoman Empire*, p. 56. According to Shtober, the Alexandrian customs collectors were the 'whales' among the Jewish tax collectors in Ottoman Egypt: Shtober, "Customs Collectors", p. 86. See also Cohen, *Jews Under Islam*, pp. 141-45.

unduly impressed by the fulsome praise which was lavished on the two Castros in the Hebrew literature of their time.[58] We must remember that in the sixteenth century Levant such hyperbole was common currency. But above all, we must keep in mind that such men, who were capable of conquering positions of great power in the upper echelons of the Ottoman high finance, and of retaining them in the face of the ruthless power struggles and intense rivalries which characterized the politics of the Ottoman Empire, could hardly have been pure as the driven snow. Such epithets as "saintly man of God", or "who acteth justly and speaketh truth", which were applied to one or both of our protagonists, rather than describing their great spirituality, suggest patronage, which typically evokes this sort of adulation. Much like the great capitalists of our times, who contribute lavishly to cultural and religious institutions, and whose names are commemorated with fulsome praise on brass plaques, walls and paper, our two sixteenth-century protagonists were mere mortals of flesh and blood.

---

[58] See, for example, Yehuda, "The Egyptian Scroll", p. 387 ("He was a man who spoke justly, was straight of speech, generous to the poor and a mainstay of Torah scholars and thinkers"); likewise Shochetman, "On the Life of Abraham Castro", p. 403 ("He was drawn to the Torah and the wisdom of the Kabbala, and may himself have been one of the sages of his age").

CHAPTER THREE

THE JEWS IN VENICE AND THE OTTOMAN MENACE, 1566-1571

The commercial rivalry between Venetians and Jews, which developed parallel to the growing anti-Jewish wave in Italy during the late 1560s, would have sufficed to trouble Venice's relations with it Jewish minority. But then another factor came into play, which fuelled the resentment of Venetian authorities against Jews, and finally led to the decision to expel them from Venice altogether.

Between 1541 and 1570 Venice and the Ottoman Empire were at peace with one another, but the accession of Sultan Selīm II to the Ottoman throne in 1566 was a potential threat to the Republic. The Empire's peace treaties were always made with the ruling Sultan, and had to be renewed when the ruler changed, by means of diplomatic negotiations which were normally conducted in Istanbul. Ottoman rulers liked to open their reigns with some conquest, and Selīm's intention to seize Venetian Cyprus had been known even before his accession.[1] Now disturbing rumours about his bellicose intentions began to reach Venice.[2]

The relations between the Viziers surrounding Sultan Selīm II were characterized by ferocious rivalry, which was reflected in their conflicting opinions on foreign policy. Among the most influential Viziers, Mustafā Pasha and Piyāle Pasha favoured Selīm's plans to conquer Cyprus, while the Grand Vizier, Mehmed Sokollu, opposed the idea

---

[1] W. Andreas, "Eine unbekannte venetianische Relation über die Türkei (1567)", *Sitzungsberichte der Heidelberger Akademie der Wissenschaften. Philosophisch-historische Klasse*, 5 (1914), p. 10; *Relazioni*, ed. Albèri, ser. III, Appendice, Florence, 1863, p. 389 (Barbaro's second report, 1574). The *Bailo* Barbaro returned to Venice in the spring of 1574 (see C. Yriartre, *La vie d'un patricien de Venise au XVe siècle*, Paris, 1884, p. 174). His report could not therefore have been presented in 1573, as stated by Albèri.

[2] *E.g.* ASV, Sen., Disp. CP, filza 2, ff. 135 (10 July 1567), 396 (19 Jan. 1568), 453 (3 Feb. 1568); ASV, Capi X, Lett. CP, busta 3, Nos 135 (2 Feb. 1568), 141 (11 May 1568).

of going to war with Venice.[3] Don Joseph Nassí, Selīm's favourite already since before his accession, belonged to the party of Mustafā and Piyāle Pasha.[4] Nassí was a legendary figure in his own lifetime, and a mythical aura still clings to his memory.[5] The legend which grew around him, though not totally unfounded, was made up of various elements, all of them somewhat exaggerated. Since it had direct repercussions on Venice's attitude to Jews in general, and to the *Levantini* Jewish merchants in particular, it deserves further clarification here.

In Venice during those years it was believed that Nassí was an outright enemy of the Republic, motivated by personal vendetta.[6] This belief was supported by such facts as Nassí's previous Italian adventures, which had caused him to be banned by the Venetian Council of Ten; by his being a Portuguese *Marrano*, who moved to Istanbul in order to embrace the Judaic faith; by his being a companion of Sultan Selīm, who bestowed upon him the Duchy of Naxos, previously held by the Crispo family under Venetian protection; by his alliance with Mustafā and Piyāle Pasha; and by his attempt to induce the Duke of Savoy to stake his claim to the Cypriot crown with Ottoman support. In other words, he could not be viewed otherwise but as a determined enemy of Venice.[7] A curious booklet, entitled "Dialogue between Selīm and

---

[3] Barbaro's Letter-book, I, ff. 275-76 (21 Jan. 1570); *ibid.*, II, f. 8 (9 Apr. 1570); *Relazioni*, ed. Albèri, ser. II, vol. I, p. 410 (Garzoni's report, 1573); *ibid.*, p. 331 (Barbaro's report, 1574), pp. 390-91; *ibid.*, pp. 390-91 (Barbaro's second report, 1574).

[4] Roth, *The House of Nasi: The Duke of Naxos*, pp. 17-18, 42, 49-51, 139-40; Grunebaum-Ballin, *Joseph Naci*, pp. 134-35. On the relations between Nassí and Selīm see also the report of the Venetian ambassador Badoer (1573) in *Relazioni*, ed. Albèri, ser. III, vol. 1, p. 361. On the rivalry between Sokollu and Nassí, see Barbaro's Letter-book, I, ff. 271v (Jan. 1570), 327v-328 (Feb. 1570), 338 (Mar. 1570).

[5] Of the books listed above, those written by Roth were strongly influenced by the myth, whereas that of Grunebaum-Ballin, though far from exhaustive, is rather more balanced.

[6] Roth, *The House of Nasi: The Duke of Naxos*, pp. 14, 38, 145-46.

[7] On Nassí's condemnation by the Council of Ten, see Grunebaum-Ballin, *Joseph Naci*, pp. 52-53; C. Rose, "New information on the Life of Joseph Nasi, Duke of Naxos: The Venetian Phase", *Jewish Quarterly Review*, 60 (1970), pp. 330-44; B. Ravid, "Money, Love and Power Politics in Sixteenth Century Venice: The Perpetual Banishment and Subsequent Pardon of Joseph Nasi", in *Italia Judaica. Atti del I Convegno internazionale (Bari, 1981)*, Rome, 1983, pp. 159-81. M.P. Pedani recently

Joseph the Jew", by Manoli Blessi, which appeared in Venice in 1571, following the loss of Cyprus and the naval victory at Lepanto, reflected this established image. In this Dialogue Sultan Selīm complains to Joseph (obviously Joseph Nassí), that he had prompted him to launch a war which proved to be too costly. For his part, Joseph the Jew tries to convince the Sultan that after all the results were not bad.[8] The booklet reflects the opinion, common not only in the ruling class, but throughout Venetian society, that Nassí had a central role in persuading the Sultan to launch the war which finally wrested from Venice its biggest and richest overseas colony.[9]

Behind this widespread belief lay two firm, though unproved, assumptions: an exaggerated idea of Nassí's role in determining or influencing the principal moves of Ottoman foreign policy, and a conviction that he was animated by a hatred for Venice. In reality, judging from the reports of various Venetian *Bailos* in Istanbul, who were generally acute observers of Ottoman politics, the main foreign-policy decisions resulted from the power struggle among the various Pashas, and could only be indirectly influenced by a courtier such as Don Joseph Nassí.[10] As for his animosity towards Venice, though he had good reasons for it, and though some of his moves could be interpreted this way, others were by no means compatible with outright

---

discovered important archival documents regarding the earlier phases of this affair, none of which have been used in the above-mentioned studies, see M.P. Pedani, *In nome del Gran Signore. Inviati ottomani a Venezia dalla caduta di Costantinopoli alla guerra di Candia*, Venice, 1994, p. 156 and n. 128. On Nassí's return to Judaism in Istanbul, *ibid.*, pp. 70-71; on the Duchy of Naxos, *ibid.*, p. 91; on his proposal to the Duke of Savoy, see C. Roth, "Joseph Nasi, Duke of Naxos, and the Counts [sic] of Savoy", in *The Seventy-Fifth Anniversary Volume of the Jewish Quarterly Review*, eds. A.A. Neuman and S. Zeitlin, Philadelphia, 1967, pp. 460-72.

[8] Manoli Blessi [pseudonym of Antonio Molin, called "Il Burchiella"], *Dialogo de Selin con Giosuf ebreo* etc., Venice, n.d., cited by Grunebaum-Ballin, *Joseph Naci*, p. 144.

[9] See, for instance, A. Calepio, "Vera et fidelissima narratione del successo dell'espugnatione et defensione del Regno di Cipro", in E. de Lusignan, *Chorografia et breve historia universale dell'isola di Cipro*, Bologna, 1573, p. 93. The same belief was expressed by Nineteenth-century historians, see J. von Hammer-Purgstall, *Geschichte des Osmanischen Reiches, 2nd ed., vol. 2, Pest, 1840*, pp. 400-401; H.H. Graetz, *Geschichte der Juden*, vol. 9, Leipzig 1866, pp.408-409.

[10] Andreas, "*Eine unbekannte Relation*", pp. 10, 12 (Cavalli's report, 1567); *Relazioni*, ed. Albèri, ser. III, vol. 1, pp. 319-22 (Barbaro's report, 1574).

ill-will. We may doubt the sincerity of his declarations of fidelity to Venice, expressed on various occasions.[11] We may question his intentions when he warned the *Bailo*, as early as 1567, against a possible Ottoman attack on Cyprus.[12] But we must also ask why he asked Venice to grant him an absolute remission from the ban imposed upon him by the Council of Ten, a request which was met by favourable response in April 1567.[13] Moreover, having the lease of the duty on wine in Istanbul, his income depended to a large extent on wine imported from Venetian Crete, where he also kept a few agents.[14] Finally, on the eve of the Cypriot war, Nassí was already past the zenith of his power. According to the reports of the French and Venetian envoys in Istanbul, and the contents of the secret versions of the 1569 French capitulations, he was deep in debt, or actually bankrupt.[15] In such a situation, the income from the duty on wine, for instance, must have been an important factor in his considerations. Furthermore, prior to the Cyprus war Nassí was engaged in a bitter conflict with the French crown, following the refusal of the Most Christian King to honour an old debt of 150,000 ducats. Nassí persuaded the Sultan to seize French vessels and goods in Alexandria in order to compensate himself for the unpaid loan. But since this operation resulted in a decrease of trade in Alexandria and of customs revenues there, Nassí tried to encourage Venice, in September 1568, to increase its own trade with Alexandria, to compensate that

---

[11] *Relazioni*, ed. Albèri, ser. III, vol. 2, pp. 66-67 (Bonvizzo's report, 1565); ASV, Sen., Disp. CP, filza 2, f. 163 (2 Aug. 1567), ff. 200-200v (8 Sept. 1567); Roth, *The Duke of Naxos*, pp. 37-38; Grunebaum-Ballin, *Joseph Naci*, p. 83. See also Nassí's letter to the Jewish merchants in Venice in the Appendix.

[12] ASV, Sen., Disp. CP, filza 2, f. 137 (10 July 1567).

[13] For Nassí's request, see *Relazioni*, ed. Albèri, ser. III, vol. 2, pp. 66-67 (Bonvizzo's report, 1565); for his absolution, see ASV, Cons. X, Secreti, reg. 8, f. 82v (9 Apr. 1567). See also *Nunziature di Venezia*, vol. 8, ed. A. Stella, Rome, 1963, p. 203 (12 Apr. 1567). One month later, Nassí expressed his gratitude to the *Bailo* for his absolution, see ASV, Capi X, Lett. CP, busta 3, No 114 (11 May 1567).

[14] Barbaro's Letter-book, I, ff. 252v-253 (8 Dec. 1569), 256 (21 Dec. 1569); ASV, Cons. X, Secreti, filza 18 (30 Aug. 1574) and reg. 11, f. 34v (20 Oct. 1574); Roth, *The Duke of Naxos*, pp. 46-47; Grunebaum-Ballin, *Joseph Naci*, p. 163; H. Inalcik, "Capital Formation in the Ottoman Empire", *The Journal of Economic History*, 29 (1969), pp. 122-23.

[15] Grunebaum-Ballin, *Joseph Naci*, pp. 123, 125, 128; Barbaro's Letter-book, I, ff. 175v (14 Sept. 1569), 338v (Mar. 1570). For Nassí's financial difficulties in the 1570s, see Baron, *A Social and Religious History*, vol. 18, p. 104.

port for the losses incurred by French withdrawal.[16] These consider-ations must have caused Nassí to adopt a conciliatory attitude towards Venice in the years before the war. Nevertheless, his association with Piyāle and Mustafā Pasha probably drove him to become Venice's enemy, whether he wanted to or not.[17] In any case, both his ability to influence events, and his motivation to harm the Republic, were much less than is generally thought.

Another element in the complex myth surrounding Joseph Nassí was the belief that he headed some kind of international organization of espionage and sabotage, which was especially active in the territories of the Venetian state. Paradoxically, the decisive proof for its existence and efficiency lay in the fact that it was never possible to find any evidence for it in all the acts which were being attributed to its opera-tion.[18] Yet even in the twentieth century, some scholars have been reluctant to abandon this conviction.[19]

A third element of Nassí's myth was the belief that he was a kind of Jewish 'king', or 'president' (as could be inferred from the name Nassí). In 1568, the Council of Ten declared that "we see the immense respect in which the entire Hebrew nation holds this Joseph Nassí, particularly following his nomination as Duke of Naxos, being considered as principal head (*capo principale*) of these Jews, with whom he

---

[16] Barbaro's Letter-book, I, ff. 44v-45 (11 Dec. 1568), 47 (23 Dec. 1568), 48v (23 Dec. 1568), 95 (30 Apr. 1569), 103v-104 (14 May 1569), 119-119v (10 June 1569), 175v (14 Sept. 1569); *Nunziature di Venezia*, vol. 8, pp. 484-85 (19 Jan. 1569), 491 (2 Feb. 1569); Roth, *The House of Nasi: The Duke of Naxos*, pp. 23-32, 62-74; Grunebaum-Ballin, *Joseph Naci*, pp. 121-22, 131. For Nassí's business interests in Venice see also Baron, *A Social and Religious History*, vol. 18, p. 475, n. 44.

[17] This ambiguous position is reflected in the *Bailo*'s dispatches, see Barbaro's Letter-book, I, ff. 338-338v (8 Mar. 1570).

[18] Baron, *A Social and Religious History*, vol. 18, p. 90. For a few examples of such unproven cases, see below.

[19] See, for instance, the somewhat anti-Semitic article by A. Arce, "Espionaje y ultima aventura de José Nasí (1569-1574)", *Sefarad*, 13 (1953), pp. 257-286. In spite of its title and Arce's affirmations about Nassí's "vast espionage organization" covering the entire Mediterranean world, not a single direct proof is cited by Arce for the existence of such an organization or acts of espionage directed by Nassí. See esp. *ibid.*, p. 263, where Arce writes about "the caste of spies" in reference to Jewish activity in this field.

maintains communication everywhere."[20] Reports about his activities on behalf of his brethren, for example the initiative (attributed to him, but actually Doña Gracia's) to settle Jews in Tiberias or in his Duchy of Naxos, helped to spread this image.[21] It was also supported by his influence on Jews throughout the Ottoman Empire, and his wide connections with Jews outside Ottoman territories. It should be noted, however, that Nassí's position among his Jewish brethren was not undisputed. He also had opponents among the Ottoman Jews, as was demonstrated on various occasions, such as in the rabbinical dispute following the burning of *Marranos* at Ancona, when the position of Nassí and Doña Gracia favouring the boycott of Ancona was disputed by several communities and rabbis; the dispute about the excommunication of the physician Daud, who had been used by the French in order to defame Nassí; and the rivalry between Nassí and Solomon

[20] ASV, Cons. X, Secreti, reg. 8, f. 121 (12 June 1568), cited in S. Romanin, *Storia documentata di Venezia*, vol. 6, Venice, 1925, p. 316, n. 2 and in Schiavi, "Gli ebrei in Venezia e nelle sue colonie", p. 494; See also *Relazioni*, ed. Albèri, ser. III, vol.1, p. 361 (Badoer's report, 1573); Roth, *The House of Nasi: The Duke of Naxos*, pp. 22, 110, 161-63; Baron, *A Social and Religious History*, vol. 18, p. 112. Interestingly, a similar conviction can also be found in Ottoman sources; see Gerber, *Economic and Social Life*, p. 23 and n. 56. I am grateful to Minna Rozen for the latter reference.

[21] On the Tiberias project, see Roth, *The Duke of Naxos*, pp. 110-35; Grunebaum-Ballin, *Joseph Naci*, p. 79; J. Braslavsky, *Studies in our Country, its Past and Remains*, Tel Aviv, 1954, pp. 180-215 [Hebrew]; U. Heyd, *Ottoman Documents on Palestine 1552-1615. A Study of the Firman according to the Mühime Defteri*, Oxford, 1960, pp. 139-42; *idem*, "Turkish Documents on the Rebuilding of Tiberias in the Sixteenth Century", *Sefunot*, 10 (1966), pp. 193-210 [Hebrew]; Baron, *A Social and Religious History*, vol. 18, pp 109-118. Baron writes that after 1563, Nassí apparently became the moving spirit behind the Tiberias project, *ibid.*, pp. 114-115. For contemporary attribution of the Tiberias project to Don Joseph, see, for instance E. Charrière, *Negociations de la France dans le Levant*, vol. 2, Paris, 1850, pp. 735-37 (report of The French Ambassador in Istanbul, 1563), and Joseph Hacohen, *Emek Habacha* [The Vale of Tears], tr. M. Wiener, Leipzig, 1858, pp. 127, 129. On the idea to obtain an island from Venice for Jewish settlement: Grunebaum-Ballin, *Joseph Naci*, p. 49. According to a report of the papal nuncio in Venice, a ship carrying 200 Jews on their way to the Duchy of Naxos was captured by pirates in Oct. 1567, see *Nunziature di Venezia*, vol. 8, pp. 277, 286, 337.

Ashkenazi.[22] The following is a passage from a letter of Rabbi Joshua Soncino to the Duke of Urbino, regarding the proposal to boycott Jewish trade with Ancona and transfer it to Pesaro in that Duchy: "...Because there is no king of the Jewish people, it is impossible to achieve uniformity of opinion and to compel the merchants to carry out the condition which the refugees [from Ancona] made with him..."[23] According to a dispatch of the Venetian *Bailo* of 1579, Nassí's death caused great satisfaction to many Jews.[24]

Without taking this discussion further beyond our main subject, we should keep in mind that the myth itself was an historical reality which affected the attitudes of Venetians towards the Jews in their midst. In fact, it reinforced the collective image of the Jew, by then already well developed, as a perfidious and traitorous creature.[25] In other words, since Nassí was held to be an implacable enemy of the Republic, the head of an international network of spies and saboteurs, and the acknowledged chief of the Jews, it was a short step to blaming all Jews for any treachery or disaster.

These ideas were probably sustained by the belief in ecclesiastical circles that the Jews nurtured messianic hopes connected with the vision of Rome's destruction by the 'Turks'.[26] Jews were traditionally accused

---

[22] On the disputes around the boycott on Ancona, see Roth, *The House of Nasi: Doña Gracia*, pp. 158-168; A.Toaff, "Nuova luce sui marrani di Ancona (1556)", in *Studi sull'ebraismo italiano in memoria di Cecil Roth*, ed. E. Toaff, Rome, 1974, pp. 261-280; M. Saperstein, "Martyrs, Merchants and Rabbis: Jewish Communal Conflict as Reflected in the *Responsa* on the Boycott of Ancona", *Jewish Social Studies*, 43 (1981), pp. 215-228. On the affair of the physician Daud, Roth, *The House of Nasi: The Duke of Naxos*, pp. 71-72; on the rivalry between Nassí and Ashkenazi, see below.

[23] Saperstein, "Martyrs, Merchants and Rabbis", p. 224.

[24] Grunebaum-Ballin, *Don Joseph Naci*, p. 165. For a different opinion, see Baron, *A Social and Religious History*, vol. 18, pp. 106-107.

[25] L. Poliakov, *A History of Anti-Semitism*, vol. 1, London, 1974, pp. 126-27, 153.

[26] See the treatise written by Giulio Marcello Romano, lecturer at the *Studio* of Rome, which can be attributed to the period on the eve of the battle of Lepanto (1571), Biblioteca Apostolica Vaticana, Ms. Vat. Lat. 3933, ff. 18, 19. I am grateful to Dr. Nicholas Davidson of the University of Leicester for this reference.

of plotting to destroy Christendom,[27] but such beliefs became more concrete in the face of the 'Turkish' menace. From the eve of the Cyprus war and throughout the period of hostilities, in the dense atmosphere of fear and insecurity, every Jew throughout the Venetian empire became a potential suspect as a traitor. The following examples show the effect of this process.

At the beginning of 1568 news reached Venice about a plot hatched in the Jewish quarter of Famagusta, co-ordinated by Joseph Nassí, to cede the important Cypriot fortress to the Ottoman fleet. The investigations directed by the Venetian governors were fruitless, but it was nevertheless decided to expel from Famagusta all the Jews who were not natives of the island.[28] When I first investigated this affair in the late 1970s, the fact that the native-born Jews were not expelled led me to conclude that Venice was guided by pragmatic considerations, not by anti-Jewish policy as such.[29] I am now convinced that matters stood differently at that time. The period was characterized by great fears, easily channelled into anti-Jewish attitudes, which were sometimes translated into actions. In March 1568, when fire broke out near the *Bailo*'s residence in Istanbul, it was rumoured that the Jews had done it.[30] In May that year the *Bailo* wrote that he did not wish to see the Venetian empire fall into the hands of "[Turkish] dogs through the treacherous perfidy of Jewish dogs".[31] While measures were being taken against the Jews of Famagusta, Venetian magistrates at Corfu and Crete were ordered to keep the Jews under control and to search their mansions.[32] On 12 June 1568, the Council of Ten decided to oust all the Jews living within the Republic's "fortresses in the Levant", basing its decision on the great esteem in which the Hebrew nation held Joseph Nassí, "considered as principal leader (*capo principale*)

---

[27] J. Trachtenberg, *The Devil and the Jews. The Medieval Conception of the Jew and its Relation to Modern Anti-Semitism*, Cleveland, New York and Philadelphia, 1961, pp. 12-13, 40, 102-103, 184-185.

[28] B. Arbel, "The Jews in Cyprus: New Evidence from the Venetian Period", *Jewish Social Studies*, 41 (1979), pp. 28-29.

[29] *Ibid.*, pp. 29-30.

[30] *Nunziature di Venezia*, vol. 8, ed. A. Stella, Rome, 1963, p. 372.

[31] ASV, Capi X, Lett. CP, busta 3, No 135 (9 May 1568).

[32] ASV, Cons. X, Secreti, reg. 8, ff. 117-118 (4 June 1568), 121 (12 June 1568). Similar instructions were sent to Crete and Cyprus early in 1570, see *ibid.*, reg. 9, ff. 50-50v (25 Jan. 1570).

of those Jews, with whom he maintains contacts everywhere."[33] According to a Venetian chronicle, the Jews of Zara were also expelled during that year.[34]

The belief in the existence of a Jewish plot against the Republic, which appeared early in 1568, continued to influence Venetian attitudes and policy during the following years. In September 1569 a fire caused great damage to the Venetian arsenal. Once again, suspicion fell on Nassí and the Jews.[35] Abraham Benveniste, known as Righetto *Marrano*, a distant relative of Joseph Nassí, was arrested in 1570 in Venice, suspected of having transmitted information to Istanbul. Unable to prove his guilt, the Ten turned him over to the Inquisition.[36] As far as I know, proofs of such secret contacts were never discovered, but in those days proofs were not essential. In January 1570, the Council of Ten ordered the governors of Crete and Cyprus to keep a vigilant eye on the Jews in these colonies, particularly on the agents of Gioan Miches (Joseph Nassí) and their correspondence.[37] The ruling circles, and not only they, were disposed to believe any rumour associating Jews with acts of treachery.

Also noteworthy is the connotation given to the Hebrew language in that context. Joshua Trachtenberg has already written on the image of Hebrew as a magic language, or a sorcerer's tongue, in Christian belief.[38] Just before and during the war of the 1570s Hebrew was regarded as a kind of secret code, used by the anti-Venetian network directed by Nassí. Some letters written by Jewish merchants, which were found floating in a Venice canal at the beginning of March 1570, were brought before the Council of Ten, the chief body responsible

---

[33] ASV, Cons. X, Secreti, reg. 8, f. 121v (12 June 1568).

[34] BNM, Ms. It VII 213 (8836), Cronaca Lippomano, f. 289v.

[35] Von Hammer did not hesitate to adopt this version four centuries later with no evidence at hand, see Hammer-Purgstall, *Geschichte des Osmanischen Reiches*, vol. 2, p. 401.

[36] Pullan, "A Ship with Two Rudders", p. 45 (His consignment to the Inquisition is recorded on 26 Sept. 1570); *Nunziature di Venezia*, vol. 9, p. 61 (18 July, 1571).

[37] ASV, Cons. X, Secreti, reg. 9, f. 50 (25 Jan. 1569 *m.v.*). The governors of Cyprus reported on 11 March having carried out these orders; see ASV, Capi X, Lett. busta 290, Nos 280-81 (11 Mar. 1570).

[38] Trachtenberg, *The Devil and the Jew*, pp. 61-63.

for public security, to be translated there.[39] Likewise, the papal nuncio,
who complained in the *Collegio* that the Venetian fleet had seized ships
sailing between Ancona and Ragusa, was told that letters written by
Jews were found in one of those ships.[40] It was not deemed necessary
to refer to their contents. It was enough that they were written in
Hebrew.

Turks and Jews, they were the enemies.[41] The former used armies
and galleys, the latter the weapons of perfidy, an attribute which the
deep-rooted Christian myth viewed as an outstanding characteristic
of Jewish nature.[42] The theme of Jewish treachery in general, and
its particular connection in the sixteenth century with the 'Turkish'
menace, was widespread throughout Christian Europe. But as demonstrated in other cases, it was more acute in the regions which were
in direct conflict with the Ottoman Empire. Similar accusations led
to the expulsion of the Jews from Bohemia in 1541, and from various
parts of Austria in 1544, 1572 and 1602.[43] In Venice they were poten-
tially more susceptible to such charges, not only because Jews resided
in many Venetian territories in the eastern Mediterranean, close to

---

[39] ASV, Capi X, Lett. CP, busta 5, No 66 ("traduttione di lettere de hebrei trovati
in aqua, per liquali si vede che sono in timore per questa guerra et dicono che li soi
si ritirino da Patras in Lepanto per maggior sicurtà, 7 martii 1570").

[40] *Nunziature di Venezia*, vol. 9, ed. A. Buffardi, Rome, 1972, pp. 419 (30 Dec.
1570), 434-35 (21 Jan. 1571).

[41] Turks and Jews are often mentioned together as enemies in the contemporary
diplomatic correspondence; see, for instance *Corrispondenza da Madrid di Leonardo
Donà*, eds. E. Vitale and M. Brunetti, Venice-Rome, 1963, pp. 132, 184-86; *Nunziature
di Venezia*, vol. 9, p. 456. Even after the peace settlement, the Council of Ten warned
the *Bailo* not to put too much trust in "Turks and Jews": ASV, Cons. X, Secreti,
reg. 11, f. 44v (25 Jan. 1575).

[42] ASV, Sen. Disp. CP, filza 2, No 63 (18 Oct. 1567), No 79 (7 Dec. 1567),
No 86 (Nov. 1568), No 100 (7 Feb. 1568); A. Valerio, *Dell'utilità che si può tirare
delle cose operate dai veneziani*, Padua, 1787 pp. 357-59 (a contemporary testimony,
referring to Alvise Grimani's speech in the Senate about 1569); ASV, Cons. X, Secreti,
reg. 8, f. 104v (13 Feb. 1569); *Nunziature di Venezia*, vol. 10, ed. A. Stella, Rome,
1977, pp. 279 (13 Sept. 1572), 303 (18 Oct. 1572); ASV, Sen. Secreti, reg. 11, f.
141v (3 Oct. 1577); ASV, Capi X, Lett. CP, busta 4, No 127 (24 Jan. 1581).

[43] Trachtenberg, *The Devil and the Jews*, pp. 185-86.

the Ottoman centres of power,[44] but chiefly because the city of Venice itself was host to Jews who were Ottoman subjects.

***

When the Cypriot war became inevitable, the Levantine Jewish merchants in Venice found themselves in a dangerous position. It should be remembered that in spite of formal prohibitions, Levantine Jews had lived in Venice for many years together with their families. The escalation which led up to the war went on for many months, but though the Jews had enough experience of exile, expulsion and escape, no doubt they still hoped for a last-minute turn for the better. Nevertheless, like the Muslim Ottoman subjects who remained in Venetian territories during the war, but unlike the Christian ones, they were detained at the beginning of March 1570, and their property, money and credits, were all confiscated.[45] The arrest of Muslim and Jewish subjects of the Ottoman Empire, and the confiscation of their goods, was meant to apply all over the Venetian dominions, particularly in the overseas colonies, as well as on the high seas.[46] The wording of the decree, proposed by the *Collegio*, did not justify this measure in detail, stating

---

[44] In 1538, during the previous war between Venice and the Ottomans, the Jewish quarter of Candia, the capital of Venetian Crete, was ransacked on suspicion that Turkish spies were harboured there, see *Statuta iudaeorum Candiae*, eds. E.S. Artom and H.M.D. Cassuto, Jerusalem, 1943, pp. 121-24, cited by Trachtenberg, *The Devil and the Jews*, p. 185.

[45] ASV, Senato, Mar reg. 39, ff, 163v-164 (6 Mar. 1570). The original decree referred to "Turchi, Hebrei levantini et altri sudditi turcheschi". For the decision to exclude Christian Ottoman subjects from these measures, see *ibid.*, f. 164 (11 Mar. 1570). The arrest of the *Levantini* and the confiscation of their merchandise on 4 March 1570 was reported by the papal nuncio on the following day; the Senate's decision, therefore, probably followed the actual seizure of the Jews and their property, see *Nunziature di Venezia*, vol. 9, p. 226. On 8 April, the Senate reiterated a clause of the original decree obliging all debtors of the detained to deposit the sums owed to them at the office of the *Governatori delle entrate*, see ASV, Senato, Mar, reg. 39, f. 195v (8 Apr. 1570).

[46] The decree stated that it applied "in cadauna ... terra et luogo del stato nostro". Its dispatch to the Venetian governors in Crete, Cyprus, Corfu, Cefalonia, Zante and Dalmatia, is recorded in the margin of the decree.

only that it was done for reasons "well-known to this council".[47] The large number of detainees necessitated a special arrangement for their confinement. It was therefore decided to put them in the public granaries (*magazeni*) of Terranova, behind the *Procuratie Nuove*, "where the *Gabioni* used to be" (*ove solevano esser li Gabioni*).[48] The detainees had to declare all property and credit which they had in Venice. People who held property belonging to the detainees, or who were indebted to them, were obliged to transfer everything to the *Governatori delle entrate*. On 8 March the Senate issued another decree, stating that there were in Venice many debtors of the "Turks and Jews who were Turkish subjects", and reiterating the obligation to transfer this capital to the office which had been appointed for the purpose.[49] On the same day, the *Governatori delle entrate* were instructed to sell those properties at a public auction and to deposit the income in the Mint.[50] Three days later the Senate ordered that a Venetian citizen be elected to guard the "Jews and the Turkish subjects", with the assistance of four "good and sufficient men".[51]

How many people did this operation entail? A Jew who managed to escape from Venice to Istanbul in December 1570 claimed that 75 Muslims and 87 Jews had been arrested and were held in prison in miserable conditions. According to him, the confiscated property, amounting to about 400,000 ducats, was sold by the Venetian authorities at half its value.[52] No information has been found regarding the fate

---

[47] Venetian historians later claimed that the Ottoman subjects had been detained in retaliation for a similar act by the Ottomans against Venetian subjects and their property; see G. Hill, *A History of Cyprus*, vol. 3, Cambridge, 1948, pp. 885-86. The claim is repeated in Ravid, "The First Charter", p. 191. But I have found no confirmation for it in the Senate's deliberation, or in the *Bailo*'s correspondence preceding the Senate's decree of 6 March 1570.

[48] The significance of the term *Gabioni* in this context is not quite clear. It could either signify great cages, or implements used for hydraulic defence.

[49] ASV, Sen., Mar, reg. 39, ff. 195v-196.

[50] *Ibid.*, f. 196.

[51] *Ibid.*, f. 200v (11 Apr. 1570).

[52] ASV, Sen., Disp. CP., filza 5, No 68, f. 307 (16 Dec. 1570). The claim that Venice sold the merchandise belonging to Jewish merchants at derisory prices was later repudiated by the Venetian special envoy to Istanbul, Giacomo Ragazzoni, who purported that only perishable goods had been sold at good prices in public auction and with the consent of the owners, that the money derived from the sale was kept for the owners in a secure place, like the other goods belonging to them; see Albèri,

of the merchants' wives, children and other relatives, during those years. Even if they were not arrested, the separation from the heads and providers of their families must have been a hard trial. It should be noted that the order was supposed to be applied in all Venetian territories, particularly those of the *stato da mar*. There are indications that Jewish merchants were, in fact, arrested in Crete.[53] The above-mentioned report, mentioning 87 Jews and 75 Muslims, apparently only referred to the operation in Venice. The overall number of detained Jews and Muslims must, therefore, have been larger.

Part of the capital confiscated from the Ottoman merchants was used for their upkeep. A *responsum* given by R. Samuel de Medina after the war refers to Venice's use of the property and capital of the detained Jewish merchants to cover the cost of their maintenance under lock and key. Somewhat later, those among the detainees whose property and capital were used in this way to support the entire group, tried, but did not succeed, to obtain compensation from their brethren, who had either been lucky enough to avoid confiscation, or had no property of their own.[54] In March 1571 the Council of Ten approved a request by the detained Ottoman merchants to allot 10 ducats to each out of the sequestrated capital for their daily expenditures.[55]

Inevitably, the same capital served other purposes too. For example, on 16 September 1570, the Senate ordered the *Governatori delle entrate* to pay 1329 ducats and 21 grossi to a certain Coggia Ali, described as *turco da Tauris*, who was a subject of the *Signor Suffi* (the Ruler of Persia), as compensation for a sum owed him by the Dolfin bank. The *Governatori* were later to be credited for the sum in the account of the same bank.[56]

The arrest of the Jewish and Muslim merchants was accompanied by other anti-Jewish measures and by violent manifestations against them. The Venetian fleet operated against foreign vessels which transported Jews, and goods belonging to Jews, across the Adriatic, with the pretext that "Jews were the main instigators of this war", which

---

Relazioni, ed. Albèri, ser III, vol. 2, p. 84.

[53] See below, n. 60, and p. 83.

[54] Samuel de Medina, *Responsa*, Ṭur Ḥoshen Hamishpaṭ, New York, 1959, No 70 [Hebrew].

[55] ASV, Cons. X, Secreti, reg. 9, ff. 148-148v (9 Mar. 1571).

[56] ASV, Senato, Mar, reg. 39, f. 273.

the Turks had been driven to launch "by the espionage and mischief of the Jews", as explained by the Doge on two different occasions to the papal nuncio.[57] In August 1570, the Venetian governors of Corfu forbade Jews to leave the island, evidently because they were suspected of treason.[58] A ship transporting Jewish refugees from the Papal States was caught by the Venetian fleet commander near Ragusa. Women, aged persons and children were set free, but the able-bodied men were sent to row in the galleys.[59] Lower functionaries in Venetian Crete felt free to commit acts of violence against Jews.[60] A French ship anchored at Candia was pillaged when a rumour spread that there were Jews on board.[61] As might have been expected, anti-Jewish hostility intensified in Venice too. Jews were stoned when they passed by the Greek quarter of San Giovanni in Bragora.[62] The storehouses of the Levantine Jews at Rialto were plundered.[63] In various pamphlets, prognostics and prophesies published in Venice during the war, Jews

---

[57] *Nunziature di Venezia*, vol.9, pp. 292 (17 June 1570), 368-69 (14 Oct. 1570).

[58] *Stampa delli signori priori o siano presidenti del Collegio degl'Intervenienti di Corfù al taglio contro li capi dell'università degl'Ebrei di Corfù* [place and date unspecified], p. 45. I am grateful to Dr. Cesare Vivante for putting a photocopy of this rare publication at my disposal.

[59] Joseph Hacohen, *Emek Habacha*, p. 108. The Hebrew chronicler only mentions the month in which this incident took place (March). Jews were expelled from the Papal States in May 1569, and Paul V died in May 1572. The incident must therefore have occurred sometime between 1570 and 1572. On these events, see D. Carpi, "The Expulsion of Jews from the Papal State under Paul V and the Trials against the Jews of Bologna (1566-1569)", in *Scritti in memoria di Enzo Sereni*, eds. D. Carpi, A. Milano and U. Nahon, Jerusalem, 1970, pp. 145-64 [Hebrew].

[60] Solomon Ashkenazi complained that his agent in Crete died while being tortured by officials in the colony during the war, see ASV, Capi. X, Lett. CP, busta 3, No 265 (Feb. 1571); a request presented to the Venetian authorities by Joseph Nassí stated that Venetian functionaries sold Jews as slaves in order to gain from their subsequent deliverance; see ASV, Cons. X, Secreti, filza 18 (30 Aug. 1574).

[61] ASV, Capi X, Lett. Candia, busta 285, No 157 (11 Mar. 1571).

[62] Pullan "A Ship with Two Rudders", p. 55.

[63] ASV, Cons. X, Secreti, reg. 11, ff. 24-24v. See also the documents in the Appendix, regarding the goods stolen during the war from the warehouses of Joshua Davizzolo and Joseph Marzan.

figured as God-killers, traitors and enemies.[64]

Jews also became embroiled in the rivalry between the Papal States and Venice over the East-West trade across the Adriatic. In the midst of the common struggle against the Ottoman enemy the Papacy and Venice were still at loggerheads on this issue, and the cause of the incidents which brought the two Christian powers into conflict were again the Jews, or so it seemed to the two allies. It is therefore not surprising to discover that from June 1570 discussions were held on the proposal to expel all the Jews from Venice and Ancona alike. The latter city, we should recall, was the only one in the Papal States other than Rome where Jews were still permitted to live at this time. Significantly, these discussions did not refer only to the *Levantini*, but to Jews in general.[65] The fact that Venice was considering more than the expulsion of Ottoman Jews received another confirmation in February 1571, when the Republic refused to negotiate the renewal of the *condotta* of the Ashkenazi Jews.[66] Even if some patricians favoured renewing the official permit, they must have felt that the moment was inauspicious for such an attitude.

***

Generally speaking, the detention of the Ottoman merchants, and particularly of the Jewish ones, seems to have been detrimental to Venice's financial position. This is borne out in a decision of the Senate on 21 November 1570, which practically opened Venice's foreign trade to any Christian person for the duration of the war.[67] This was a radical step for a Republic which had always carefully restricted this lucrative activity to particular groups and maintained continuous control over it.

It is noteworthy that Venetian merchants apparently fared better

---

[64] *E.g.* Giovanni Battista Nazari, *Discorso della futura e sperata vittoria contra il turco etc*, Venice, 1570, p. 15; Cosimo Filiarchi, *Trattato della guerra e dell'unione de' principi Cristiani contra i Turchi e gli altri infedeli*, Venice, 1572 [but written before Lepanto], pp. 6, 63.

[65] *Nunziature di Venezia*, vol. 8, p. 213; *ibid.*, pp. 144, 154, 295-96; Pullan, *The Jews of Europe*, p. 182.

[66] Ravid, "The Socioeconomic Background", p. 41.

[67] ASV, Senato, Mar, reg. 39, f. 295v (21 Nov. 1570).

in the Ottoman Empire than did the Ottoman merchants in Venice. At the beginning of March 1570, probably on the very days when the *Levantini* were being arrested in Venice, Venetian merchants in Egypt appeared to be facing similar treatment. A boat belonging to the Venetian ship *Dolphina* reached Cyprus on 14 March 1570, or a little earlier. The men on board reported that they escaped by the skin of their teeth, having been warned by the interpreter of the Venetian consulate in Cairo, who also told them about the detention of the consul and other Venetians in the Egyptian capital.[68] Yet, subsequently, the situation in Egypt must have improved, since at the beginning of December 1570, the captain of the *Barbara*, a Venetian ship which had been mobilized in Egypt to carry supplies to Istanbul, reported to the Venetian *Bailo* that all Venetian merchants in Egypt were well and were able to trade and move around freely.[69] In the Ottoman capital too, though the Bailo was confined to his mansion for the duration of the war, Venetian merchants were free to move about and even to engage in trade. The only limitation on their movements seems to have been a restriction to Ottoman territory, at least legally, as long as the war lasted.

When the news about the arrest of the *Levantini* and the Muslim merchants in Venice, and the sequestration of their goods, reached Istanbul, the Jewish entrepreneurs in the Ottoman capital began lobbying at the Porte, to secure the liberation of the Ottoman subjects detained in Venice. In his letter of 10 August 1570, the *Bailo* reported that "this Hebrew nation has made public a letter signed by many Jews, according to which all subjects of this Seigneur, Turks and Jews alike, who are in Venice, have been harshly confined, their goods confiscated and sold in favour of the public treasury". The *Bailo*, who must have been unaware of developments back home, tried to find out the date of that report. Finding that the letter was undated, he took advantage of it to claim that all Ottoman subjects had in the meantime been released. He went so far as to add a warning, that unless they stopped their machinations, all the Jews and their possessions were in grave danger.[70]

Thereafter Barbaro was left in peace for some time, but the fact

---

[68] ASV, Sen. Disp. da Cipro, filza 4 blue, 14 Mar. 1570.

[69] "Ciascuni di essi trafficava et faceva liberamente i fatti suoi", ASV, Sen., Disp. CP, filza 5, No 68, f. 307 (16 Dec. 1570).

[70] *Ibid.*, f. 192 (10 Aug. 1570).

that Jewish and Muslim merchants were still detained in Venice could not be kept secret much longer. In December 1570 Barbaro reported that the Grand Vizier showed him a petition presented to the Sultan by a Jew who had escaped from Venice and brought to Istanbul a detailed description of the hardships suffered by the Sultan's subjects in Venice, with a request to arrest all the Venetians in Ottoman territories in reprisal. The petition was brought to the *Bailo* by a *Çavuş*, who told Barbaro that the Sultan had noted in his own hand in the margin: "If our subjects are suffering in this manner, while these [Venetians] live here with all their goods, it is not right." The Grand Vizier suggested that Barbaro should consider the implications of this note. Four days later the Vizier informed Barbaro about another petition, similar to the former, which had been presented to the Sultan. Curiously, Ibrāhīm Bey, the interpreter of the Porte, who in this affair was the Vizier's messenger to the *Bailo*, told him that the Sultan's intention to retaliate by arresting all the Venetians had been reversed by Sokollu. According to this report, Sokollu obtained a religious opinion from the *Mufti* of Istanbul, that those who came to the Empire in good faith should not be made to suffer, and that if Venice had unjustly arrested the Sultan's subjects, Muslims must not imitate such evil actions. It seems that the prudent Vizier, who was interested in bringing the war to an end, determinedly pressured the *Bailo* to secure the release of the Ottoman merchants, while preventing harsh actions against the Venetians in the Ottoman Empire.

It must have been obvious to the *Bailo* that, unless he helped to bring about the release of the *Levantini* in Venice, the fate of Venetians throughout the Ottoman Empire might take a turn for the worse. He therefore expressed his readiness to negotiate a mutual exchange of merchants. Sokollu suggested that the *Bailo* should send his interpreter, accompanied by another messenger, to Venice to examine the possibilities of such an agreement. The *Bailo*'s interpreter being an Ottoman subject, the Vizier saw him as a reliable envoy.

And so, on the 21 February the papal nuncio in Venice reported to Rome that Matheca, the *Bailo*'s interpreter, had arrived in Istria to negotiate the liberation of the Jewish merchants (curiously, the Muslims were not mentioned in this report) with their merchandise, in return for the release of goods belonging to Christians in Ottoman territories.[71] The Senate responded swiftly, and on 3 March announced that Matheca Salvego had been sent by the *Bailo*, following the proposal made by Mehmed Pasha, in the Sultan's name, to exchange the "Jews and Turks", who were imprisoned in Venice, with their goods, with the Venetians in Istanbul. But Matheca, not being an Ottoman official, was not empowered to negotiate. He was only a confidential messenger. The Senate moved cautiously: it resolved to send to Istanbul not an official envoy, but a private citizen with commercial interests in Istanbul, to negotiate the matter with the Ottomans. The *Collegio*, which was empowered to chose the envoy, selected Giacomo Ragazzoni, a non-patrician citizen.[72] Before his departure, in addition to official instructions, Ragazzoni was given a detailed document which had been presented by Venetian entrepreneurs with interests in Istanbul, Syria, Alexandria and other Ottoman territories. It should be noted that during the same period, Venetian Famagusta was still holding out against its siege, and the battle of Lepanto was yet to come. It seems as if the interests of trade were stronger than the mutual animosity between the two states even at the height of the war.

But the true purpose of Matheca's mission was apparently not revealed even to the Senate. It was the Council of Ten which received the most secret message brought by the *Bailo*'s interpreter. Mehmed Pasha actually proposed to enter into peace negotiations. This is explicitly stated in the letter of the Council of Ten to Barbaro, voted upon on 2 March 1571, that is, only a day before the above-mentioned deliberation of the Senate. The *Bailo* Barbaro was authorized to negotiate the peace terms with the Vizier, and even to use the services of Giacomo Ragazzoni, the citizen appointed to negotiate the exchange of merchants, who also took the Ten's instructions to the *Bailo* in Istanbul.[73] The issue of the exchange of merchants was, therefore, used by Mehmed Pasha to advance his efforts for peace. The attempt proved to be premature, but the exchange of merchants, or at any rate, the release of the Ottoman merchants in Venice, was to be realized within a few months. The secrecy of this mission must have been well kept, since the papal nuncio in Venice, reporting about Ragazzoni's mission in

---

[71] *Nunziature di Venezia*, vol. 9, pp. 448-449 (21-24 Feb. 1571).

[72] ASV, Sen., Delib. CP, reg. 4, f. 36 (3 Mar. 1571).

[73] ASV, Cons. X, Secreti, reg. 9, ff. 141-143v (2 Mar. 1571); *ibid.*, ff. 144v-145 (Instruction given to Ragazzoni, 7 Mar. 1571).

a letter to Rome on 7 March, was apparently unaware of the hidden motives behind this initiative.[74]

Ragazzoni must have arrived in Istanbul some time in April 1571, and departed on the 18th of the following month.[75] An interesting record concerning Ragazzoni's mission and the efforts to liberate the *Levantini,* is an unpublished and undated letter of Joseph Nassí to the Jewish merchants detained in Venice. The reference to Ragazzoni's stay in Istanbul enables us to date this document to the period of April-June 1571 or a little later. The letter, preserved in an Italian version, indicates that Nassí had been approached by the detained merchants (in what way we do not know), who asked him to intervene on their behalf. In his reply, Nassí mentioned his own efforts in trying to persuade Venice to free his detained brethren, "as you can learn from Ragazzoni, who came here to negotiate the release of Christian merchants and their goods." He regretted that he had failed to get results, and asked them to bear their suffering patiently, since they would be compensated for all their losses. "Venice", he added, "can bar your way back to Constantinople, but not the way to Heaven, which is smoother the greater our suffering on earth." In the same letter Nassí reiterated that he had never acted against Venice, and that it was most unjust to punish the Jews in Venice because of acts attributed to him. He went on to say that Venice would never have treated members of other nations in this way. He hoped, however, that with the help of the Ottoman ruler they would soon be delivered from such persecutions by returning to their promised land.[76]

According to a report written by the papal nuncio in Venice, on 16 May 1571, the 'Turkish' merchants in Venice, who had been under arrest, were transferred to the Venetian mansion of the *Bailo* Barbaro, and were also allowed to trade at Rialto. The reason for this change of policy, according to the nuncio's report, was that "the Venetians

---

[74] *Nunziature di Venezia,* vol. 9, p. 456.

[75] ASV, Sen., Disp. CP, filza 5, ff. 387 (4 May 1571), 434 (June 1571). His presence in Istanbul is recorded on 26 April 1571 in the diary [erroneously?] attributed to the *Bailo*'s *Maestro di Casa,* see ASV, Collegio, Relazioni, busta 4, "Diario del Maestro di Casa di Marcantonio Barbaro in Constantinopoli", f. 1v. Cf. Bertelè, *Il palazzo,* p. 138, n. 88. A final report (*relazione*) on Ragazzoni's mission was presented to the Senate on 16 August of the same year; see *Relazioni,* ed. Albèri, ser. III, vol. 2, p. 77 ff.

[76] For the entire text of this letter, see the Appendix.

in Constantinople remain free and are allowed to engage in trade."[77]
The prospect that all the Venetian merchants throughout the Ottoman
Empire might be detained must have moved the Venetian authorities
to release the Jewish and Muslim merchants in Venice. Apparently
the Republic preferred to reach a *de facto* arrangement of this kind
even before it was informed about a formal agreement on this issue
in Istanbul, since on 16 June (*i.e.*, before Ragazzoni's departure from
Istanbul), the Senate wrote to the *Bailo* to continue negotiating about
the exchange of the merchants, "in case this matter was not already
settled."[78] In his report, the nuncio did not mention the location of
Barbaro's house where the oriental merchants were to lodge. Nor is
it currently known whether the *Bailo* was consulted about the settlement
of so many Jewish and Muslim merchants in his private mansion back
home.

Were the Jewish *Levantini* released together with the 'Turkish'
merchants? At this stage there is no reason to doubt that this was the
case. But such a turn for the better was not destined to last very long,
since the anti-Jewish atmosphere in Venice was rife with anti-Jewish
feelings as long as the war continued.

***

The process of anti-Jewish hostility reached its climax on 18 December
1571, when the Venetian Senate decided, during the religious fervour
which accompanied the victory over the Ottomans at Lepanto, to expel
all the Jews from Venice.[79] Historians writing about this affair, though

---

[77] *Nunziature di Venezia*, vol. 9, p. 152 (16 May 1571). I have been unable to
find in the Venetian archives any official decision regarding the release of the detained
merchants.

[78] ASV, Sen., Delib. CP, reg. 4, f. 38v (16 June 1571).

[79] ASV, Senato, Terra, reg. 48, ff. 180-185v. The text has only partially been
published in A.A. Viola, *Compilazione delle leggi [...] in materia di offici e banchi
in Ghetto*, V/2, Venice, 1786, p. 224. For an English translation, see Ravid, "The
Socioeconomic Background", pp. 42-43. The dates of this resolution given by Ravid
("The Socioeconomic Background", p. 47), Roth (*Venice*, p. 88) and Milano (*Storia
degli ebrei in Italia*, p. 280) are inaccurate. The decision was not immediately abrogated,
as claimed by Grendler, but remained in vigour until 1573, cf. P.F. Grendler, "The
Destruction of Hebrew Books in Venice, 1568", *Proceedings of the American Academy
for Jewish Research*, 45 (1978), p. 120. It regarded only the Jews in Venice, and

referring in general terms to the circumstances related to the war with the Ottomans, have tended to deal with it from the perspective of the Ashkenazi Jewish money-lenders.[80] However, we have already seen how the idea to expel the Jews from Venice occasionally surfaced during the 1560s in the context of the controversies with the Levantine Jews. The decision was the climax of a process in which the negative image of the Jew was built up during the years preceding the Cyprus war. The result is reflected in the wording of the edict of expulsion, stating that "Since the Lord has conceded grace to all Christendom, and especially to this Republic, by granting such a felicitous and conspicuous victory over the Turk by defeating his fleet, it is appropriate to demonstrate our gratitude towards Jesus Christ, our blessed defensor and protector, by acting against those who are the enemies of his Holy Faith, as are the Jews", The decree referred to "all the Jews, of whatever status, grade, sex and condition". It emphasized both "the fraud, extortions, deceit and dishonesty towards the poor", obviously attributed to the Ashkenazi money-lenders, and the "treacheries and rebellions against the state", which must have referred to the *Levantini*. Consequently, all the Jews, not only the Ashkenazis, were forbidden to remain in Venice after the two years which were left to the expiration of the old *condotta*. The general character of the decree may also be deduced from the permission given in November 1572 to the Jews of Corfu to come to Venice, as a special dispensation from the decree of December 1571.[81]

A few Venetian leaders were disposed to take more extreme measures. Four days after the decree of expulsion was passed in the Senate, the papal nuncio received a communication in which the Venetians renewed the offer to expel all Jews from all the territories of the Republic, provided the Pope also expelled the Jews from Ancona, so as to "purge

---

not those in the rest of Venetian territories, as claimed by Roth (*Venice*, p. 313) and Milano (A. Milano, *Storia degli ebrei italiani nel Levante*, Florence, 1949, p. 77).

[80] E.g. Ravid, "The Socioeconomic Background", pp. 41-47; Pullan, "A Ship with Two Rudders", p. 55.

[81] *A stampa dell'università degli Ebrei di Corfù* [place and date unspecified], p. 44 (referring to a *Ducale* of 24 Nov. 1572) [I am grateful to Dr. C. Vivante for putting this publication at my disposal]; J.A. Romanos, "Histoire de la communauté israélite de Corfou", *Revue des Etudes Juives*, 23 (1891), p. 67; Roth, *Venice*, p. 313; Milano, *Storia degli ebrei italiani nel Levante*, p. 77.

this dominion and Ancona of the Jews."[82] The papal representative
saw immediately what it was that preoccupied the Venetians: Venice
was likely to pay heavily for the decision to expel all its Jews, including
the Levantine merchants. The trade with the East could easily pass
from Venice to nearby Ancona. There were only two ways to prevent
this eventuality: to persuade the Pope to expel the Jews from Ancona,
or to retract the decree of expulsion, which had been adopted in a
moment of religious fervour without regard to its economic implications.

In the end, the general expulsion from the Venetian state did not
take place. According to Roth, however, many Jews were leaving
Venice, and it looked as if Jewish presence on the lagoon was gradually
coming to an end.[83] In the following chapters we shall see how Jewish
involvement in the world of international trade, and the role played
by a Jewish physician at the Porte, finally led Venice to repeal this
drastic anti-Jewish enactment.

---

[82] *Nunziature*, vol. 10, pp. 167 (22 Dec. 1570), 168 (29 Dec. 1570), 173 (5 Jan.
1572). For earlier contacts concerning a simultaneous expulsion, see above, p. 68.
[83] Roth, *Venice*, pp. 89-90. As usual, Roth does not supply any reference to this
assertion.

CHAPTER FOUR

MEDICINE, DIPLOMACY AND TRADE: SOLOMON ASHKENAZI AND VENETIAN-OTTOMAN RELATIONS, c. 1564-1573

Early in 1571, in the midst of one of the bloodiest wars between Venice and the Ottomans, when Famagusta was still in Venetian hands, tentative contacts were taking place about a possible political settlement.[1] These contacts continued almost without a break until the signing of the peace treaty between Venice and the Sultan in March 1573. Venice's final decisions were made at home, specially by the Council of Ten, but the negotiations were conducted in far-away Istanbul by the *Bailo*, who had to carry out as best he could the Signory's directives. On the Ottoman side, the situation was less clear. The final decision belonged, of course, to the Sultan, but the Grand Vizier, Mehmed Sokollu, directed and influenced, more than anyone else, the contacts with foreign powers. On the other hand, Sokollu's rivals in the Ottoman ruling circle did everything in their power to put obstacles in his way.[2] The war notwithstanding, Sokollu was viewed as rather friendly to Venice. He had received, on various occasions, presents and large sums of money for his cooperation.[3] During the war he could not meet the *Bailo*, or he would risk having his enemies accuse him of treason. The *Bailo* Barbaro, on the other hand, was forbidden to leave his home in Galata, across the Golden Horn, for nearly three years.[4] In order to conduct the serious negotiations, in which both sides were interested, it was therefore necessary to find a trustworthy and discreet intermediary.

---

[1] ASV, Cons. X, Secreti, reg. 9, ff. 141-141v (2 Mar. 1571).

[2] See above, pp. 55-56 and n.3.

[3] *E.g.* ASV, Cons. X, Secreti, filza 12 (7 Dec. 1565); *ibid.*, reg. 8, ff. 75 (28 Jan. 1567), 104v (13 Feb. 1568), 136v (5 Jan. 1569); *ibid.*, reg. 9, f. 2v (2 Apr. 1569).

[4] Barbaro was put under house arrest (not "thrown into prison", as stated in Roth, *Venice*, p. 91) on 7 May 1570; see Barbaro's Letter-book, II, f. 27v. He was released on 13 March 1573; see *ibid.*, f. 415v.

Fortunately for both parties concerned, the best person for the job was readily available—it was the Jewish physician Solomon Ashkenazi.

Solomon Ashkenazi has been the subject of many studies, most of which deal with his involvement in Ottoman foreign policy.[5] In the present chapter we shall briefly mention some highlights of his biography, and focus on his role in re-establishing the peace between the Porte and Venice, and, his involvement in the maritime trade, while his role in bringing about the readmission of the Jews to Venice in 1573 will be discussed in the following chapter.

Ashkenazi's name points to a German origin, but according to his own testimony, he was born at Udine and could therefore be regarded as a Venetian subject, a fact which he liked to mention to Venetian interlocutors.[6] He completed his medical studies at the University of Padua, and then, probably after the expulsion of the Jews from Udine in 1556, started on his peregrinations. For a while he practiced his profession at the court of King Sigismund II Augustus at Cracow, and in the 1560s he settled in Istanbul.

Jewish physicians were by then occupying important positions in the Ottoman court, often beyond their professional functions.[7] When

---

[5] The main studies dedicated to Solomon Ashkenazi are: Graetz, *Geschichte der Juden*, vol. 9, Note 7, pp. lxix-lxxiii; L. Luzzatto, "Un ambasciatore ebreo nel 1574", *Il Vessillo Israelitico*, 41 (1893), pp. 245-246; M. Soave, "Un ambasciatore ebreo nel 1574", *Il Corriere israelitico*, 17 (1878-79), p. 607; M. Diena, Rabbi Scelomò Askenazi e la Repubblica di Venezia", *Atti del Regio Istituto veneto di Scienze, lettere ed arti*, ser. 7, vol. 9 (1897-98), pp. 616-37; C. Roth, "Dr Solomon Ashkenazi and the Election to the Throne of Poland (1574-75)", *Oxford Slavonic Papers*, 9 (1960), pp. 8-20; *idem*, "Ashkenazi, Solomon", in *Encyclopaedia Judaica*, Jerusalem, 1971, vol. 3, pp. 731-33; A. Aschkenasi, "L'étonnante carrière d'un médecin juif au XVIe siècle: Solomon Aschkenasi", *Revue d'Histoire de la Medicine Hébraïque*, 32 (1979), pp. 5-10, 27-32.

[6] ASV, Capi X, Lett. CP, busta 3, No 256 (31 Jan. 1571); Barbaro's Letter-book, II, f. 439v (7 May 1573).

[7] T. Bertelè, *Il palazzo degli ambasciatori veneti e le sue antiche memorie*, Bologna, 1932, p.142, n. 111; A. Galanté, *Médecins juifs au service de la Turquie*, Istanbul, 1938; F. Babinger, "Ja'qûb Pascha, ein Leibarzt Mehmed's II. Leben und Schiksale des Maestro Iacopo aus Gaetà", *Rivista degli studi Orientali*, 26 (1951), pp. 87-113; B. Lewis, "A Privilege granted by Mehmed II to his Physician", *Bulletin of the School of Oriental and African Studies*, 14 (1952), pp. 550-63; U. Heyd, "Moses Hamon, Chief Jewish Physician to Sultan Süleymān the Magnificent", *Oriens*, 16 (1963), pp. 152-70; M. Benayahu, "The Sermons of R. Yosef b. Meir Garson as a Source for the History of the Expulsion from Spain and Sephardi Diaspora", *Michael*, 7 (1981),

Ashkenazi arrived there were apparently no Catholic physicians in the Ottoman capital and the Western residents also used the services of Jewish doctors.[8] From the mid 1560s, Ashkenazi's clientele included the Venetian *Baili* Bragadin, Soranzo and Barbaro, who served in Istanbul between 1564 and 1574. The last-named must have introduced Ashkenazi to the influential Ottoman Grand Dragoman, who for his part introduced him to the Grand Vizier Sokollu. The Pasha must have noticed the personal qualities of the Jewish physician and took him under his protection.[9] Before long Ashkenazi had become an important member of the Grand Vizier's entourage.

With the outbreak of war between Venice and the Ottoman Empire Ashkenazi found himself in the position of intermediary between the *Bailo* and the Grand Vizier, since both of them, despite the hostilities, wanted to maintain open lines of communication. Ashkenazi was one of the few persons allowed to enter the *Bailo*'s house during the war period, ostensibly as the *Bailo*'s personal physician, but in fact to enable him to communicate with the outer world, particularly with Sokollu.

Ashkenazi was eager to serve the cause of peace between the two powers, and ready to expose himself to great dangers in serving the *Bailo* Barbaro. Some Venetian merchants who had been held up in Istanbul during the war sailed away in his own vessel.[10] He also saw to it that the *Bailo*'s letters reached Venice by smuggling them out of Barbaro's residence in his shoes, and later sent them to Crete, together with his own correspondence, in vessels which he chartered for the purpose.[11] On one occasion, the agent who carried out this mission died accidentally in the Duchy of Naxos. The officials of Don Joseph Nassí seized the secret correspondence and sent it to their master in Istanbul, who did not hesitate to communicate them to the authorities. Consequently, Ashkenazi was arrested, and might have ended his life on the hook, according to local custom. He was saved by Sokollu, probably thanks to his indispensability in the contacts with the Venetian

---

pp. 124-132 [Hebrew]. I am grateful to Minna Rozen for the latter reference.

[8] Bertelè, *Il palazzo*, p. 142, n. 111.

[9] *Relazioni*, ed. Albèri, ser. III, Appendice, Florence, 1863, p. 400 (Barbaro's second report, 1574); Bertelè, *Il palazzo*, p. 137, n. 85.

[10] ASV, Cons. X, Comuni, filza 121 (14 July 1574).

[11] ASV, Capi X, Lett. CP, busta 3, No 256 (31 Jan. 1571); *Relazioni*, ed. Albèri, ser. III, Appendice, p. 400 (1574).

Bailo.[12]

Evidently, the frightful prospect of ending his life on the hook did not demoralize Ashkenazi or diminish his readiness to risk his life. The Ottoman court spent the winter of 1571-72 in Edirne. Sokollu, unwilling to dispense with Ashkenazi's services, brought him along with him on the pretext that he was treating his wife. Sokollu's enemies, aware of his contacts with the *Bailo,* thought that this was the appropriate moment to attack. Ashkenazi was again arrested and interrogated about his functions as intermediary, but Sokollu succeeded in saving him again.[13] At the same time, the merchants of the Jewish Segura family persuaded the Sultan to issue an order to arrest the *Bailo* and the Venetian merchants, who were still free in Istanbul, and to compensate the Segura for the losses they suffered in Venice.[14] At that delicate moment the Grand Vizier, who did not wish to appear as a protector of the Venetians, induced Ashkenazi to try to persuade the influential Ahmed Pasha to get the order abrogated. Ashkenazi did not know Ahmed Pasha, did not have the capital necessary to back up such a request, and did not even know if the *Bailo* would repay him. Sokollu not only encouraged him to carry out this mission, but also lent him the money to grease his colleague's palm. The mission was finally crowned with success.[15]

Except for an interval of a few months in 1572, during which the Republic preferred the mediation services of the French ambassador in Istanbul—which produced no results—Ashkenazi was the central figure, the main hinge, of the negotiations between Mehmed Sokollu and Marcantonio Barbaro.[16] It was also Ashkenazi, together with the Grand Dragoman 'Alī Bey—who had actually been chosen by Ashkena-

---

[12] Barbaro's Letter-book, II, unbound letter at the beginning of the volume, ff. 4-5v; Bertelè, *Il palazzo,* p. 137, n. 85. However, Bertelè confuses Dr. Solomon Ashkenazi with another Jew of the same name. See also the sixteenth-century illustration of execution on the hook in *Life in Istanbul, 1588. Scenes from a Traveller's Picture Book,* Bodleian Library Picture Books, Oxford, 1977, No 24.

[13] Barbaro's Letter-book, II, ff. 251-53.

[14] On the Segura and their business interests in Venice, see below, Chapters Six and Seven.

[15] *Ibid.,* ff. 248v-256v.

[16] On the French mediation, see A. Tenenti "La Francia, Venezia e la Sacra Lega", in *Il Mediterraneo nella seconda metà del Cinquecento alla luce di Lepanto,* ed. G. Benzoni, Florence, 1974, pp. 400-407.

zi's intervention—who drafted the text of the peace treaty which was finally signed in March 1573, despite the enormous difficulties which beset the negotiations until the last moment.[17] After the signing, the *Bailo* Marcantonio Barbaro wrote to Venice:

> ...I am really unable to describe the extent to which Rabbi Solomon has exerted himself in these negotiations, the trials and dangers he faced, which were such that I cannot understand how he summoned so much integrity and sound judgement, and how he did not go out of his mind, since this affair was conducted by all parties so vigorously that I am afraid that if I described it, it would hardly be believed. I am confident that your Serenity, according to your usual courtesy, will not forget the continuous and important services rendered by him throughout this war, with so much damage and risk to himself, and how bravely, lovingly and prudently he strove for this conclusion..."[18]

What drove Solomon Ashkenazi to such utter devotion? The letters of the *Bailo* Marcantonio Barbaro, which are the principal source for our information, reveal the great mutual respect between the three main protagonists of this drama, Sokollu, Barbaro and Ashkenazi, despite the differences in their respective status and power. Judging from the letters, which naturally reflect Barbaro's impressions, Ashkenazi's conduct was not driven by coercion or fear. It is true that the Jewish physician derived some material benefits from his services to Venice. In 1571, he was appointed physician of the Venetian Community in Istanbul. Occasionally he received gifts amounting to several hundreds of ducats from Venice,[19] and other favours were to follow after the conclusion of the peace treaty. But all these benefits together seem disproportionate to the dangers to which he had exposed himself, the expenses which he incurred by his activities, or the personal tragedies which he had to suffer.[20] Beside the satisfaction which he might have

---

[17] *Relazioni*, ed. Albèri, ser. III, Appendice, pp. 413-407.

[18] Barbaro's Letter-book, II, f. 413.

[19] *Ibid.*, f. 247v; ASV, Cons. X, Secreti, reg. 9, f. 177v (27 Sept. 1571); *ibid.*, reg. 10, f. 118 (19 May 1573).

[20] On 7 Feb. 1572, the *Bailo* reported that one Ashkenazi's vessels had sunk, and that his brother, who had been on board, died; see Barbaro's Letter-book, II, ff. 247v-248.

drawn from his involvement in the Porte's high politics, his conduct
seems to have resulted from a sincere attachment to his native country,
where he had passed his childhood and youth, was trained as a physician,
and where several of his relatives were still living.[21] In fact, he made
a great effort to obtain permission for his children to live in Venice,
and even expressed a wish to return to his homeland to pass his final
years there.[22]

***

From our point of view, it is also interesting to see how Solomon
Ashkenazi used the opportunities open to Jews in the maritime trade
of the Ottoman Empire. The first relevant piece of evidence is a letter
dated 21 December 1569, sent to Venice by the *Bailo* Marcantonio
Barbaro. This is also the earliest direct reference to Ashkenazi which
I have so far been able to trace in Venetian sources. Its date and contents
clearly show that the physician's involvement in international commerce
preceded his rise to prominence in Sokollu's entourage. Barbaro wrote:

> ...A certain Rabbi Solomon Ashkenazi, a physician from Udine, has been
> in regular attendance at the house of your Serenity's *Baili*. I believe he
> is a discreet and honest person and an avowed friend of the Baili. Having
> various commercial investments in Crete, constituting the greater part of
> his capital, he was interested in information on the plans regarding Cyprus.
> Being on familiar terms with Gioan Miches [Don Joseph Nassí], he tried
> several times to learn from him whether it would be safe to send his capital
> to Crete, considering these disturbances...[23]

Obviously, the doctor's involvement in mercantile enterprise had already
been going on for some time before the clouds of war threatened to
disturb it. The rumours which circulated in the eastern Mediterranean

---

[21] For Ashkenazi's family relations, see B. Arbel, "Salomone Ashkenazi, mercante
e armatore", in *Il mondo ebraico. Gli ebrei tra Italia nord-orientale e Impero asburgico
dal Medioevo all'Età contemporanea*, Pordenone, 1991, p. 16 and note 15, as well
as the genealogical tree on p. 128.

[22] ASV, Senato, Lettere e scritture turchesche (hereafter: LST), filza 3, Nos 157-58
[blue numbering] (Feb. 1577); Barbaro's Letter-book, II, 439v (7 May 1573).

[23] Barbaro's Letter-book, I, f. 256.

regarding an eventual Ottoman invasion of Cyprus justly worried him, being afraid of finding himself unprepared with most of his investments in enemy territory.

Unfortunately for Ashkenazi, his fears proved to be well founded. In another letter written by the *Bailo* on 31 January 1571, we find the sequel of the affair:

> ...Dr. Rabbi Solomon Nathan Ashkenazi, our house physician and your Serenity's subject, originating from Udine, who indeed, with great care and affection, and not without considerable risk to himself, has always promptly served our affairs, as you may already know by reading those of my letters which have reached their destination... About a month ago he told me that he was informed by people who came from Candia, where he has much money and goods, that the authorities there have arrested his agent and brother-in-law, and that several of his small vessels (*caramussalini et bergantini*), as well as a ship which he had sent there in order to purchase wine for the most serene king of Poland, have been sequestrated. He complained that since these vessels were sailing with the *Bailo*'s letters of recommendation, and being himself a subject of your Serenity, to whom he has already proved his good will and servitude, it is most unfortunate that such damage has been inflicted upon him...

According to this letter, Ashkenazi incurred a debt of 1500 ducats as a result of these events. The *Bailo* transmitted Ashkenazi's request to send his goods on the same *brigantino* which also carried the *Bailo*'s letter.[24] It seems as if the Venetian officials on Crete had not been aware of Ashkenazi's importance for Venice's interests and treated him, as well as his Jewish relative and agent, as enemy subjects, and their goods as enemy property.

This letter not only reveals that Ashkenazi was investing his capital in commercial enterprise, it also shows that his business activities were substantial, since he was in possession of several small vessels, and exported Cretan wine to Poland through Istanbul. His high connections in the Ottoman capital must have been useful in business affairs of this kind. It is also possible that Ashkenazi's earlier contacts in the Polish court were used for this purpose. Another document reveals

---

[24] ASV, Capi X, Lett CP, busta 3, No 256.

that a brother of his actually lived in Poland.[25] Evidently Ashkenazi's commercial ventures were supported by a network of kinsmen, spread over a large geographical area, including Venice, the Venetian mainland, Crete and Poland. [26]

To follow Ashkenazi's business affairs: the Council of Ten received the *Bailo*'s letter, and as could be expected, ordered the governors of Crete to release the goods, the money and the ships and restore them to Ashkenazi's agent.[27] But they had meanwhile answered the *Bailo* directly, claiming not to have sequestrated any goods, on the basis of Barbaro's recommendations. According to their letter, the goods were in the hands of the executor of the deceased agent of Solomon Ashkenazi. As for the vessels, the governors excused their actions by the special circumstances of the war.[28]

In spite of the war and the risks involved, Ashkenazi tenaciously advanced his commercial ventures. Unable to cope from afar with the problems of his Cretan business affairs, he decided to send his brother, who was then in Poland, to look after them, at the same time asking the *Bailo* to back him in the new endeavour. And indeed, on 10 April 1571, the Ten sent new instructions to Crete, with orders to consign the money, goods and ships to Ashkenazi's brother. Special mention was made of a ship of 300 *botti*, belonging to the Jewish physician, which had been sequestrated by the Venetian authorities in Crete. The governors were also instructed to allow Ashkenazi's brother to sell the goods on the island and invest the proceeds in Malmsey wine and lemon juice. This merchandise would then be sent to Venice with an official safe-conduct.[29] It should be recalled that while Ashkenazi was enjoying such favourable treatment by the Council of Ten, Jewish merchants in Venice and throughout the Venetian dominions were being held in custody and their goods were sequestrated by the state.

Unfortunately, Ashkenazi was unable to rejoice in this special favour.

---

[25] Arbel, "Salomone Ashkenazi, mercante e armatore", pp. 123-125, n. 15.

[26] *Ibid.*

[27] ASV, Cons. X, Secreti, reg. 9, f. 138 (21 Feb. 1571).

[28] ASV, Capi X, Lett. CP, busta 3, No 265; *ibid.*, Lett. da Candia, busta 265, No 134 (27 Feb. 1571). It seems that the news about the death of his agent and brother-in-law, mentioned in the governors' letter, had not reached Ashkenazi's when he complained to the *Bailo*.

[29] ASV, Cons. X, Secreti, reg. 9, f. 156v and filza 15.

According to another letter written by the *Bailo* on the following 7 February, a ship belonging to Solomon Ashkenazi, loaded with merchandise, foundered off Crete. His brother, who was on board, met his death on that occasion.[30] In all likelihood this was the same ship and the same brother mentioned above, who were on their way to Crete.

After this notice the Venetian documents do not supply any further information on Ashkenazi's business affairs for some time. Obviously, our physician's involvement in international politics did not leave him much time for other activities. Yet, on the eve of the Day of Atonement (*Yom Kippur*) 5333 [in the autumn of 1572], a few months before the final conclusion of the peace treaty, Ashkenazi again used the *Bailo* and the Venetian Council of Ten to convey a message to his Cretan agent. The letter was addressed to Sabati Cassam, described as the physician's brother-in-law. Was it the same brother-in-law who was reported as dead in one of the previous letters? For the time being, this question remains unanswered. In any case, Cassam was instructed to send to Ashkenazi the proceeds from the sale of his goods, or other goods acquired on Crete, preferably apples and cloth. In case he could not send them to Istanbul, Ashkenazi asked that they be sent to Venice, to Andrea Gradenigo, *Bailo* Barbaro's brother-in-law, who lived near the Ghetto.[31] Gradenigo was supposed to send the goods, or an appropriate letter of exchange, to Ashkenazi via Ragusa. The *Bailo*'s letter to which Ashkenazi's instructions were attached specified that the Jewish physician was still deep in debts, and was hoping to extricate himself from his financial difficulties with a final settlement of his investments in Crete.

Research in the Venetian archives for documents regarding the sequel to this affair has borne no fruit. It is possible that the conclusion of peace helped to solve the problem in a satisfactory manner—though, as we have seen, not without human and material losses. In any case, this seems to be just one case in a wider range of commercial activities, which must have begun in earlier years and, as our sources imply, continued later too.[32] Of special interest here is Ashkenazi's activity,

---

[30] Barbaro's Letter-book, II, ff. 247v-248.

[31] ASV, Cons. X, Secreti, reg. 10, f. 97 (21 Feb. 1573). For the translation of Ashkenazi's letter, see *ibid.*, filza 16. The letter was sent to Crete in Italian translation with the Ten's instructions to offer every possible assistance to its addressee.

[32] *E.g. ibid.*, reg. 11, ff. 178v-179v (10 Jan. 1579).

directed from Istanbul but spread over an extensive area, connecting Crete with the Polish court at Cracow. Ashkenazi's subsequent intervention in the election of the king of Poland in 1574-5, which cannot occupy us here, could have also been motivated by his personal business interests, not only by his advisory functions at the side of the Grand Vizier.[33] It should be emphasized that Ashkenazi's involvement in maritime commerce, though helped in some phases, especially during the war, by his good relations with the Venetian regime, originated before his rise to prominence. The opportunities opened before the Jews of Istanbul and other commercial centres of the Ottoman Empire in the sixteenth century, were not overlooked by those who had an enterprising spirit, including such persons as Ashkenazi, who cannot be described merely as merchants.

---

[33] On Ashkenazi's role in the election of the king of Poland, see C. Roth, "Dr. Solomon Ashkenazi and the Election to the Throne of Poland", cited above in n. 5.

CHAPTER FIVE

THE EASTERN TRADE, SOLOMON ASHKENAZI AND THE READMISSION OF THE JEWS TO VENICE IN 1573

The war between Venice and the Ottomans changed the political scene in the eastern Mediterranean. Cyprus was lost to Venice and became an Ottoman province in 1571, and the Christian naval victory at Lepanto, though it destroyed the myth of the invincible Turk, did not reestablish the former balance of power in the region. After these events, Venice's keenest interest was to return to peaceful relations with the Ottomans, in order to stop squandering its resources and start rebuilding its trading network in the East.[1] The contacts which finally led to the conclusion of the peace treaty in March 1573 have been dealt with in the previous chapter. Here we shall focus on the impact of these developments on the Jewish presence in Venice.

On 29 June 1573, i.e., about 18 months after the decree of expulsion, and about three months after the conclusion of the peace with the Ottomans, the two State Attorneys (*Avogadori di comun*) asked the Venetian Senate to abrogate that decree, arguing that it was incompatible with Venetian law. They based their argument on a decision taken by the Council of Ten in 1524, which prohibited any attempt to establish a *Monte di Pietà* in Venice without previous authorization from the Council of Ten.[2] Following the Senate's approval of the *Avogadori*'s appeal, the *condotta* of the Ashkenazi Jews was renewed, and the way was also opened for the return of the *Levantini*.

What did this strange legal procedure mean? Expelling the Jews not only caused problems for Venice's foreign trade, it also created a vacuum in the area of credit for the poor. The substitute for the Jewish pawnbrokers of the Ghetto Novo was the Christian *Monte di Pietà*, an institution which had been introduced in several towns of the Venetian *terraferma* to replace the Jewish bankers. But was the State Attorneys'

---

[1] Braudel, *The Mediterranean*, vol. 2, p. 1125.

[2] Ravid, "The Socioeconomic Background", pp. 47-48.

initiative really connected with a firm policy to prevent the creation of the Christian substitute to Jewish credit? and why did it take the Attorneys so much time to find the original decision invalid according to Venetian law?

Jewish contemporary sources do not seem to have taken the official argument very seriously. The chronicler Joseph Hacohen, in his famous *Vale of Tears*, attributed the abolition of the decree of expulsion to the intervention of Solomon Ashkenazi.[3] We shall see presently that this was not mere conjecture. Another view, which appears in the anonymous sequel to that chronicle, was later adopted by the nineteenth-century historian Graetz. According to it, the abrogation was the result of the intervention of the Venetian *Bailo* in Istanbul, Soranzo [*sic*]. On Soranzo's return to Venice from Istanbul, so writes the anonymous chronicler, he was moved by the lamentations and tears of the Jews who were about to leave Venice. He then succeeded in persuading the Council of Ten, in an eloquent speech which focused on the damage which the expulsion of the Jews would cause, to abrogate the 1571 decree.[4] The latter explanation does not, however, conform with historical reality. Jacopo Soranzo had been *Bailo* in Istanbul during the years 1566-68, and later served as ambassador to the Sultan in 1575, neither of which missions can be directly related to the circumstances of the abolition of the decree.[5] Moreover, no other *Bailo* or ambassador returned from the Ottoman capital just before the abrogation. Cecil Roth partially adopted the version the anonymous chronicler, attributing, however, the return from Istanbul and the speech before the Council of Ten to Francesco Barbaro, son of the *Bailo* Marcantonio Barbaro, who was sent home by his father in March 1573 with the text of the peace agreement.[6] But this conjecture too is rather implausible, in view of the fact that the *Bailo*'s son was only twenty-seven at the time, and Venice was notoriously gerontocratic. It is highly improbable that the elderly senior statesmen in the Council of Ten—which, it should be remembered, also included the Doge and his Councilors—would

---

[3] Joseph Hacohen, *Emek Habacha*, p. 110.

[4] *Ibid.*, p. 121; cf. Graetz, *Geschichte der Juden*, vol. 9, p. 416. *Cf.* also Schiavi, "Gli ebrei in Venezia e nelle sue colonie", p. 496.

[5] Bertelè, *Il palazzo*, p. 414.

[6] Roth, *Venice*, p. 91.

let themselves be persuaded by a twenty-seven year old youth.[7] As we shall see, though his diplomatic bag included a petition on behalf of the Jews, it was not Francesco Barbaro who brought about the switch in the Venetian policy.[8]

In recent years historians who returned to this issue have also differed about the reasons for the shift in Venice's policy. Benjamin Ravid, the only historian who devoted a long and detailed study to these events, accepted the official reason given in the Senate's proceedings. He wrote that, even if the peace with the Ottomans moderated the anti-Jewish climate in Venice, the change in the Republic's position was essentially dictated by the need to assure credit to the poor, which was traditionally extended by the Jews of the Ghetto Novo.[9] But Ravid fails to explain the logic behind the constant and firm refusal to consider the Christian alternative to this arrangement, nor does he dwell on the rather strange procedure of abrogation. Brian Pullan holds an opposite view. Though conceding that the Jews provided a convenient solution to the problem of credit for the poor, in his opinion, what finally decided the issue was Venice's preoccupation with its trade with the Levant, the considerable influence of certain Jews in Constantinople, and the new prospect of involving "Western" Jews (*Ponentini*) in the Venetian trading system.[10] This view seems to me more plausible. Without underestimating the importance of Jewish pawnbrokers in the social life of Venice, at that particular moment of summer 1573, the Venetian leaders had weightier and more urgent problems on their agenda, problems directly related both to the relations with the Ottoman Empire and to Venice's trade with the East.

***

The first serious attempt to persuade Venice to abrogate the decree

---

[7] R. Finlay, "The Venetian Republic as a Gerontocracy: age and politics in the Renaissance", *Journal of Medieval and Renaissance Studies*, 8 (1978), pp. 157-178. The minimum age for election to the Council of Ten was forty, but according to Finlay, it was rare for a person to be elected before the age of fifty; see *ibid.*, p. 160.

[8] Francesco Barbaro reached Venice at the beginning of March 1573, see M. Barbaro, *Arbori de' patritii veneti*, ASV, Miscellanea Codici, 894, f. 199.

[9] Ravid, "The Socioeconomic Background", pp. 50-51.

[10] Pullan, *Rich and Poor*, pp. 538-39; *idem*, "A Ship with Two Rudders", pp. 55-56.

of expulsion seems to have been made by Solomon Ashkenazi. As long
as the war lasted, he could do nothing about it. But once peace was
established, he started to exert pressure on the Venetians. In the same
letter in which he announced the conclusion of the peace agreement,
Bailo Barbaro included the request of the Jewish physician:

> ...Rabbi Solomon has asked me to supplicate your Serenity to show your
> good will (*usar ogni cortese dimostrazione*) towards the Hebrew nation,
> saying that although there are Jews of bad nature, the others, who are good,
> should not suffer on their account. It is therefore possible to punish the
> scoundrels and open the door of grace (*la porta della gratia*) to the rest...

Moreover, Ashkenazi did not hesitate to insinuate that a favourable
response to his request would also benefit Venetian interests in Istanbul.[11] It is quite possible that Francesco Barbaro, the *Bailo*'s son who
brought the text of the peace agreement to Venice, also brought a
personal petition to the Venetian authorities written by Ashkenazi. When
the young Barbaro returned to Istanbul at the beginning of May 1573,[12]
Ashkenazi must have learned that his first attempt had not borne fruit.
But he was not a man to be easily deterred. Returning to Barbaro, he
persuaded the *Bailo* to include another appeal in his new report to
Venice: "...Acts of treachery were not perpetrated by Jews, who had
never been involved in matters of that kind," started Ashkenazi's
renewed request, included in Barbaro's letter. "And if on some occasion
of lesser gravity, some of them behaved badly, they should be justly
punished, but the rest, who are innocent, do not deserve punishment."
Ashkenazi knew very well that he did not possess any official or legal
standing to put forward such a request. Nevertheless, "he could not
resist the obligation [to help] his own nation" (*non l'havea potuto far
resistenza all'obligo della sua natione*).[13]

What weight, what effect could such a request have in Venice, where
the Doge himself was boasting himself of its hostility to the Jews?[14]
It should be noted that at that stage, the stability of the newly-signed
peace agreement was a matter of some concern. Moreover, the peace

---

[11] Barbaro's Letter-book, II, f. 413v (13 Mar. 1573).
[12] *Ibid.*, f. 434v (6 May 1573).
[13] *Ibid.*, f. 439v.
[14] See above, p. 1.

treaty did not immediately resolve all the problems resulting from the war. Venice was still hoping to regain some foothold on Cyprus, several territories in Dalmatia were still disputed, prisoners of war had not yet been exchanged, goods sequestrated during the war had not yet been restored, and the Porte was trying to press Venice into an anti-Spanish alliance.[15] In all these matters, Solomon Ashkenazi could be of great help to the Republic. True, the *Bailo* was no longer confined to his house, and was therefore much less dependent on the mediation of the Jewish physician. But Ashkenazi remained one of the Grand Vizier's closest advisors, a position which made his cooperation indispensable, as was explicitly affirmed by several Venetian representatives in the Ottoman capital.[16] Nearly all the letters written by the *Baili* during that period make reference to Ashkenazi's opinions and advice. His services at the centre of Ottoman power were vital to Venetian interests, and must have been considered in Venice when the issue of the Jewish presence in the city came up.[17]

But Ashkenazi was not the only influential Jew who exerted pressure on Venice at this time. We have mentioned Venice's worry about losing its predominnce in the trade with the East to Ancona. The *Levantini* merchants knew how to take advantage of these worries. Following the conclusion of peace they came up with two projects to which Venice could not remain indifferent. On 13 May 1573, the *Bailo* reported from Istanbul that a few of the leading Jews in Istanbul approached Solomon Ashkenazi with the proposal to negotiate with Venice the transfer of all their commercial activities from Ancona to Chioggia, the town on the southern edge of the Venetian lagoon.[18] The proposal was favourably received by the Council of Ten, which authorized the *Bailo*

---

[15] The necessity to reinforce the peace was emphasized in the *Bailo*'s letter announcing its conclusion, see Barbaro's Letter-book, II, f. 414. On Venice's hopes to receive rights in Cyprus and its renunciation of these attempts because of Ottoman pressure to involve the Republic in an anti-Spanish league, see ASV, Cons. X, Secreti, reg. 10, ff. 119v-120 (10 Jun. 1573), ff. 129v-130 (10 Jul. 1573). Negotiations on the borders in Dalmatia, and on redemption of prisoners taken into slavery, lasted for along time after the conclusion of peace.

[16] *E.g.* Barbaro's Letter-book, II, ff. 414-14v; *Relazioni*, ed. Albèri, ser. III, Appendice, (Barbaro's second report, 1574), f. 401; *ibid.*, ser. III, vol. II, pp. 188-89 (Antonio Tiepolo's report, 1576).

[17] *Nunziature* di Venezia, vol. 9, p. 474.

[18] Barbaro's Letter-book, II, f. 445; ASV, Capi X, Lett. CP, busta 3, No 7.

to negotiate its terms with the Jews in Istanbul. Significantly, the authorization was issued only a few days after the abrogation of the act of expulsion.[19]

Another project which arose after the war, and probably before the readmission of the Jews to Venice, was a suggestion to settle in Venice Jews of Spanish and Portuguese origin in order to revive the Republic's international trade, which had suffered greatly during the war. Daniel Rodriga, known as the originator of the *Scala* of Spalato and of later initiatives to settle the *Ponentini* in Venice,[20] contacted the *Bailo*'s son on his return from Venice early in May, probably in order to further this project.[21] The substance of this proposal can be deduced from the resolution of the Venetian Council of Ten in December 1573, which must have been the outcome of negotiations on Rodriga's proposal.[22] This was a virtual charter, inviting Jews of Spanish and Portuguese origin to settle with their families in Venice. They were guaranteed protection against persecution on account of their past actions or identity, provided they live as Jews in a separate quarter. They were also offered immunity against any claim arising from debts incurred before their settlement in Venice. They were likewise given the right to build their own synagogue and to print and circulate Hebrew books. But the last clause of what might have become the first charter of the *Ponentini* proved to be decisive in postponing its realization for another sixteen years. It subordinated its implementation to its approval by the Senate, which, apparently, did not have the opportunity to discuss the matter at that stage. Nevertheless, several perspectives were opened for a renewed collaboration between Venice and different groups of Jewish merchants in the trade between Western Europe and the eastern Mediterranean. All this had direct repercussions on the future of Jewish presence in Venice.[23]

***

[19] ASV, Cons. X, Secreti, reg. 10, f. 131v (10 Jul. 1573).

[20] See above, p. 7 and n. 22.

[21] Barbaro's Letter-book, II, f. 445 (13 May 1553).

[22] ASV, Cons. X, Secreti, reg. 10, ff. 159v-160 (23 Dec. 1573).

[23] For Venice's commercial considerations regarding the settlement of the *Ponentini*, see Pullan, "A Ship with Two Rudders", p. 56; Ravid, *Economics and Toleration*, pp. 32-33.

These, and not the Jewish credit for the poor, were the great issues on Venice's agenda at that moment. The decree of expulsion was abrogated because the relations with the Ottoman Empire were connected in various ways with the fate of the Venetian Jews. The latter had no doubt as to who was to be credited for the abrogation. In 1574, when Solomon Ashkenazi reached Venice as an official envoy of the Porte in order to negotiate problems relating to the borders in Dalmatia, he was received in the Ghetto with great enthusiasm.[24] A special prayer was composed in his honour, which went as follows:

> He who blessed our Forefathers Abraham, Isaac, Jacob, Moses, Aaron, David and Solomon, will bless and preserve the exalted and honourable physician, who was sent during the week of *Shelaḥ lekha* in the year 5334 [1574] by the King Sultan Selim to the glorious Dominion of Venice. He is a leader and a prince in Israel, Rabbi Solomon, may God preserve him, son of Rabbi Nathan, of blessed memory, since he was aided by the Celestial Throne to assure the welfare of the people of Israel and our own good, after the exile was decreed here in Venice in 5333 [1573], as everyone knows, and through his intervention the decree was annulled. For such merit the Almighty will preserve him from every mishap, will increase his greatness and grant his wishes, will prosper his voyages and bless him in every matter. Amen.[25]

The readmission of the Jews to Venice, so greatly influenced by commercial considerations, naturally brought about the renewal of the collaboration with the *Levantini* merchants. In order to persuade them to return, Venice had to compensate them for their losses in Venice and throughout her empire during the war. Indeed, when peace was concluded, the Jewish merchants immediately moved to regain their properties and fortunes, which had been confiscated or lost during the previous three years. A petition presented by a group of eighteen *Levantini* merchants in August 1573 may indicate that despite the repeal, at least some of the Jewish merchants had no desire to stay in Venice,

---

[24] Hacohen, *Emek Habacha*, pp. 110, 123; Roth, *Venice*, pp. 93-94; The event was also recorded on the last page of a *Shulhan Arukh*, printed in Venice in those days, see S.A. Rosanes, *History of the Jews in Turkey and the Lands of the East*, Sophia, 1938, vol. 2, p. 101, n. 12 [Hebrew].

[25] Luzzatto, "Un ambasciatore ebreo", pp. 245-46.

but were eager to return to the East after being duly compensated for
their losses.[26] During his stay in Venice in 1574 Solomon Ashkenazi
helped some Jewish merchants to solve their disagreements with the
Venetian authorities concerning the claims resulting from their detention
during the war.[27] It seems that Venice demonstrated its goodwill by
promptly restoring the merchandise and compensating for lost fortunes.
In a letter addressed to the Sultan in 1583, the Signory claimed to
have disbursed after the conclusion of peace as much as 200,000 ducats
in compensation for damages suffered by Ottoman subjects from the
confiscation of their goods (*per robbe loro trattenute*), which most
likely referred to this settlement, though not exclusively to the Jewish
merchants.[28] In any case, the door was again open for Jewish traders
to settle in Venice and to participate in the Republic's trade with the
East.

[26] ASV, Senato, Terra, filza 61 (22 Aug. 1573).
[27] See the group of documents pertaining to this issue in the Appendix.
[28] ASV, Senato Delib. CP, reg. 6, f. 126 (17 Mar. 1583).

CHAPTER SIX

THE PANDORA BOX OF ḤAYYIM SARUQ'S BANKRUPTCY

The relations between Venice and the Levantine Jewish merchants about the time of the Cypriot war have been outlined in the previous three chapters. In the following two chapters we shall see how they were reflected in the life of one Jewish merchant. But the story of Ḥayyim Saruq, the main protagonist of these chapters, not only highlights the problems discussed above—the activities of this hitherto rather anonymous merchant also influenced Venice's attitudes and policy towards the *Levantini* merchants during that time.

The name of Ḥayyim Saruq is hardly known today among historians of the early modern Mediterranean.[1] So far, only one very short article in Hebrew and a few occasional references have been devoted to him. The interest of scholars of Jewish history in Ḥayyim Saruq originally stemmed from his sponsorship of the publication of religious literature in Venice during the 1560s and 1570s. In the year 5326 (1565/6), he printed in Venice a sumptuous edition of Rabbi Joseph Caro's *Tur Oraḥ Ḥayyim* (The Column of the Way of Life), and eight years later (1576/7), Caro's *Ḥeleq Yoreh De'ah* (The Knowledge-Instructing Part). These were two parts of his encyclopaedic work, *Beit Yosef* (The House of Joseph), which, after the ban on the Talmud in Italy in 1554, became the main Talmudic text among Italian Jews. The proofreader of the latter publication, one Rabbi Yaḥia ben Abraham from Fez, in a note at the end of the book described Ḥayyim Saruq in the following words: "a man of many achievements, whose name was known among ancient kings and famous men, the illustrious master the honourable Rabbi

---

[1] Saruq himself signed his name in Hebrew as חיים סרוק or as סרוק חיים 'ן (see the Appendix). In the *Encyclopaedia Judaica* the family name of our protagonist (who is not specifically mentioned there) appears in various forms: Saruk, Sarug and Saruq. I have opted for latter form, which conforms with the general principles of Hebrew transliteration adopted in this book. In the Venetian documentation, the name is generally spelled Saruch, whereas the first name of our protagonist is spelled in many forms, such as Cain, Caim, Haim, Chaim, Caym or Cayn.

Ḥayyim ben Saruq, may God preserve him". He went on to express the hope that Saruq's great influence would enable him to bring about the abolition of the prohibition "to print the Oral Law". Saruq also sponsored the printing of "Questions brought before the sage Rabbi Shaul Hacohen of Candia", published in Venice in 5334 [1574].[2]

Meir Benayahu, who referred to Saruq in various publications, first surmised that Saruq originated from Egypt, where members of his family were numbered among the leaders of the Cairo community.[3] Somewhat later, Benayahu suggested that Saruq might have originated from Salonica, where there were prominent persons with the same name.[4] He also mentioned a letter of an Egyptian rabbi, Ḥayyim Caphusy, from about 1600, who vehemently attacks Ḥayyim Saruq for falsely announcing in a letter from Venice to the Jewish community in Egypt [Cairo?] that a number of Jews who had been captured in 1599 by pirates on their way to Safed had been ransomed. Benayahu concluded from these data that by the middle of the sixteenth century Ḥayyim Saruq was probably one of the leaders of the *Levantini* in Venice. In support of this conclusion he published the following *Haskama*, or "agreement", resolved by the leaders of the *Levantini* in Venice, which was included in a *responsum* of the Salonican rabbi, Samuel de Medina (1506-1589):

> We, the undersigned officials and leaders of the holy community of the *Levantini*, considering the load of custom duties on certain goods which are not a matter of state legislation (אשר לא מדינא דמלכותא המה), such as the *quarantesimo* (קוארינטיישמו), and the custom imposed on saffron, and many similar ones, as well as several additional burdens and difficulties which suffocate the merchants, and which both they and us are unable to overcome, fully or in part, we have agreed among ourselves that for our own sake, and for the sake of the goods and the merchants

---

[2] M. Benayahu, "Further Evidence on Ḥayyim ben Saruq in Venice", *Oẓar Yehudei Sefarad (Tesoros de los Judios Sefardies)*, 8 (1965), p. 135 [Hebrew]; *idem, Relations between Greek and Italian Jewry*, Tel Aviv, 1980, p. 92 [Hebrew].

[3] The Egyptian Rabbi Isaac Saruq was involved in 1564/5 in the copying of *Sefer Ha-Rimon* (The Book of the Pomegranate) by Rabbi Moses de Leon, see Benayahu, "Further Evidence", p. 135.

[4] A Salonican rabbi also called Isaac Saruq, who appears in a *Haskama* of 1583/4 and a merchant called Joseph ben Saruq, killed in 1617, see Benayahu, *Relations*, pp. 91-92.

that are at present, and will be in future, here in Venice, to ask the honourable and wise Rabbi Ḥayyim [Ib]n Saruq, may God protect and preserve him, for succour by God's help, and to obtain relief from the Signory and the customs-officers, and reach a solution of the said matters by reducing the impositions on goods and merchants as far as God would allow. And of any part which he would succeed in reducing, as appears in the list (נוטה) issued by the customs officers (דו"אגירי), the said honourable Rabbi Ḥayyim Saruq will receive one half for a period of ten consecutive years, as his reward. The said Rabbi Ḥayyim has agreed to undertake these matters and to be available to us for any question and demand, on condition that every merchant be obliged, and each merchandise be mortgaged, for the said period of ten years, to give to the said honourable Rabbi Ḥayyim half of everything which would be included in the reductions and favours accorded to the merchants in the said customs and dues.

Therefore, we, the officials and leaders of the holy community of the *Levantini*, by the authority which we have from the whole of the said holy community, do decide by unanimous agreement and opinion, and by the force of all other decisions (*haskamot*) of the holy community, may God protect and preserve it, that every merchant be obliged, and each merchandise mortgaged for the payment of one half of any reduction obtained by Rabbi Ḥayyim from the customs, impositions and their payments, as mentioned above, in the course of ten consecutive years, starting from the day in which the impositions on the arrears would be raised. And anyone who would refuse to give and pay the said half to the said honourable Rabbi Ḥayyim the said half, will be considered a transgressor of the bans and provisions of the holy community, and will be proclaimed accordingly as a transgressor of one of the existing and binding provisions of the holy community, may God protect and preserve it. And may those who honour this provision be blessed.[5]

The matter was brought before Rabbi Samuel de Medina following a refusal of some merchants to pay half the reductions as stipulated in the contract. Since the famous Salonican Rabbi decided in favour

---

[5] See the original *responsum* in *Maharashdam* [Rabbi Samuel de Medina], *Responsa*, Part IV: *Ṭur Ḥoshen Hamishpaṭ* ["The Breastplate's Column"] , New York, 1959, No 99. For Benayahu's version, see Benayahu, "Further Evidence", p. 136, citing two different editions, the first presumably of 5344 (1583/4), and the second of 5355 (1594/5).

of Saruq, obliging the merchants to honour their commitment, we may assume that Saruq had succeeded in obtaining the reductions from the Venetian authorities. This *responsum* is, as usual, undated. Benayahu attributed it to the beginning of the second half of the sixteenth century. Goodblatt, for some unknown reason, dated it to 1571.[6] Salo Baron, who mentioned this *responsum* very briefly, mistakenly describes it as an attempt made during the war of Cyprus (1570-73) by the leading Salonican Jews to get Ḥayyim Saruq to release their merchandise confiscated in Venice, by promising him 50% of its value.[7] In fact, the agreement had nothing to do with goods confiscated during the war, but rather, as Benayahu rightly noted, with an attempt to reduce customs tariffs. As to its dating, I believe it should be dated later, probably the late 1570s or early 1580s, as will be explained below.

The issue treated in this *responsum* is worthy of further consideration. In the Venetian Republic, fiscal tariffs were not normally subject to the whims of customs officers, but to decisions of the governing councils. Moreover, the *quarantesimo* (or *quadragesimo*), mentioned in the document, was one of the earliest imposts on goods reaching Venice from the Italian mainland.[8] Yet the agreement explicitly refers to customs tariffs "which were not a matter of state legislation", a distinction which I am unable to explain. In fact, the subject of customs organization in Venice is still largely unexplored. Normally, in order to obtain a reduction in the tariffs, Saruq would have had to lobby the appropriate councils and cause a process of legislation to reach a successful conclusion. I have been unable to find traces of such a reduction of tariffs in the decisions of Senate, the Council of Ten, or any other council, either in the period indicated by Benayahu or in the following decades. It should be noted, however, that organized pressure by various groups on the Venetian political and administrative system was probably not unusual. The following case may serve as an example: on 7 November 1570, four Florentines and one Genoese signed an agreement before the notary P.G. Mamoli, according to which

---

[6] M.S. Goodblatt, *Jewish Life in Turkey in the XVIth Century, as Reflected in the Legal Writings of Samuel De Medina*, New York, 1952, p. 51.

[7] Baron, *A Social and Religious History*, vol. 18, p. 244, but without any specific reference to the source.

[8] *Documenti finanziari della Repubblica di Venezia*, ser. I vol. I. *Bilanci generali*, ed. F. Besta and F. Visentini, Venice, 1912, p. liv.

one of them, the Florentine Marco Lachi, would obtain within a year a law confining the commerce in bills-of-exchange exclusively to bill-brokers. Lachi was also granted an unspecified amount of money, with the declared purpose of covering his expenses and as a remuneration for his efforts. If he succeeded, he would receive an additional sum. And in fact, Lachi succeeded in bringing about an appropriate act on 24 October 1571.[9] Saruq's ability to obtain a reduction of tariffs could therefore be seen as part of a broader spectrum of pressures exerted on the Venetian administration by various interest groups. Naturally, his success proves his connections in the Venetian state system.

It is to be expected that the social standing of such a person would be fairly high. Indeed, the many marks left by Ḥayyim Saruq in sixteenth-century Venetian sources from the 1560s on indicate that his position was considerable. During that period his name occurs time and again in notarial documents, in the acts of the most important Venetian councils, such as the Senate and the Council of Ten, in Venice's diplomatic correspondence, in judicial records, and in the acts of the Venetian Inquisition. We shall try to present Ḥayyim Saruq's story by means of a detailed chronological analysis of these records. The purpose is not only to unfold the story of a Jewish merchant in sixteenth-century Venice, to explore the new possibilities open to Jewish entrepreneurs in the eastern Mediterranean, and the intricate relationship between Jews, Venetians and Ottomans in that context, but also to illustrate the ample possibilities offered by the Venetian archival sources in this field.

Ḥayyim Saruq must have arrived in Venice from Salonica in 1560, or a little earlier.[10] The documents of a Venetian notary, Zuan Battista Monte, offer what is so far the earliest discovered record of Ḥayyim Saruq's presence in Venice. On 2 January 1561 Saruq presented a legal notification (*intimatio*) to a certain Simonetto, master of the ship *Lazarona*, which unloaded in Venice, instead of Ancona, 32 sacks of wool and 691 pieces of leather which had been sent by Joseph, son of Aaron di Segura, from Constantinople to Abraham Codara (or Codaro) in Ancona. Saruq was acting as Codara's agent, and demanded

---

[9] G. Corazzol, "Varietà notarile: scorci di vita economica e sociale", in *Storia di Venezia, vol. 6: Dal Rinascimento al Barocco*, eds. G. Cozzi and P. Prodi, Rome, 1994, p. 775.

[10] For Saruq's provenance from Salonica, see the next chapter, p. 160.

delivery of the merchandise in Ancona within five days, or payment of the damages. Six days later the ship's owner announced that the vessel had been prevented from unloading in Ancona by bad weather, and that on 18 December 1560, Saruq had already paid for the freight and duty.[11] We may therefore assume that Saruq was already in Venice by mid December 1560. The same notarial document also reveals Saruq's business connections with the powerful Segura family, led by Aaron di Segura, a central figure among the Jewish entrepreneurs of the Ottoman capital.[12]

From 1561 on, Zuan Battista Monte seems to have been Saruq's trusted notary, and in the following years there is scarcely a register of this notary which does not contain documents touching upon Saruq's manifold business activities.[13] Saruq had business connections with Jewish and non-Jewish partners in Venice and other centres, such as Constantinople, Ferrara, Ancona and Salò, importing from the Ottoman Empire wool, leather (*cordovani*), camlets (*zambellotti*) and alum, conducting credit operations, issuing powers-of-attorney, going to arbitrations, and acquiring bonds of the *Grand Parti* of Lyons, the banking organization that gave credit to the French crown.[14] He was also engaged in buying, or becoming part owner of small and medium vessels (a few *brigantini*, a galleon, a *navetta*, a *grippo* or *saytia*). Some of the latter were especially built for Saruq in the shipyards on

---

[11] ASV, AN, busta 8248, quaderno I, ff. 14-15.

[12] In 1558, Aaron di Segura had organized the boycott of Jewish merchants of Istanbul against the Venetian merchants, whereas in 1560 he is said to have leased, in association with Joseph Nassí, the alum mines of Phocaea, Simon, "Contribution", pp. 990-91 and n. 59.

[13] Z.B. Monte's extant documents cover the period 1556-1579, see ASV, AN, buste 8244-8274. No trace of Hayyim Saruq has been detected in the *buste* containing material preceding the above-mentioned document. I am most grateful to Gigi Corazzol for completing the survey of buste Nos 8244-8251 for me.

[14] *E.g.* ASV, AN, busta 8248/II, f.1 (17 Feb. 1561); *ibid.*, busta 8249/IV, f. 18 (20 Apr. 1562); *ibid.*, busta 8249/V, f. 18 (12 Aug. 1562); *ibid.*, busta 8250/I (8 Jan. 1563); *ibid.*, busta 8250/IV, f. 33-33v (7 July 1563); *ibid.*, busta 8250/V, ff. 39-39v (22 Sept. 1563); *ibid.*, 8250/VI, ff. 49-49v (20 Dec. 1563); *ibid.*, busta 3251/I, ff. 32-32v (9 Feb. 1564); *ibid.*, busta 3251/II, ff. 3-3 (29 Feb. 1564); *ibid.*, busta 8251/II, f. 4 (1 Mar. 1564); *ibid.*, busta 8251/II, f. 19 (10 Mar. 1564); *ibid.*, busta 8251/III, f. 9v (12 May 1564); *ibid.*, busta 8251/IV, f. 16v (8 Aug. 1564); *ibid.*, busta 8251/V, f. 31v (6 Nov. 1564). I am grateful to Gigi Corazzol for sending me abstracts of these documents.

the Venetian island of Curzola in Dalmatia, with Saruq himself supplying the necessary credit to the shipbuilders.[15] The acquisition of a great quantity of paper in January 1565 could have been related to his involvement in the publishing of Jewish religious literature.[16] During that period he was also apparently active in Ferrara.[17] The overall impression arising from the notarial documentation pertaining to the early 1560s is of a fairly active merchant disposing of many thousands of ducats, whose sphere of action ranged from Lyons to Constantinople, though mainly focusing on the axis Venice-Constantinople. Hayyim Saruq's brother, Isaac, was also involved in his affairs. He is mentioned in a notarial document of 5 October 1562 as Saruq's agent who negotiated at Pastrovich the acquisition of half a *brigantino* from Thoma Guchia of Pastrovich for the price of 200 ducats.[18] In September 1564, when Saruq concluded a four-year partnership with Joseph di Segura of Constantinople, the contract stipulated that the only person in the Ottoman Empire to whom he would be entitled to send money beyond the framework of the partnership was his brother Isaac, though not more than 500 ducats.[19]

The earliest mention of Hayyim Saruq which I have been able to find in Venetian official records is a decision of the Council of Ten of May 1566 on an affair of contraband in which Saruq had been involved in 1563. The interest of the Council of Ten in this matter

---

[15] ASV, AN, busta 8249/VI, ff. 44-44v (5 Oct. 1562); *ibid.*, busta 8250/I, ff 27-27v (1 Feb. 1563); *ibid.*, busta 8250/II, f. 44 (20 Mar. 1563); *ibid.*, busta 8250/III ff. 33v-34 (7 May 1563); *ibid.*, busta 8250/V, ff. 27v-28 (27 Aug. 1563); *ibid.*, busta 8251/II, ff. 24v-25 (17 Mar. 1564); *ibid.*, busta 8251/III, ff. 46-46v (18 July 1564); *ibid.*, busta 8253/I, ff. 11-11v (11 Mar. 1566), ff. 36-37 (22 Mar. 1566), f. 39v (23 Mar. 1566). Among Saruq's business partners in this sector figure several persons from Pastrovich, the Dalmatian 'republic' dependent on Venice. For a more detailed discussion on Saruq's activities in this field, see Chapter Eight.

[16] ASV, AN, busta 8252/I, f. 9v (4 Jan. 1565). On another occasion, an arbitration decided in favour of Saruq served as a security for the printing of Caro's *Hoshen Hamishpaṭ*, see *ibid.*, busta 8253, last fascicle, f. 45 (24 Dec. 1566).

[17] Saruq's presence at Ferrara is attested in 30 Nov. 1563, see ASV, AN, busta 8250/VI, ff. 49-49v. Cf. also below, p. 160.

[18] ASV, AN, busta 8249/VI, ff. 44-44v (5 Oct. 1562). Pastrovich (Pastrovići) was a community in southern Dalmatia under Venetian protection.

[19] ASV, LST, busta 2, f. 199v (blue), 18 *Tishri* 5325 (24 Sept. 1564). For the full Hebrew text of this contract, see Illustration No 1 on p. 102 and the transcript in the Appendix.

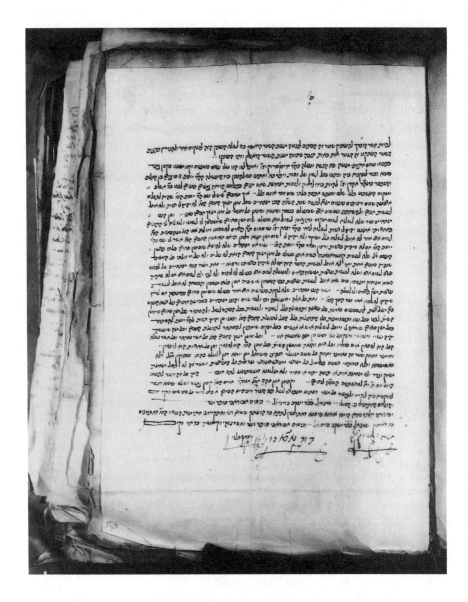

1. Contract between Ḥayyim Saruq and Joseph di Segura, 18 Tishri
5325 (24 Sept. 1564) [paper, 21x30.5 cm.]

points to its importance in the eyes of the Venetian authorities. It was claimed that the merchandise seized as contraband had actually belonged to the Grand Vizier in Istanbul. Clearly Venice did not wish to antagonize the Vizier. Consequently, while making an effort not to infringe upon legal norms, the Ten took the necessary measures to reach a quick solution which would satisfy the Ottoman Pasha. On 10 May 1566 the Council of Ten resolved to send to the Republic's representatives in the Ottoman capital a resumé of an enquiry carried out in that matter, and adding further instructions. The merchandise confiscated as contraband from Saruq (whom the resolution does not name) included 17 pieces of cloths of various colours, such as scarlet (*scarlati*), red (*paonazzi*) and black (*cuppi*), amounting to 957 *brazza* in all. According to Venetian law, merchandise confiscated as contraband was forfeited to the state. But following an appeal by Saruq, the State Attorneys (*Avogadori di comun*) consented to release half the goods as a goodwill gesture (*per gratia*), though subtracting the costs and other dues which were customarily deducted in such cases for charitable institutions and various offices. Consequently, of the original 17 pieces, there were only 4 pieces and a few remainders left, 282 *brazza* in all. It was decided to dispatch this to Istanbul with the first passage, accompanied by instructions to the Venetian *Baili* to compensate the Vizier for the rest, with as little cost and damage to the Republic as possible.[20] But the affair had meanwhile developed into a diplomatic crisis. The Venetian *Bailo*, Jacopo Soranzo, wrote on 21 June of that year from Istanbul that, although his predecessor had promised to restore the cloth to the Pasha, the latter carried out his earlier threats, arrested the *Bailo*'s interpreter, Marucini, and prevented the *Bailo* himself from leaving Istanbul at the end of his term of office. The Ottoman authorities made it clear that this situation could change only on condition that the *Bailo* undertake formally before the Kadi of Pera (the quarter across the Golden Horn where the *Bailo*'s residence was situated) that the cloth would arrive on the first Venetian ship sailing to Istanbul. Soranzo

---

[20] ASV, Cons. X, Secrete, reg. 8, ff. 57v-58r (10 May 1566). See also the copy of the journal of the *Avogaria* (State Attorneys Office) of 20 October 1563: "per panni scarlati et chupi de 60 [?]... e paonazi ...tolti per Paulo Turchetto Capitano de Colfo a contrabando ... sopra li qual panni fu formato processo nell'officio nostro et fatto sentencia contra Cain Saruch ebreo, e levato [?] per lo Exellentissimo consiglio de Quaranta Civil Vechio, *ibid.*, filza 12.

made no bones about whom he blamed for these complications. "Unfortunately", he wrote in his dispatch of 21 June 1566, "the insolence of these Jews is great, and I have heard that they have caused many troubles to your Serenity's *Baili* in these parts; nevertheless, they live in Venice in comfort, and so, according to reports, does Hayyim Sarug [*sic*], the cause of all this trouble." Moreover, Soranzo reported that Saruq was the real owner of the confiscated merchandise, but after it was seized, he donated part of it to Ottoman statesmen, expecting them to compensate him as they saw fit.[21]

The affair of the confiscated cloth was hardly over when Saruq became involved in another, much bigger, scandal. On 20 July 1566 the *Bailo* Giacomo Soranzo reported from Istanbul about the bankruptcy in Venice of Hayyim Saruq, who acted as the agent (or probably as a partner) of Aaron (Haron) di Segura. The latter, a leading Jewish entrepreneur in the Ottoman capital who belonged to one of the most prominent Jewish families of Spanish descent, had the lease of the Sultan's alum mines and was well connected in the Ottoman court.[22] Since Saruq had in his possession a consignment of alum belonging to the Ottoman Sultan, the Grand Vizier asked the *Bailo* not to let Saruq's creditors in Venice lay their hands on this merchandise, which, he maintained, actually belonged to the Sultan. The *Bailo* described the pressure exerted on him by the Pasha and by Segura's envoys (Segura himself was bedridden, suffering from gout). Segura was about to send his son, Joseph, to Venice to settle the affair, but fearing that Saruq would escape, he had asked the *Bailo* to see to it that Saruq be held custody, so as to enable the younger Segura to sue him. Segura claimed that the alum was not held in partnership between himself and Saruq, but was part of a separate account which belonged to the Sultan. The gravity in which the matter was viewed by the Porte was shown by

---

[21] ASV, Capi X, Lett. CP, busta 3, Nos 59-61 (21 June 1566). On 18 July, the Ten decided to pass the information contained in the *Bailo's* letter to the Senate, see ASV, Cons. X, Secreti, reg. 8, f. 62.

[22] Moses di Segura was president of the *Sinagoga Mayor* in Istanbul in the 1550: Roth, *The House of Nassí: Doña Gracia*, p. 165; the physician Judah di Segura is mentioned in one of the sermons of Rabbi Moses Almosnino (c. 1515-c. 1580), as one of the influential Jewish figures who helped obtain the charter of liberties for the Jews of Salonica (1567): Moses Almosnino, *Sefer Meamez Koah (Reinforcing Strength)*, Venice, 1588 (reprint: Westmead, 1969), p. 7 [Hebrew]. I owe the latter reference to Minna Rozen. On the lease of the alum mines, see below.

the Pasha's request that the Council of Ten should secretly receive Segura's envoy,[23] and by the decision to send a special official envoy, or *Çavuş*, with Joseph Segura. The *Bailo* disliked this move, because Venice wanted to avoid transforming a private business litigation into a diplomatic crisis.[24] Nevertheless, the *Çavuş* was sent to Venice, bearing Sultanic letters which are still preserved, together with a Venetian translation, in the State Archives. The first of these letters was a *firmān* of Sultan Süleyman II from the beginning of the month of Safar 974 AH (the last third of August 1566), addressed to the Venetian Doge. This document, probably one of the last of its kind issued by Sultan Süleyman, stated that the Jew Aaron (Harun), leaseholder of the alum mines of Māronia and Kedūs (Kudūs, Kadūs, Kidūs ?) [in the translation: Maronia et Giedir], who became heavily indebted to the Sultan's treasury, claimed that the creditors of Ḥayyim Saruq, a Jewish subject of the Sultan, intended to lay their hands on 15,000 *kantar*s [about 846 metric tons] of Sultanic (*miri*) alum, which had been sent by the said Aaron through his son Joseph, to Saruq and Joseph David, also called Segura, in Venice. The Sultan claimed that the alum belonged to him and that Saruq who, like his partner Segura, was supposed to act as the Sultan's agent in marketing the alum, was fraudulently hiding the goods. The Sultan announced the dispatch of a special envoy, the honourable Ḥaydar, a *sipāhī*, or 'feudal' cavalryman, who together with Joseph di Segura was dispatched to Venice to settle the affair. The Sultan demanded that the accounts between Joseph Segura and Ḥayyim Saruq be settled by a group of senators (*dil corpo di Pregai*) and that the proceeds of the alum be sent to Istanbul. He also demanded that in the event Saruq was unwilling or unable to honour his debt to Segura, Venice would send him, an Ottoman subject, to Istanbul.[25] The second document is a letter of recommendation for Joseph Segura, signed by Sultan Selīm shortly before his accession as the heir of Sultan Süleyman. It stated that the Jew Aaron

---

[23] ASV, Capi X, Lett. CP, busta 3, No 64 (20 July 1566).

[24] ASV, Sen., Disp. CP, filza 1, No 44 (31 Aug. 1566). A copy of the *Bailo*'s letter of recommendation to Joseph Segura is attached to his letter to the Senate.

[25] ASV, LST, filza 2, f. 195 [blue enumeration], with the corresponding translation on ff. 189-190. See also the abstracts compiled by Alessio Bombaci, ASV, Documenti turchi, Indice Bombaci (hereafter: IB), No 408. This must have been one of the last firmans bearing the *tuğra* of Süleyman II.

(Harun), a relative of the "Frankish Bey" Joseph Nassí, had sent alum
to Venice and was sending his son Joseph in order to settle the matter
in court, asking that the Signory see to the settlement of this case
according to Venetian laws and customs.[26]

It is no coincidence that the highest Ottoman authorities intervened
in this case. The alum affair was related to important economic developments. During the sixteenth century Venice became one of the most
important industrial cities of Europe. Its industries: shipbuilding, glass,
silk and especially wool, enjoyed a spectacular rise. Some of these
industries depended on the importation of alum, a product used in large
quantities as a mordant in textile finishing, as well as in many other
industries, such as glass, paper and leather.[27] One of its main sources
were the alum mines of Phocaea (Foglia), in western Anatolia, as well
as others also in areas ruled by the Ottomans. Jean Delumeau has
estimated that about the middle of the fifteenth century, the alum trade
was probably the most important component of the Western trade in
the Levant.[28] In 1462 it was estimated that Westerners paid the Ottomans 300,000 gold ducats a year for alum.[29] In earlier times Genoese
entrepreneurs had been prominent in exploiting these mines and
transporting the product to the West. After the Ottoman conquest,
however, the Venetians apparently obtained the leasehold of the Phocaea
mines for an unspecified period.[30]

The seizure of Phocaea by the Ottomans stimulated the search for
alternative sources in the West. Following the discovery in 1462 of

---

[26] ASV, LST, filza 2, f. 194, and the corresponding translation on f. 206-7. See
also the abstract in IB, No 409. Selīm II acceded the throne on 14 August 1566.

[27] J. Delumeau, *L'alun de Rome, XVe-XIXe siècle*, Paris, 1962, pp. 13-14.
Eighteenth-century sources also mention the use of alum in the sugar industry, in
the desalination of codfish, in the candle-making, silver plating and medicine. Heyd
also mentions the use of alum by illuminators, painters, and gilders; see W. Heyd,
Histoire du commerce du Levant au Moyen Age, Leipzig, 1886, p. 570; See also Singer,
The Earliest Chemical Industry, op. cit.

[28] Delumeau, *L'alun de Rome*, p. 18.

[29] *Ibid.*, p. 21.

[30] M.L. Heers, "Les Génois et le commerce de l'alun à la fin du Moyen Age",
Revue d'Histoire Economique et Sociale, 32 (1954), pp. 30-53. The Venetians obtained
the leasehold of Phocaea in 1461: *ibid.*, p. 51. Heers, who used only Genoese sources,
wrongly supposed that after 1458 Ottoman alum practically disappeared from Western
markets.

the alum mines at Tolfa, in the Papal States, the Papacy made great efforts to impose a monopoly on Christendom, notably by applying religious sanctions on states and individuals who continued to import alum from the infidels. Delumeau, who studied this issue, came to the conclusion that after the rise of Tolfa, though Turkish alum continued to reach Western markets on occasion, it was of marginal importance.[31] The limited quantitative data which may be gleaned from the Venetian documentation presented in this study, though too fragmentary to allow a general evaluation, suggest that the importation of Ottoman alum to Venice in the 1560s was far from negligible. Segura's claim of having shipped 15,000 *kantar*s to Saruq in Venice should be compared with the 15,800 *kantar*s annually produced at Phocaea in the middle of the fifteenth century,[32] and with the 36,000 *kantar*s produced annually at Tolfa between 1566 and 1578.[33] Evidently, papal sanctions were not much heeded in Venice, at least in this matter. The growth of industrial production and the expanding markets for Venetian products must have increased the demand for Ottoman alum. Moreover, these imports supported the exportation of Venetian industrial products to the East. Venetian textiles were known for their high quality, and together with other luxury goods found favourable marketing opportunities at the heart of the Ottoman Empire, which was then at its most vigorous. We shall see presently that the capital involved in these transactions in the 1560s was considerable.

The Jewish entrepreneurs in the East took advantage of this trend. They themselves leased alum mines,[34] and they are often mentioned, both in the East and in Venice, as prominent in the international alum trade. The concentration of alum imports in the hands of the *Levantini*

---

[31] *Ibid.*, p. 54.

[32] *Ibid.*, p. 18.

[33] *Ibid.*, p. 53. As can be expected, the *kantar*, a volume measure used at Ottoman Phocaea was similar to the one used during the former Genoese administration. According to Inalcık, the Ottoman *kantar* was equivalent to 56.443 kg, see H. Inalcık, "Introduction to Ottoman Metrology", *Turcica*, 15 (1983), p. 320; according to Delumeau, the Genoese and the Roman *cantaro* was approximately 50 kg.; see Delumeau, *L'alun de Rome*, p. 17, n. 4.

[34] For the mines of Phocaea, see above, n. 12; The mines of Maronia, mentioned in the cited *firmān*, were situated in Thracia, to the west of the mouth of the Maritsa river, see Heyd, *Histoire du commerce du Levant*, vol. 2, p. 567. I have been unable to locate Goduz, the other toponym mentioned in the same document.

was also convenient to Venice—it enabled the Republic to assume solidarity with the Church (since the *Levantini* were not Venetian subjects), while assuring a sufficient supply of the important material for its expanding industries.[35] Hayyim Saruq's involvement in this activity is, therefore, of some importance.

***

Before returning to Hayyim Saruq's financial predicament, it will be useful to dwell briefly on some Venetian legal procedures regarding bankruptcies. After being officially declared bankrupt, a person had to deposit the appropriate documentation and the list of his creditors at the court of the *Sopraconsoli*, which during this period was normally responsible for cases of bankruptcy.[36] The creditors usually formed a group, three of them becoming 'Heads' (*capi*) or 'Representatives' (*deputati*) of the collective body. The next step usually was to issue an *intromissione*, or sequestration of the property of the bankrupt person, a judicial act serving as security for the payment of the debts. If an agreement was reached and corroborated by the appropriate court, such a sequestration could later be cancelled.

Venetian law tended to encourage persons who were unable to honour their debts to reach a settlement with their creditors, enabling repayment within an agreed period. If the bankrupt person remained in Venice and was not suspected of trying to evade his responsibilities, the law was more lenient in his regard. He was then regarded as *gravato di debiti*, and could obtain a *fida*, or safe-conduct, from the court of *Sopraconsoli*, which enabled him to negotiate the terms with his creditors. However, if he fled, or even if his creditors suspected that he might try to flee, or if he hid in Venice in order to evade his obligations, he was publicly declared as 'fugitive' (*fugitivo*), which aggravated his legal status. In such cases, the bankrupt person could be arrested so as to safeguard the interests of the creditors. A general and final sequestration was carried out only as a last resort, followed

---

[35] P. Preto, *Venezia e i Turchi*, Florence, 1975, pp. 59-60.

[36] Other magistracies, such as the *Consoli dei mercanti*, could also handle cases of this kind.

by a public auction of the debtor's goods.[37]

Similar procedures were at first implemented in Saruq's case, but, as we shall see, the political complications arising from his bankruptcy necessitated some extraordinary measures.

A batch of documents preserved in the *filze* of the Senate's delibera-tions, where the background material for official decisions is kept, sheds some light on the events around Saruq's bankruptcy. Readers without great interest in the legal mechanism regarding bankruptcies in sixteenth-century Venice may find the following details tedious. I have nevertheless decided to describe this batch of documents as an illustration of the procedures in such cases. It will also reveal the complexity of these situations, which were probably not uncommon, when merchants found themselves in financial straits.[38]

The first document is a copy of a notarial contract, dated 22 March 1566, between 'Ser Chain Saruch', son of the late Solomon, described as a Levantine Jew, and 'Ser Joseff Segura', son of the late David, also a Levantine Jew, on the one hand, and a certain *messer* Paolo Cicero (described in another document as a 'mercer under the sign of the compass'), on the other hand.[39] The two Levantine Jews, appar-ently acting as partners, pledged merchandise loaded on the ship *Colomba*, which was supposed to reach Venice from Constantinople, as security for bills of exchange. Saruq pledged merchandise to the value of 6,000 ducats, and Segura pledged goods valued at about 1,600 ducats.[40]

A second document in the same batch is a copy of a *strida*, or public announcement preceded by a fanfare,[41] made on 1 June 1566 at Piazza San Marco and at Rialto, in which the said contract was made public.

---

[37] On Venetian law and procedures regarding bankruptcy, see G. I. Cassandro, *Le rappresaglie e il fallimento a Venezia nei secoli XIII-XVI*, Turin, 1938, pp. 89-136.

[38] ASV, Sen., Delib. CP, filza 3, documents pertaining to the Senate's decision of 5 July 1569.

[39] ASV, AN, busta 8253/I, f. 26v (15 Jan. 1566).

[40] For the original version of this act, see ASV, AN, busta 8253/I, f. 39, where a statement, dated 29 July 1566, is appended to this act, whereby Cicero renounced his claims to the above-mentioned merchandise following an agreement (*accordo*) signed by all the creditors. In a previous act of the same notary Saruq gave Angelo de Georgiis q. Pietro power of attorney to collect 1140 ducats from Paolo Cicero; see ASV, AN, busta 8250/V, ff. 39-39v (22 Sept. 1563).

[41] G. Boerio, *Dizionario del dialetto veneziano*, Venice, 1856, p. 715.

The public announcement signified that Saruq and Segura were unable to honour their commitments, made more than two months previously before the notary Monte, and that their creditor, or creditors, had started legal procedures to proclaim them as 'fugitives' (which did not necessarily mean that they had actually escaped).

Next in chronological order is a copy of a document entitled *sonvention e intromission*, taken from the registers of the court of *Consoli dei mercanti*. Saruq, at this stage, must have been declared a 'fugitive' debtor, since the term *sonvention*, or *sovvention*, signified a legal procedure in favour of the creditor, making it possible to arrest a bankrupt who was suspected of flight.[42] This document, dated 10 September 1566, stated that Saruq was under obligation to pay the 'Representatives of the creditors' (*deputadi de credittori*) of Ser Paulo Cicero dal Compasso, by force of a *sovvention* of 6,000 ducats and their expenses. The court's bailiff (*fante*) declared that he had put under sequestration everything which the 'Representatives' of Ḥayyim Saruq's creditors were holding, or which was supposed to come into their possession, for the payment of the said debt. The three 'Representatives' of Saruq's creditors then declared that they would keep anything they could get, but two of them stated that they already had to deal with another *intromission*. It now transpires that Paulo Cicero, to whom Saruq had pledged his merchandise in the earlier document, had also gone bankrupt. The 'Representatives' of Cicero's creditors obtained a legal authority (*sovvention*) to collect Cicero's credit to Ḥayyim Saruq from Saruq's 'Representatives'.[43]

Another document in the Senate's file (*filza*), entitled *intromission a lezze*, is a copy of a document of 27 September 1566, taken from the registers of the *Corte dell'esaminador*, a magistracy which was responsible, among other things, for sequestrating and sealing the

---

[42] D.F.N.A.E. [Filippo Nani], *Prattica civile delle corti del palazzo veneto*, Venice, 1694, p. 256; P.G. Pivetta, *L'arte di ben apprendere la pratica civile e mista del foro veneto*, vol. 2, Venice, 1791, p. 155; Cassandro, *Le rappresaglie*, pp. 94, 96, 103, 124, 130, 133, 135, 143.

[43] Cf. D.F.N.A.E., *Prattica civile*, pp. 259-260. The 'representatives' of Saruq's creditors were Ser Luca di Albici, ser Zuan Vais and ser Pelegrin Brunacini.

property and income of debtors (*interdetti a legge*).⁴⁴ This document stated that a sequestration order was announced on 27 September 1566 with regard to Saruq's property and income, which were held by the same three 'Representatives' of the creditors of Hayyim Saruq mentioned in the previous document, at the request of the aforesaid 'Representatives' of Paulo Cicero's creditors.

Saruq's bankruptcy clearly involved conflicting claims by different individuals and groups who were all trying to lay first claim to his property and capital. These must have been available and could compensate Saruq's creditors, if only in part. The above documents, though constituting only fragments of what must have been a voluminous package of legal instruments, still indicate that the ordinary courts of Venice, such as the *Consoli dei mercanti* and the *Giudici dell'esaminador*, were beginning to deal with the various claims according to normal Venetian bankruptcy procedures. We shall see that another court, the *Cinque savi alla mercanzia*, which generally dealt with the Levantine Jews, was meanwhile dealing with the dispute between Saruq and Aaron di Segura.

For the time being Saruq remained at liberty. He probably obtained a *fida*, allowing him to try and reach agreements with his various creditors within a given time limit. The notarial acts of Zuan Battista Monte enable us to catch a glimpse of Saruq's efforts to disentangle himself from his financial difficulties by submitting himself to arbitration, selling his vessels, transferring his own credits to his creditors, and reaching agreements with others. Thus, on 18 June 1566, Saruq agreed with the owners of the ship *Peliciaria* to submit their dispute in two cases of freight charges from Constantinople to Venice to arbitration. The arbitrators were Luca de Albici, son of the late Antonio and Benevento de Beneventi.⁴⁵ On 8 August Saruq turned over to Antonio de Ambrupsio, a merchant from Mal[ines?], a credit of 150 ducats and 19 *grossi*, which he was claiming from Gasparo and Zuane Ribero, resulting from an arbitration about eight months before. He turned

---

⁴⁴ A. Da Mosto, *L'Archivio di Stato di Venezia. Indice generale*, 2 vols, Rome, 1937-1940, vol. I, pp. 92-93; M.F. Tiepolo, "Archivio di Stato di Venezia", in Ministero per i Beni Culturali e Ambientali. Ufficio Centrale per i Beni Archivistici, *Guida generale degli archivi di stato italiani*, Rome, 1994, pp. 989-990.

⁴⁵ ASV, AN, busta 8253/VI, f.18 (18 June 1566). Luca di Albici was also one of the 'representatives' of Saruq's creditors; see above, n. 41.

over another credit, amounting to 100 ducats, which was owed him by a certain Ser Maximilian, called Ghedalia Cohem [sic], a Jew, resulting from a document (scritto) dated 5 June 1564.[46] A week later, Saruq transferred to messer Zuane, son of the late Battista, a shipmaster (patron di nave), all his claims upon Master Mathio, son of the late Zuane, shipbuilder (marangon) at Curzola, and his claims upon Master Francesco de Vicenzo, likewise from Curzola, on account of a vessel (navetta) built for Saruq on that island, and various agreements made with those persons, including its outfit, cords, sails, anchors, etc. In return, Zuane promised to pay Saruq 1,700 ducats within fifteen days.[47] On 26 of August, Saruq ceded his right to those 1,700 ducats to messer Piero di Pagani, a broker (sanser) at Rialto, to satisfy various creditors.[48] In two similar acts of 30 August 1566, Saruq ceded his rights to a galleon built on Curzola by master Francesco de Zuane de Rado, to Nicolo de Semeno of Corfu for the sum of 1,175 ducats, which Nicolo promised to disburse in two installments on the following 15 September and 15 October.[49] On 3 September, Saruq submitted to arbitration his dispute with Severinus Cicero, son of the late Andrea, of Como.[50] Three days later, Saruq was involved in another arbitration, this time as the agent of a certain Samuel Talmit, son of the late Abraham, in his dispute with Moses (Moise) Papo, son of Abraham.[51] Though seemingly unrelated to Saruq's own affairs, it is likely that this case was connected, at least indirectly, with his difficulties. On 11 April 1567 Saruq authorized Ioannis Pastrovich, residing in Venice, to collect debts owed him by Luca Buchia and Damian de Cattaro on account

---

[46] ASV, AN, busta 8253/VII, f. 12v (8 Aug. 1566). On Gaspar and João Ribeiro, Portuguese merchants suspected of marranism, see B. Pullan, "The Inquisition and the Jews of Venice: The Case of Gaspare Ribeiro, 1580-1581", Bulletin of the John Rylands University Library of Manchester, 62 (1979), pp. 207-231. Was Maximilian, alias Ghedalia Cohen, another Marrano, whose double identity was public knowledge?

[47] ASV, AN, busta 8253/VII, ff. 22-22v (2 acts, dated 15 Aug. 1566).

[48] Ibid., ad datam 26 Aug. 1566.

[49] ASV, AN, busta 8253/VII, ff. 32-32v (30 Aug. 1566).

[50] Ibid., f. 37v (3 Sept. 1566). The arbitrator chosen by Cicero was the draper Bernardo Gasparis, while Saruq chose Augostino di Antonio Albici, q. Nicolai.

[51] Ibid., busta 8253/VI, f. 2 (6 Sept. 1566). Samuel Talmit also figures, beside other Jews, in a promissory note of Hayyim Saruq on 13 Sept. 1564, attached to a power of attorney given to Abraham Sarfatti, to collect a debt of 400 ducats from Hayyim Saruq; see ASV, AN, busta 8254/I, f. 5v (8 Jan. 1567).

of two small vessels (*brigantini*).[52] A similar power-of-attorney was given on 21 July 1567 to Ioanettu Baptista de Tassis, to collect Saruq's debts, particularly from Nicola and Marco de Horio.[53] Finally, on 8 January 1568, Saruq gave a general power-of-attorney to his brother Isaac, who was authorized to act in his name in any matter. The latter document attests that despite all his efforts, Hayyim Saruq's situation had deteriorated, since this act was signed at the Doge's palace, in the chamber of the Doge's *scalco*, or mayordomo.[54] In fact, as we shall see, Hayyim Saruq had by then spent several months in jail.

Another notarial document concerns the repercussions of Saruq's bankruptcy on his own family. In this document Hayyim Saruq's wife, Donna Letitia, daughter of the Levantine Jew Moses (Moise) Alfandari, empowered her father and a certain Isaach [sic] Cogiati, son of the late Abraham, to claim her dowry and counter dowry (*dote et contradote*) from Hayyim Saruq's assets.[55] According to Venetian law, dowries took precedence over any other claim on the assets of a bankrupt person.[56] Saruq's wife was protecting her rights, perhaps even in collusion with her husband.

***

While Saruq was desperately trying to solve his financial difficulties by settlement, the Ottoman pressure on Venice for the repayment of Saruq's debt to the Segura was also gaining momentum. Venetian diplomatic representatives in Constantinople endured some very difficult moments on this account. By the end of September 1566 the *Bailo*'s dispatches from Constantinople reflected the nervousness in the Ottoman

---

[52] ASV, AN, busta 8254/III, f. 4v (11 Apr. 1567).

[53] *Ibid.*, busta 8254/V, f. 25 (21 July 1567).

[54] ASV, AN, busta 8255/I, f. 20 (8 Jan. 1568). *Cf.* a previous power of attorney given to Isaac Saruq by his brother on 3 April 1567, when he was still free: *ibid.*, busta 8254/II, f. 42v.

[55] ASV, AN, busta 8252/VIII, f. 11 (3 [4?] Oct. 1566). Moyse Alfandari appears in another dispute with Hayyim Saruq and Joseph Segura, which was arbitrated by Rabbi Moyse Cabillo and Rabbi Caym [sic] Gachi, son of the late Abraham. The latter, described as a Levantine Jew from Angora (Ankara), having to leave Venice, declared he was ready to endorse any decision taken by his colleague, see ASV, AN, busta 8254/II, f. 28v (20 Mar. 1567).

[56] Cassandro, *Le rappresaglie*, pp. 106-107.

capital about the consequences of Saruq's bankruptcy. In one of his letters the *Bailo* added some remarks in cipher, writing that "the Jews here are generally very well considered, and particularly these [the Segura], since they are very closely related (*congiuntissimi*) to Zuan Miches". The latter, according to the *Bailo*, was on friendly terms with the Sultan, and the two frequently entertained each other.[57]

The presence of an official Ottoman envoy in Venice undermined the Republic's intention to treat Saruq's case as an ordinary commercial litigation. Thus, in accordance with Segura's demand, backed by official Ottoman *firmāns*, the case was transferred from the court of the *Cinque savi alla mercanzia* to the *Dieci savi del corpo del senato*, a body of ten senators which had been instituted in 1529 to deal with appeals in fiscal matters, but also with special cases delegated to it by the Senate.[58] The latter function became increasingly frequent in the 1560s. It is interesting to see this tendency reflected in an official Ottoman *firmān*, with its explicit request to put Saruq's case before this body. Obviously, this request had come from the Segura family which, thanks to its connections in Venice, was acquainted with the Republic's judicial practice. Trying the case in the Court of ten senators would not only emphasize its political implication, but would also prevent Saruq from appealing to a higher court.[59] The fact that the Venetian authorities agreed to this demand shows their reluctance to antagonize the Porte, and their awareness of the influence of the Segura in Ottoman high circles. When the presidents of the senatorial court later decided that the law did not authorize them to deal with part of the material pertaining to contracts, the entire matter was declared by the Council of Ten to be an 'affair of state' (*causa di stato*), thus enabling the *Dieci savi del corpo del senato* to continue their work on this delicate case.[60] Apparently, legal technicalities seemed irrelevant at that point and were easily swept aside. As we shall see, the senatorial court dealt not only

---

[57] ASV, Sen., Disp. CP, filza 1, No 61 (27 Sept. 1566).

[58] *Collegio dei X poi XX savi del corpo del senato*, ed. G. Tamba, Rome, 1977, pp. 9-15, 20. As indicated in the title, the ten *Savi,* often reinforced by a *Zonta*, or adjoining committee, later became a court of twenty 'Sages'.

[59] See Joseph Segura's petition, attached to the Senate's decision to appoint ten *savi* to hear the case, in ASV, Sen., Mar, reg. 37, ff. 237-237v (2 Nov. 1566); *ibid.*, filza 36 (1566).

[60] ASV, Cons. X, Secreti, reg. 8, ff. 95-95v (22 Aug. 1567).

with the Saruq-Segura dispute, but with all the other implications of Saruq's bankruptcy, previously dealt with by the ordinary palace courts (*corti del palazzo*).

I have been able to find one document concerning this case in the archive of the Court of ten senators. It is a long deposition by Saruq himself, dated 7 January 1567, in which he defended himself against all his creditors (*contra cadauno*).[61] The Segura of Constantinople are not mentioned in this document, whereas some of his creditors in Venice, who have already been mentioned, are referred to by name. Formally, at any rate, Saruq's bankruptcy was not due to his business relations with the Segura. It should be kept in mind that the official Ottoman claim was that Segura and Saruq were both the Sultan's commercial agents. Moreover, as we shall see, Saruq could prove that he and Segura were indeed partners, which put the latter in a different legal position from that of the other creditors.

In his deposition Saruq stated that his failure to honour his debts stemmed from the exorbitant interest rates on bills of exchange, amounting to 40% and even 50%, which he had to pay. By his own statement, his debts amounted to 112,000 ducats, including 40,000 ducats of interest and not including expenses. Yet, according to Saruq, he had already succeeded in repaying a large part of his debts, and given more time he would be able to honour them all. By then he had already transferred to his creditors merchandise, including camlets, alum, wool, leather, felt and cordovan leather, valued at more than 77,000 ducats. Several persons, including the very same creditors, owed him some 49,000 ducats, "including the jewels", as shown in a balance-sheet which was supposedly attached to his deposition. Saruq also wrote that Luca degli Albizzi (Albici), described as "one of the three elected ['Representatives']", actually owed him a great deal of money.[62] The same was true of Thomaso Vivaldi (or Vivaldo) and

---

[61] ASV, Dieci, poi venti savi del corpo del senato, busta 178 (7 Jan. 1566 *m.v.*). Saruq writes that his deposition was accompanied by "4 polizze et 3 depenadure", but these documents have not been found.

[62] This Albici [Albizzi] was probably the father of the writer and theologian Antonio degli Albizzi, born in Venice in 1547, where according to Spretti, Antonio's father, Luca, settled after the fall of the republican regime in Florence. Antonio later went to Germany and became a Lutheran; see V. Spretti, *Enciclopedia storico-nobiliare italiana*, vol. 1, Milan, 1928, p. 347. Litta mentions two persons bearing the name Luca Albizzi during that period: Luca degli Albizzi, son of Paolo, born in 1497, podestà

Bernardino Rotulo (or Rotollo), whose claim was based upon three documents (*scritti*) which Saruq had given to Paulo Cicer [*sic*], who was also in his debt. According to Saruq, the same was true of his other debts. By subtracting credits from debts, and reducing the part of his debts due to excessive rates of interest, he would be able to meet all his obligations.

Saruq further claimed that imprisoning him would not solve his creditors' problems. He did not flee from Venice, and was ready to honour all his commitments. Moreover, his creditors should be interested in leaving him free to settle his debts. A document he had given to his creditors in June wold show that all his goods were in their hands, and he would resume paying his debts as he collected his own credits.

Apparently none of the mentioned documents contained a full list of Saruq's creditors at that stage. Some time later the Grand Vizier complained to the *Bailo* that Venetian courts gave precedence in this case to the claims of Ferrarese and Milanese subjects over those of the Ottoman Sultan. It is possible, therefore, that as well as the Florentine Albizzi the other creditors were citizens of those Italian states. Most, though not all the creditors mentioned in documents dated about a year later were Jews or *Marranos*.[63] The sums of money mentioned by Saruq himself—who would presumably seek to minimize the extent of his liabilities—are very impressive: a debt of 112,000 ducats, a large part of which, according to Saruq, had already been repaid with a consignment of merchandise from the East: camlets, alum, wool, felt and cordovan leather valued at 77,000 ducats.

I have been unable to find the final decision (or rather decisions) of the senatorial 'Ten Sages'. A letter sent by the Senate to the *Bailo* in January 1579, recapitulating the whole affair, states that the senators had decided in favour of Joseph Segura (son of Aaron), who was

---

of Acetto in 1550; and Luca, son of Antonio Francesco, who joined the exiled Florentines who tried to "liberate their homeland" from Alessandro de Medici's rule, and was declared a rebel on 6 October 1536 [probably the one mentioned by Spreti], see P. Litta, *Famiglie celebri italiane*, 2nd series, vol. I, Turin, 1902, tavola XII and tavola XIX. Minna Rozen has kindly reminded me that Luca degli Albizzi was also the name of the Italian business correspondent of Doña Grazia Nassí in the 1550s; see Roth, *The House of Nasi: Doña Gracia*, pp.179-180. It is highly probable that we are here dealing with the same person, who continued to be engaged in business affairs with Levantine Jews.

[63] See below, pp. 136-37.

satisfied with the outcome.[64] It is possible that a document preserved in the Venetian State Archive, in which Joseph di Segura undertook half of Hayyim Saruq's debt to the banker Daniele Dolfin di Andrea dal Banco, amounting to 4,177 ducats, lire 9, while appropriating half the value of the emerald deposited by Saruq as a guarantee, refers to part of this settlement.[65] However, for some unknown reason Joseph Segura later agreed to submit his dispute with Saruq to arbitration, at the same time obtaining the repeal of the sequestration of Saruq's goods.[66] This development must have taken place sometime between 14 April 1567, when the Senate informed the *Bailo* that the judges were still dealing with this case,[67] and 11 August 1567, when the Senate referred to the arbitration in the past tense.[68] Meanwhile, however, great changes had taken place in the East.

***

On the night of 5 September 1566, in the middle of a successful military campaign in Hungary, Sultan Süleyman the Magnificent died in his tent and was succeeded by his son Selim. The accession of a new Sultan called for a Venetian ambassador to be dispatched to congratulate the new ruler and reconfirm the terms of the peace treaty between the two countries. The person chosen for this mission was a senior statesman and exemplary diplomat: Marino Cavalli, a rich patrician who had served as *Bailo* in the Ottoman capital between 1557 and 1559, and had also served as ambassador to the Papal court, to France and other capitals. During his first stay in the Ottoman capital he had presented Sultan Süleyman a Turkish translation of a work written by his maternal grandfather, Andrea Foscolo, which was actually an adaptation of Cicero's *De senectute*. He drew on his diplomatic experience to write the treatise "Information on the office of ambassador", most probably in the early 1560s.[69] But now the mission, which was meant to be

---

[64] ASV, Sen., Delib. CP, reg. 5, f. 116 (16 Jan. 1578 *m.v.*).

[65] ASV, LST, filza 2, f. 197, summarized in IB, No 416/1 (16 Jan. 1566 *m.v.*).

[66] ASV, Sen., Delib. CP, reg. 5, f. 116 (16 Jan. 1578 *m.v.*).

[67] *Ibid.*, reg. 3, f. 82v (12 Apr. 1567).

[68] *Ibid.*, reg. 3, f. 90v.

[69] A. Olivieri, "Cavalli, Marino", *Dizionario biografico degli italiani*, vol. 22, Rome, 1979, pp. 749-754.

solemn and friendly, was seriously hampered by the prolonged crisis surrounding Saruq's bankruptcy.

On 8 March 1567, while Ambassador Cavalli was on his way from Venice to the East, the *Bailo* Soranzo wrote to Venice about the renewed pressure from the Segura family, in response to the news about the sentence issued in Venice:

> ...Every day the insolence of this rabble grows so much that they permit themselves, by word and deed, to molest your Serenity's representative and infringe upon your dignity, without consideration for the many favours and advantages which they received from our nation, which, because of them, has been almost despoilt of its business in this country. Therefore, it is surely necessary that his Serenity consider taking appropriate actions to suppress their great insolence...[70]

But the diplomatic tension was to rise still higher. After Ambassador Cavalli's arrival at the Ottoman capital, on 23 April 1567, it was hinted to him that the peace terms would not be renewed unless the Saruq case was settled to the satisfaction of Segura and his Ottoman protectors. Time and again the Pasha claimed that the alum actually belonged to the Sultan, and that he could not understand how the Republic gave precedence to the private interests of foreigners over those of its ally, the Sultan. Whenever the subject was raised, the *Bailo* and ambassador replied that this was a dispute between individual litigants, and was treated as such; that there was no indication whatsoever that the merchandise sent from Aaron di Segura to Ḥayyim Saruq belonged to the Sultan; and that in spite of all this, Segura's representatives had received exceptionally favourable treatment in Venice, and had no cause to complain.[71] But when the affair dragged on through the month of June, Cavalli understood that he had to reach some agreement with Segura if he was to accomplish his official mission. On 4 July Cavalli and the *Bailo* reported about a meeting with the Pasha, in which they learned that another *Çavuş* was about to be sent to Venice to try and settle the matter. The two Venetian diplomats informed the Pasha that an agreement had meanwhile been reached between Cavalli and Segura's son-in-law, in the presence of a *Çavuş*, in which Cavalli promised that

---

[70] ASV, Sen., Disp. CP. filza 2, No 3 (8 Mar. 1567).

[71] *Ibid.*, No 24 (28 May 1567).

after his return to Venice he would make every effort to assist Segura's agents.[72]

But what seemed to the Venetians a reasonable compromise was only an illusion. On 10 July 1567 the *Bailo* and the ambassador wrote another letter to Venice describing the dramatic events of the previous days.[73] When Ambassador Cavalli came to take his leave from the Pasha, the sons of Aaron Segura intervened claiming that Cavalli had promised to release the alum and other sequestrated merchandise on his return to Venice, and that for their part they were satisfied with the arrangement; otherwise, they would insist that a *Çavuş* be sent to Venice to settle the matter. Cavalli immediately denied that he had promised to release the merchandise. According to him, he only promised to make the utmost effort to solve the affair. Since twenty senators had already been appointed to judge the case,[74] and having no current information about the proceedings of this body, the ambassador was unable to commit himself further. The Pasha noted irritably that he too had been under the impression that Cavalli had promised to see to the release of the goods. According to the letter, Sokollu then stood up angrily, and while the Jews increased their vociferations, he summoned a *Çavuş* and ordered him to lead the ambassador to court. Turning to the two patricians, he said that if the matter remained unsettled, things would take a turn for the worse.

Being led to court by a *Çavuş* through the streets of Istanbul was not a dignified prospect. Moreover, as the two diplomats explained in their letter, consignment by the Pasha to a *Çavuş* meant that they would to be held in custody until the conclusion of the case. The Venetians, therefore, tried to persuade the *Çavuş* to accompany them to their respective houses at Pera, where they would try to reach a new accord with the Segura. Finally, it was agreed that further negotiations would be carried out at the house of Ibrāhīm, the Porte's Dragoman. There, after long disputes and bargaining an agreement was reached in the presence of the *Çavuş* and six other Muslim witnesses, according to which the ambassador would be allowed to leave Istanbul, promising to make every effort in Venice in order to release the alum and the other sequestrated goods, and to have them turned over to Segura's

---

[72] *Ibid.*, No 31 (4 July 1567).

[73] ASV, Sen., Disp. CP, filza 2, ff. 115v-117.

[74] The ten *Savi* were probably joined by a *Zonta* of ten additional senators.

agents. The difference between this agreement and the former was a clause stating that, unless a settlement was reached within six months to Segura's satisfaction, the *Bailo*—who, of course, remained in Istanbul—would present himself to the Kadi for judgement.

Yet even this was not enough to bring the affair to an end. The *Bailo* and the ambassador were allowed to return to their respective mansions, but when the Venetian interpreter appeared before the Pasha, together with Ibrāhīm, his Ottoman colleague, and the *Çavuş*, to report and arrange for a farewell audience for Cavalli, the Pasha said that if the Jews were satisfied with the compromise, so was he, but he considered a verbal agreement made before witnesses as insufficient. He therefore ordered that the Kadi of Pera should prepare a proper judicial statement *(hüccet)*[75], and added that he would not receive Cavalli and the *Bailo* before this was done.

Apparently, there was nothing for it but to consent. The Venetian interpreter was sent, together with the *Çavuş*, the Ottoman interpreter Ibrāhīm and the Jews, to the Kadi, who, after a brief investigation, prepared the *hüccet*. The translation of this document was attached to the letter which Cavalli and Soranzo immediately sent to the Signory. It goes as follows:[76]

> Copy of a *sigiletto*[77] made by Mehemet son of Acmet, Kadi of Pera.
> Present before the judge: Mussa, son and representative of the Jew Haron, leaseholder of the alums; Lodovico the interpreter, representing Giacomo Soranzo, Venetian *Bailo*, and Marino di Cavalli, currently ambassador; and Cubat chiaus [*Çavuş*] of the Sublime Porte, responsible for this case.
>   The said Mussa declared that after the said Haron had sent goods valued at 110,000 ducats to Jussuf, son of Davit and Cain Saruc in Venice, those Lords (*quelli Signori*) sequestrated them, claiming that the said Cain was indebted to other persons. Therefore, since the said Haron was a debtor of the Sultan, he demands that the said goods be returned here.

---

[75] On the *hüccet*, see A. Boškov, "Die hüccet-Urkunde - Diplomatische Analyse", in *Studia turcologica memoriae Alexii Bombaci dicata*, Naples, 1982, pp. 81-87; V. Demetriades, "Some observations on the Ottoman-Turkish judicial documents (*Hüccets*)", *Balkan Studies*, vol. 26 (1985), pp. 25-39.

[76] ASV, Sen., Disp. CP, filza 2, ff. 118-118v. I have kept the spelling of names and terms as they appear in the document.

[77] *Sicil*: record of the Kadi's court.

And the said Dragoman Lodovico replied that the said Ambassador Marin di Cavalli committed himself to make every effort and use good will to release within six months the goods which had been sent to Venice in the name of the said Haron. And that if, after six months from to-day, the goods were not released, and the said Haron remained dissatisfied, the said *Bailo* Giacomo Soranzo, acting as agent for that party, would be obliged to continue the case and dispute and submit to the court's judgement.

Therefore the present note has been made at the request of the party concerned, to serve in due time if necessary.

Made in the first days of the month of Muherem [Muḥarram] 975, *i.e.*, in the month of July 1567.

Testimonies: Mustaffà, *Chiecaia*[78] of Mustafa Pasha; Hasan, *Chiaus*, son of Abdalla; Ibrahim, *Imam* of the neighbourhood of Cagicanzà;[79] Mustafa, son of Camzà; Hasan, son of Abdalla; Heder Bei, son of Murat; Hasan, son of Kasim, *Capigi* [*Kapıcı*];[80] and others present.

In conclusion, Cavalli and Soranzo apologized for having submitted to this unusual procedure, noting in cipher that the prospects were gloomy if the alum was not released, as it could hurt the interests of the Pasha and his party (*li suoi congionti*); in fact, because of the Jews' indebtedness to the Sultan's treasury, the alum sequestrated in Venice was their only chance of honouring their debt. The two Venetian envoys also noted that the Chief Treasurers (*Defterdārs*) supported the claims of the Jews before the Grand Vizier, arguing that goods owned by the Sultan's debtors, even abroad, appertained to the Sultan's treasury, since the latter always took precedence over other creditors. According to Soranzo and Cavalli, their compliance with the procedure was the only way to enable the ambassador to leave and to gain some time in order to report back home and receive new instructions.

---

[78] This may be a Venetian distortion of the term *Kâhia*, or *Kethüda*, signifying a steward, or majordomo; see J. Redhouse, *New Redhouse Turkish - English Dictionary*, 12th ed., Istanbul, 1992, pp. 582, 646. I am grateful to Minna Rozen for this reference.

[79] This seems to be the *maḥalle* of Hâce Hamza, see *Istanbul Vakıfları tahrîr defteri 953 (1546) Târîhli*, eds. O.L.Barkan and E. H. Averdi, Istanbul, 1970, *ad vocem* Hâce Hamza in the index, p. 483.

[80] A *Kapıcı* was a member of a military corps whose chief responsibility was to guard the doors of the imperial palace; see Gibb and Bowen, *Islamic Society*, p. 347.

This clash between Ottoman and Venetian justice was described in another letter from the *Bailo* to Venice, dated 2 August, in which he wrote that

> ...the legal considerations which obtain in the Christian world are not accepted here, since the Turkish legal system (*la ragion turchesca*) is totally different, unused to attorneys or legal counsellors and to written evidence (*termini di scritture*); all cases, even the most important, are here summarily dispatched by factual (verbal) evidence (*con la evidentia del fatto*). This is the system to which I shall have to submit myself in six months' time because of the promise which we have made...[81]

Apparently, the Porte did not rely too much on Cavalli's promise to support Segura's case in Venice, as towards the end of August Kubad, the *Çavuş* who had been involved in securing the agreement between the Venetians and the Segura, was about to leave Istanbul to go to Venice, to follow the developments on the spot.[82]

The official response to the quoted reports from Istanbul of 4-12 July is included in letters approved by the Senate on 11 August 1567.[83] The Signory severely reprimanded its two senior representatives for the way they had handled the affair in the Ottoman capital:

> Your reports regarding the developments in the case of the Jew Aaron di Segura have been received by us with great bitterness and displeasure, being matters touching upon the dignity and profit of our Signory. You should not have agreed to participate in the issuing a *hüccet*, which caused us disgrace and damage, since it violates the peace terms (*li capitoli della pace*), and because you had not received from us any authority to this effect...

The Senate instructed the *Bailo* to present himself immediately before the Pasha to protest in the Signory's name about the recent occurrences. Venice had dispatched a special ambassador to congratulate the new

---

[81] *Ibid.*, No 42 (2 Aug. 1567).

[82] *Ibid.*, f. 174 (the *Bailo* announces Kubad's imminent departure, 19 Aug. 1567).

[83] ASV, Sen., Delib. CP, reg. 3, ff. 90-91 (11 Aug. 1567). A somewhat inaccurate echo of the *Bailo*'s report of 12 July is included in a report sent on 9 Aug. 1567 from Venice to Rome by the papal nuncio, see *Nunziature di Venezia*, vol. 8, p. 258.

Sultan on his accession to the throne; the Senate was astounded to hear that Cavalli, together with the *Bailo*, had been so badly treated, in a manner unprecedented in the diplomatic relations between the two countries—an ambassador being forced to guarantee the debts of other persons was

> ...not only contrary to universal customs pertaining to the treatment of ambassadors and official ministers, who are generally well treated and honoured, as we ourselves have done and will always do with regard to anybody, and particularly those sent by the Sultan, as can be testified by the honourable Ibrāhīm, who was recently here; it also violates the terms of the peace which we have made with His Majesty, which on the same occasion were confirmed and sworn by him, and in which it is declared that our representatives cannot be molested for debts of other persons...[84]

The Senate expressed its conviction that it had all arisen from misinformation given to the Pasha by the interested party, or by others "who do not have the good will of the Pasha towards Venice". The Senate asked the *Bailo* to clarify to the Pasha that in the matter of Aaron di Segura nothing could be done other than what had been done by the Senate. In order to satisfy Sultan Süleyman, and later his successor, they had consigned the case to a senatorial tribunal, ordering it to resolve it as quickly as possible; they had given every assistance to Joseph di Segura, by sequestrating goods and by other means, to the point that he did not know what more he could ask for. Later he decided, of his own accord, to submit to arbitration and consented to the repeal of the judicial sequestration. The Signory never intervened, nor would it intervene in cases of this kind, except to assist Joseph, so as to honour the letters of recommendation he had been given by his imperial patron. Nothing more could be demanded from the Signory in this matter, since rulers could not be held responsible for goods imported into their territories by individuals subject to privately agreed conditions, even if they were negligent in doing so. To emphasize this point, the Senate mentioned the particular case of Joseph di Segura, who claimed that a ship of his had been lost on the high seas, causing him heavy losses. Venice could not be held responsible for incidents of this kind.

But legal arguments were evidently not enough to persuade the

---

[84] On this point, see Brown, "Venetian Diplomacy", pp. 4-5.

Ottomans to change their attitude. The Senate, therefore, added a statement suggesting that Venice was also capable of hurting its opponents. If these molestations went on, it said, the Republic would be forced to prevent those persons who caused such disturbances from trading in Venice and all its territories. Nevertheless, to demonstrate its good will, the Senate informed its representatives in the Ottoman capital that Ḥayyim Saruq had already been arrested, as demanded by the Sultan, so as to send him to Constantinople. Moreover, they had also detained Joseph di Segura, for having cancelled the sequestration, to enable the Signory to send him to the Pasha too, if asked to do so.

On that day another letter to the *Bailo* was voted upon and confirmed by the Senate.[85] In it the Senate reported the results of a detailed investigation carried out following the detention of Ḥayyim Saruq and Joseph di Segura. The examination of their papers revealed that Ḥayyim Saruq was not only the agent (*commesso*) of the said Joseph, but his partner (*compagno*)[86]; that both of them traded and contracted their merchandise at will; that Joseph had agreed to cancel the sequestration, which proved the falsehood of the claim that Venice was responsible for this move so as to ensure payment to her own merchants. Having learned the identity of the debtors of the Jewish associates, the Signory would help them to collect. It had already nominated judged and instructed them to resolve without delay the problems concerning the interest demanded from them (this may be a reference to Saruq's claim that he was forced to pay excessive interest on his borrowings). Moreover, Joseph Segura admitted that his debt to the Sultan's treasury did not exceed 40,000 ducats. Apparently being in detention made him more collaborative, since according the Senate's letter he was also ready to write to Istanbul demanding the lifting of the obligation undertaken by Ambassador Cavalli and *Bailo* Soranzo. In the margin of this document there is a very interesting paragraph about the impact of the affair on the Jewish community in Venice:

...The Hebrew nation (*la natione hebrea*) is very much afraid of being

---

[85] ASV, Sen., Delib. CP, reg. 3, pp. 91-91v.

[86] For the Hebrew contract of 18 *Tishri* 5325 (24 Sept. 1564), establishing a partnership between Ḥayyim Saruq and Joseph Segura for a period of four years, see the Appendix.

expelled from our state because of this mishap, which seems a good thing to us, for this fear may lead them to take measures to save us such trouble on their account. And they have already expressed their intention to write about this matter to their brethren...

The Senate made it very clear that the *Bailo* should do whatever was necessary to bring about the revocation of the *hüccet*. "You should raise the subject of the *hüccet* in your conversations with the Pasha as often as you deem necessary in order to bring about its suppression." The Senate was worried not only about the particular case which had led to the *hüccet*, but also by the precedent it created in the diplomatic practice. It is emphasized that not only Joseph Segura, but also others "of his nation" had expressed their willingness to help in bringing about the revocation of this document. The *Bailo* was instructed to consult "intelligent people who are loyal to Venice" about the means of obtaining this objective, and to guide the persons who were willing to cooperate how to act in this matter. Since "nothing can be of higher importance than this", the *Bailo* was called upon to devote his capabilities, energy and prudence so as to achieve a satisfactory settlement.

With Saruq and Segura behind lock and key, the Venetian authorities were able not only to exert more pressure on them, but also to seize the correspondence and documents which revealed the strategy of their opponents in Istanbul.[87] On 9 August the Council of Ten decided to convey to the Senate the contents of letters addressed to Joseph Segura which they had intercepted.[88] Some of these letters, written by a one Meir Olivaro, contained information which was immediately used in Venice's diplomatic efforts. According to the Signory's report to the *Bailo*, the contents of the letters, which were passed on to the *Bailo*'s in great secrecy, revealed "the impious way" in which the Jews intended to cheat the Venetian representative in Istanbul.[89] This kind of material could also be used for other purposes, as was demonstrated some time later, when Ambassador Cavalli himself faced charges.[90]

---

[87] On the same day, 11 August, the Senate reconfirmed the detention of Segura in the "camera del capitano grande" and of Saruq "in the same prison where he is at present", *ibid.*, f. 92v.

[88] ASV, Cons. X, Secreti, reg. 8, f. 95 (9 Aug. 1567).

[89] ASV, Sen., Delib. CP, reg. 3., f. 91v.

[90] *Nunziature di Venezia*, vol. 8, pp. 258, 267 (9 and 30 Aug. 1567).

A paraphrase of Meir Olivaro's letter which was transmitted to the *Bailo* has been preserved in the file of the Senate's deliberation.[91] We shall note only a few significant features of this long and detailed document. The letter is dated according to the Hebrew calendar, 2 of *Menahem* [*Av*] *i.e.*, July 1567. It describes the negotiations between Ambassador Cavalli, the Pasha and the Segura which had led to the issuing of the *hüccet*. The Pasha appears as most inimical to Venice, in spite of the many presents which he had received from the Republic. Aaron di Segura, who is referred to as the writer's father-in-law, is described by Olivaro, in the part dealing with the conversation with the *Bailo*, as favourably disposed towards Venice, but dragged into those disputes by his sons. Hayyim Saruq is said to be owner of three *bregantini* (small vessels), worth about 1,000 ducats each. Two very different amounts are cited concerning Segura's debt to the Sultan's treasury: according to one passage, the Pasha claimed in his dispute with Cavalli that it amounted to 305,000 ducats, whereas Olivaro, in anther passage, mentions 50,000 ducats. Joseph di Segura (the above-mentioned Joseph David, not to be confused with Aaron di Segura's son), who had been Saruq's partner in Venice, is described as a cousin of Aaron Segura. Olivaro writes how he himself pretended to be too busy to come to the *Bailo*'s house when invited, thus helping to bring about what he considered to be a favourable outcome [*i.e.*, the *hüccet*]. According to this letter, the main claim concerned a cargo of 15,000 *kantar*s of alum, shipped on four vessels to Venice, of which the Pasha received the bill to the amount of 110,000 ducats. Summing up what seemed to him a marvellous achievement, Olivaro noted that one could not have done any better if one had given the Pasha 100,000 ducats. He expressed his belief that the Republic would disburse the sum in order to placate the Sultan and secure the confirmation of the peace terms.

In another letter of 11 August the Senate asked the *Bailo* to contact Don Joseph Nassí, who had only a few months before warned the Signory that the Ottomans were considering an attack on Venetian Cyprus. The relations between Nassí and Venice have already been discussed in a previous chapter. Suffice it to say that at this point, Nassí was anxious to improve his relations with Venice, and had even succeeded in obtaining, a few months earlier, the repeal of a ban which

---

[91] ASV, Sen., Delib. CP, filza 2, appendix to the resolution of 11 Aug. 1567.

had been proclaimed against him in Venice some years before.[92] In any case, this positive turn in Nassí's relations with the Republic was also exploited by the Senate in its efforts to undo the detested document. The *Bailo* was instructed to thank the Jewish courtier for his warning, and at the same time bring to his knowledge "how justly angry we are with the Hebrew nation" on account of Aaron di Segura, and to clarify that unless a satisfactory solution was reached, Venice would have no alternative but to expel this nation from its territory, as the Republic refused to suffer such indignities on their account. The Senate also remarked that alum could be imported from many other countries. Considering that Nassí also had some interest in the alum business, and taking into account his relations with Aaron di Segura, described as a close relative of his (*suo stretto parente*), it was assumed that he too would be willing to help get rid of the *hüccet*.[93]

Nor was this all. Another letter to the *Bailo* was approved by the Senate on the same day, in which he was informed that Ambassador Marino Cavalli had been turned over to the State Attorneys (*Avogadori di comun*) for having consented to the issuance of the *hüccet*, a document so prejudicial to the Signory, without authorization and contrary to the peace terms. The *Bailo* was instructed to inform the Pasha about this procedure, and point out that this was how the Signory treated those who deviated from their instructions, as any ruler would, including the Sultan and his Pasha, if a representatives of theirs acted contrary to imperial commands.[94] This short letter obviously had a dual purpose: to demonstrate to the Ottoman authorities how gravely Venice viewed these developments; and to emphasize to the *Bailo* how essential it was to do away with the *hüccet*. A bill proposing to proceed against the *Bailo too,* on his return was passed in the Senate on 30 August, but was immediately suspended,[95] obviously so as not to hamper the *Bailo*'s efforts in Istanbul. Ambassador Cavalli was arrested on his return and charged not only with violating his commission, but also

---

[92] See above, p. 58.

[93] ASV, Sen., Delib. CP, reg. 3, f. 92.

[94] *Ibid.*, f. 92.

[95] *Ibid.*, c. 79v (30 Aug. 1567). I am obliged to Maria Pia Pedani of the Venetian State Archives for this reference.

with accepting a bribe from Segura.[96]

The Signory's severe letters, voted upon on 11-12 August 1567, had already reached the Bailo when he reported from Istanbul on 7 and 8 September. He reiterated that the *hüccet* had been unavoidable, and that the wording of the document did not match the original wording agreed between the Venetians and the Segura. The letters of Meir Olivaro, which the Signory had brought to his attention, increased his suspicion that the Segura had conspired with the Kadi to obtain a *hüccet* which would suit their interests better. Moreover, Kubad, the *Çavuş* sent to Venice to settle the affair, had also been very favourable to the Segura, and might receive some 10,000 ducats for his trouble, the customary 10% paid for such services in those parts.[97]

Of particular interest is the *Bailo*'s letter of 8 September, which sheds light on the way Venetian diplomats acted in such cases. Soranzo reported "working through a certain friend" he had learned that having received letters from Joseph Segura and notables of the Jewish community in Venice, the leading Jews of Istanbul met and deliberated at length how to deal with this crisis. According to Soranzo's informants, the Jews decided to rely on Segura's good contacts with the Pasha, refusing to believe that the Signory would prevent them from trading in Venice. The *Bailo* further reported about a meeting with Meir Olivaro and Joseph, son of David di Segura (Saruq's partner in Venice, who had meanwhile returned to Istanbul). The two Jews defended Segura's case, arguing that Saruq owned several vessels, as well as half of the ship *Mazzona*. They stated that he had conspired with his creditors in Venice, transferring to them goods of a much greater value than what he actually owed them, at the cost of what he owed the Segura. When told about the detention of Joseph di Segura in Venice, after the sequestration was repealed at his request, the other Joseph suggested that he must have been threatened, since he himself had also been threatened by a merchant in Venice, which prompted him to flee to Istanbul. The *Bailo* hinted to Olivaro that he knew about his involvement in the affair of the *hüccet*, and that such intrigues would force Venice to get rid of those who caused her so much trouble.

[96] *Ibid.*, f. 94 (29 Aug.1567), c. 84v (6 Sept. 1567). See also Marino Cavalli, *Informatione dell'ofitio dell'ambasciatore di Marino Cavalli il vecchio, MDL*, ed. T. Bertelè, Florence-Rome, 1935, p. 28, n.1.

[97] ASV, Sen., Disp. CP, filza 2 (7 Sept. 1567).

The *Bailo* then described a meeting arranged, in accordance with the Signory's instructions, between him and Joseph Nassí, at which Soranzo passed on the message he had been told to give the Duke of Naxos. But Nassí was evasive, stated that for him to intervene with the Pasha would be counter-productive, nor would Segura be pleased about it. However, Nassí had some information to offer. According to him, Segura had already received at least 80,000 ducats out of the 110,000 which he claimed, and that after subtracting the interest, the account could be said to have been balanced.[98]

But Soranzo's main concern now was to bring about the repeal of the *hüccet*, since his own political career, and probably also his personal fate, depended upon his ability to reverse what Venice regarded as a grave error in his and in Ambassador Cavalli's conduct. His long and detailed reports of 10, 14, 18 September all concerned a series of meetings between him and the Pasha during those days, in which he made great efforts to achieve this. Soranzo brought out the entire arsenal of his previous arguments, adding new ones in the hope of persuading the Grand Vizier to conciliate Venice. The Jews, he claimed, were cheating everybody, including the Grand Vizier himself. They had introduced into the *hüccet* the sum of 110,000 ducats, which had not been mentioned in their agreement with the Venetian diplomats. Their actions in Venice did not match their arguments before the Porte, as some "more honourable Jews" in Istanbul could testify.[99] At one of his meetings with Sokollu, Soranzo used the information supplied to him by Nassí, namely, that Segura had already goods valued at about 80,000 ducats, which could be ascertained by checking the registers of the Ottoman customs of the past four years. Moreover, not all the Sultan's alum reached Venice, for a substantial part had been sold in the East. The Pasha finally showed some good will. He agreed to send another *Çavuş* to Venice with instructions to Kubad not to use the *hüccet*. This, of course, did not satisfy Soranzo, who continued to press Sokollu. It was of the utmost importance to repeal the original *hüccet* altogether. The Pasha's promise that the document would not be used any more against the Venetians did not set the *Bailo*'s mind at rest. Sokollu, who must have been impressed by Soranzo's persistence, promised

---

[98] *Ibid.*, No 51 (in cipher with deciphering attached).
[99] *Ibid.*, No 52 (10 Sept. 1567).

to discuss the matter with the Kadi.[100]

Unwilling to take anything on trust, Soranzo made enquiries whether such a meeting took place, but the Pasha seemed to be in no hurry to arrange it. In the meantime, the Kadi was informed by the *Bailo*'s interpreter that his cooperation would be generously repaid. When he was finally invited to meet with the Pasha on two consecutive days, the Kadi expressed his opinion that since the *hüccet* had been prepared at the Pasha's request, it could also be repealed in the same way. Later, as the *Bailo* secretly found out and reported in cipher to Venice, the Pasha sent a *Çavuş* to the Kadi, and caused the page with the *hüccet* to be torn out of the register by the Kadi, leaving no trace of it. To make sure that this information was reliable, two of the *Bailo*'s interpreters, Mauroceni and Pasqual, were sent to look through the Kadi's registers. Having examined it page after page, and having found nothing, they were able to set the *Bailo*'s mind at rest.

But the task was not yet done, since it was also necessary to get rid of any extant copy of the dangerous document. The Pasha was again approached by Soranzo, asking for an official writ repealing the *hüccet*, but Sokollu was evasive. He tried to convince the *Bailo* that the *hüccet* would never again be used and that the only extant copy of it was in the hands of Kubad in Venice (or rather, on his way there), who had been told to ignore it.[101]

Thus it seemed that the Bailo Soranzo succeeded in neutralizing the source of his near ruin. On 13 October he wrote a long and unusually self-abasing and apologetic letter, in which he recapitulated the whole affair, justifying his and Cavalli's conduct by the difficult circumstances in which they had found themselves, and including some harsh terms, such as "those wretched and perfidious Jews" (*questi scelerati et perfidi hebrei*), in reference to his Jewish opponents.[102]

The measures approved by the Senate in mid-August reflected the great displeasure which was still felt in Venice before the arrival of Soranzo's report about his recent successes. On 2 September, when the *Bailo*'s efforts had not yet produced visible results, some of the Venetian oligarchs lost patience and proposed to send a special ambassador to convey Venice's anger about the past events, and to try to remedy

---

[100] *Ibid.*, No 53 (14 Sept. 1567).

[101] *Ibid.*, Nos 54 (18 Sept. 1567), 56 (later in the same month).

[102] *Ibid.*, No 61 (13 Oct. 1567).

them. "The sinister accidents which our ambassador and *Bailo* in Constantinople had to undergo due to the machinations and evil operations of Aaron di Segura and his dependent Jews," stated the resolution proposed on that day, "and caused such great offence to the dignity of our Signory, as everyone in this council knows, are so grave that our displeasure must be demonstrated in every possible way, and the dignity and reputation of our state must be asserted". It was therefore decided to send a new ambassador to the Porte. Though an attempt was made to postpone the implementation of this decision until further news arrived from Istanbul, a respectable Venetian statesman, Hieronimo Zane, was chosen for this mission and his commission was approved on 27 September.[103] It included a full report on the affair and detailed instructions how and what to say to the Grand Vizier about it. Great stress was laid on the information gleaned from letters of Istanbul Jews to Joseph Segura which had been intercepted by the Venetian authorities, and which, according to the commission, were "so villainous and diabolical that their writers do not deserve to live." Not only were they conspiring to cheat everybody, they also had the impertinence to meddle in state affairs, in order to arouse suspicion between friendly rulers such as "his Imperial Majesty and our Signory".[104] The importance attributed to this mission was underlined by the intervention of the Council of Ten, which saw fit, on 2 October, to add its own instructions to the new ambassador, to see to it that "the Jews" (obviously the Segura) were punished and the *hüccet* repealed in a manner which would redound to the honour of the Republic. The indignity inflicted on Venice had to be expunged, and a deterrent established for future generations. Zane was authorized to pay the Pasha 25,000 ducats for this purpose, later increased to 30,000 ducats.[105] Apparently, the Ten had still not received the *Bailo*'s reports of 10-18 September, describing the measures taken in Istanbul following his own efforts to quash the *hüccet*.

Zane must have left Venice on his way to Istanbul in the third week of October. In spite of the Senate's intensive occupation with this affair until it approved Zane's commission on 27 September, the record of its deliberations contain no reference to the affair, or to anything else

[103] ASV, Sen., Delib. CP, reg. 3, f. 94 (2 Sept. 1567), f. 94v (5 Sept. 1567).
[104] *Ibid.*, f. 99v.
[105] ASV, Cons. X, Secreti, reg. 8, ff. 96-96v (2 and 7 Oct. 1567).

to do with the Ottoman Empire until 22 October. On that date, evidently after the arrival of the new dispatches from Istanbul,[106] the Signory sent new instructions to Ambassador Zane, who was already on his way East:

> Having received the *Bailo*'s reports of 23 September, referring to the results of his negotiations with the Pasha, and considering what you have reported us in your letter of 20 October, you are instructed to return immediately to the nearest Venetian territory and feign illness. You should remain there while waiting to recover and pending our new instructions.[107]

Zane's mission was clearly less important or urgent after the good news from Istanbul. And, indeed, his mission was later cancelled.[108]

While Venice was instructing its special ambassador to Istanbul, unaware that his main mission had already been accomplished by the *Bailo*, a parallel diplomatic mission was prepared in Istanbul for Kubad, the *Çavuş* who was given the task of obtaining the release of the goods sent to Hayyim Saruq which had been blocked in Venice following his bankruptcy.

It should also be noted that while all this was going on, Ambassador Marino Cavalli remained under arrest and interrogation in Venice.[109] The dispatches of the papal nuncio from Venice to Rome reflect the interest of political circles in the investigation of this senior statesman. If he were found guilty, Cavalli's case would have been a major scandal and would have damaged the good, almost mythical, reputation of

---

[106] In those days, it normally took about a month for an official message sent from Istanbul to reach Venice. See, for instance, ASV, Sen., Delib. CP, reg 3, f. 90 (32 days); *ibid.* reg. 4, f. 12v (35 days); *ibid.* Cons. X, Secreti, reg. 8, f. 95v (25 days).

[107] ASV, Sen. Delib. CP, reg. 3, f. 101v (22 Oct. 1567).

[108] On 4 December the *Bailo* was instructed to inform the Pasha that Zane had been taken ill at Liesina, and that it was doubtful whether he would be able to continue his mission; see ASV, Sen. Delib. CP, reg. 3, f. 104v. Apparently, Zane remained at Liesina for several months, as on 7 February 1568 a resolution was presented to the Senate to order him to resume his mission to the Porte. However, though it obtained a majority, the *parte* does not seem to have passed, since it is not marked by a cross, as usual in such cases; see *Ibid.*, f. 110. *Cf.* Bertelè, *Il palazzo*, p. 414.

[109] *Nunziature di Venezia*, vol. 8, p. 290 (18 Oct. 1567).

Venetian diplomacy. Eventually, however, Cavalli was acquitted.[110]

***

In the meantime, the legal procedures surrounding Saruq's bankruptcy were continuing. The Senate reported to the *Bailo* on 5 September that the dispute between Joseph di Segura and Hayyim Saruq was being sorted out by the judges assigned for this purpose, the accounts pertaining to the dispute being examined by "two competent merchants nominated by them, and other two Jews of good condition, also chosen by them."[111] This passage probably referred to the arbitration, to which Segura and Saruq had agreed to submit, which had already been described in the Senate's letter of 11 August. The *Bailo* also referred to the four arbitrators at his meeting with the Grand Vizier, on which he reported to Venice on 18 October 1567.[112] But judging from what followed, it seems that this first attempt, in the summer of 1567, to arbitrate the dispute between the two Levantine Jews failed to produce a satisfactory solution.

The *Çavuş* Kubad reached Venice towards the end of October and was officially received by the Signory on the 31th.[113] His presence in Venice stimulated the Signory's efforts to bring the affair to an end. A resolution of the Senate of 4 November illustrates the complexity of the situation and Venice's eagerness to reach a settlement:[114]

A large amount of goods and monies belonging to the Jews Joseph, son of Aaron, and Hayyim Saruq, is in the hands of their debtors in our city, while other possessions are hidden, either in our city or elsewhere, or have been sequestrated at the request of persons who lay claims to them, and still others are in the possession of these Jews [Segura and Saruq]. Moreover, several sentences have been pronounced by the college which was instructed to hear the cases of these Jews, and others are yet to be pronounced. Considering that the implementation of the established proce-

---

[110] *Ibid.*, pp. 258 (9 Aug. 1567), 267 (30. Aug. 1567), 290 (18 Oct. 1567), 296 (1 Nov. 1567), 298 (8 Nov. 1567), 310 (29 Nov. 1567).

[111] ASV, Sen., Delib. CP, reg. 3, f. 97 (5 Sept. 1567).

[112] ASV, Sen., Dispacci CP, filza 2, No 63 (18 Oct. 1567).

[113] *Nunziature di Venezia*, vol. 8, p. (1 Nov. 1567).

[114] ASV, Sen., Delib. CP, reg. 3, ff. 101v-102 (4 Nov. 1567).

dures of our city in all these difficulties and legal proceedings would take much time and would not satisfy the *Çavuş* recently arrived here from Constantinople, ... in order to enable his prompt departure, it is necessary to find a way to collect the said money and to recover and secure the said goods, those which are now in the possession of these or other Jews, as well as the those which have been hidden or sequestrated; likewise, to put into effect the sentences already issued and others which would be issued by the said college from here on, so that this council can decide what to do with these goods. It is therefore decided that by the authority of this council, the delegation made by our *Collegio* to our noblemen Marcantonio Barbaro, *Savio di terraferma*, and Alvise Grimani, who was also recently *Savio di terraferma* and was entrusted by the *Collegio* to deal with these cases, and is also very well informed in all these matters, should be approved and confirmed. In order to enable them to bring to a satisfactory conclusion all the above-mentioned matters, they are given liberty, by the authority of this council, to liquidate everything necessary: make payments by transfer in bank accounts (*far scriver partita di banco*) in order to carry out sentences already issued or which would be issued, or for any other reason, receive claims concerning concealed goods and other frauds committed, examine witnesses, sequestrate any goods anywhere which pertain to this case and do whatever they see fit to bring this matter to an end. All that will be as valid as if it had been decided upon by the present council.

The two noblemen were further authorized to oblige anyone who had handled the said goods to give a full report about it, and to transfer the matter to persons whom they trusted to carry out such an assignment, if they felt that the previous handling had been unsatisfactory. Finally, instructions were given to keep a separate record in which all the operations to do with those goods and monies could be clearly seen. In contrast to all normal judicial procedures, the two noblemen were granted the authority of the Republic's highest governing bodies—a very unusual procedure, which reflects the urgency of the situation in the eyes of the Venetian senators.

Nor was the *Çavuş* idle during this time. He asked the Signory that Joseph Segura and Hayyim Saruq—who, it should be remembered, were still in custody—be sent to his residence on the *Giudecca*, to enable him to inform himself on the affair so as to report to Istanbul. The Senate agreed, but ordered that Alvise Grimani, one of the two noblemen appointed to manage the affair, should brief the *Çavuş* before his meeting with the two disputants. The Senate also decided that Saruq would be accompanied by the accountants (*ragionati*), Jews and Christians, with all the relevant documents. The Heads of the *Dieci savi del corpo del senato* also proceeded to make every effort to conclude those matters which were still pending in their court. The deliberations at the *Çavuş*'s residence could go on for several days, but at the end of each day the two Jewish disputants were to be returned to prison.[115]

These extraordinary measures proved to be successful, as an agreement was reached on 19 November. Saruq and Segura agreed to nominate four arbitrators who were to give the final verdict on their disputes. Two of the judges were Christians—Francesco Bonaldo and Giacomo Ragazzoni—and the other two—Giosef [Joseph] Amigo and Moisè [Moses] Botton—were described as "Jews who are Turkish subjects".[116] It is not entirely clear how this arbitration was connected with the previous one, before Kubad's arrival in Venice. It should be recalled that according to Venetian law, arbitration decisions could not be appealed, so that if the former procedure was concluded, the validity of the later one (if indeed there were two different arbitrations) was doubtful. A similar question hangs over the sentence of the *Dieci savi del corpo del senato*, which, in principle, could not be appealed either. Apparently, in the case of Saruq's bankruptcy and its aftermath, Venice was willing to disregard its own established legal procedures. However, the absence of any reference to the former arbitration suggests that the same arbitrators, who had dealt with the affair the previous summer, were reappointed, this time at the presence of the Ottoman representative, so as to preclude any future claims by the Porte. This possibility is supported by the fact that the four arbitrators reached their verdict on 24 November 1567, a mere five days after their nomination.

Compared with the huge sums originally demanded by Segura in Constantinople and Venice, the decision of the four arbitrators could be seen as favourable to Saruq. It stated that Saruq's debt to Segura

---

[115] *Ibid.*, f. 102 (5 Nov. 1567).

[116] ASV, LST, filza 2, No [blue] 191, summarized in IB, No 416/2 (19 Nov. 1567). An agreement in Ladino, signed in Venice in 5327 (1567), which seems to be an earlier attempt to settle the disagreement between Saruq and Segura, apparently did not solve the matter; see *ibid.*, No [blue] 192.

amounted to 25,979 ducats, at lire 6 soldi 4, "taking into account the exchanged goods, about 15,300 *kantar*s of alum, as well as Rabbi Meir's pitch."[117] On 4 December the Senate reported to the *Bailo* about these results, stating that "one can see how wicked those Jews have been," since a debt which they claimed to be 110,000 ducats turned out to be much lower.[118] In fact, Saruq's indebtedness to Segura was established at less than a quarter of the latter's original claim. It should be noted, however, that Saruq went bankrupt before this dispute with Segura, so that the full extent of his debts must have been much bigger. Nevertheless, Saruq was able, in a matter of a few weeks, to raise 10,190 ducats, which were given to the *Çavuş* in two installments on 10 [11?] and 23 of December. Kubad's official receipt stated that the *Çavuş* was taking the money into the imperial treasury, to cover Segura's debt to the Sultan.[119]

The amount of the debt quoted in the sentence served as a basis for a number of arrangements between Saruq, Segura and their various business associates. Some of these arrangements reveal business connections of Saruq's which had not been mentioned in the earlier documents, and also shed some light on Kubad's commercial activities in Venice. On the first of January 1568, in response to Alvise Grimani's demand, Saruq submitted a formal statement naming the persons with whom he was still disputing in Venice itself. Among them were eight Levantine Jews: Giacho [Jacob] Chohen [Cohen], Joseph Amatto, Moise [Moses] Papo, Moise Chavaler, Mair [Meir] Chasch[a], Mattia son of Moise, Moise Alfandari [Saruq's father-in-law?] and Cardiel Moise; and four Christians who were not Venetian subjects: Ribero, Chusani,

---

[117] ASV, LST, filza 2, No [blue] 183. Bombaci's summary is mistakenly dated 24 September; *cf.* IB, No 416/3. The reference to Rabbi Meir's pitch is clarified by a Senate's letter to the *Bailo*, dated 4 Dec. 1567, mentioning a claim by Meir Olivaro against Ḥayyim Saruq of 150,000 aspers, on account of pitch (*pegole*) sent by Olivaro to Saruq: ASV, Sen., Delib. CP, reg. 3, f. 104.

[118] ASV, Sen., Delib. CP, reg. 3, ff. 103v-104v (4 Dec. 1567).

[119] See the receipts for the sums of 7,000 ducats and 3,190 ducats, respectively, paid by Hayyim Saruq on 10 [?] and 22 Dec. 1567, on account of his debt of 25,979 ducats, ASV, LST, filza 2, Nos [blue] 187 and 222 (with translation in No 221), and 187 and 238 (with translation in No 237); the summaries appear in IB, Nos 416/4-5.

Benvenuto and Gian [Giovanni] Vai.[120] On 4 January, as a result of another arbitration, which apparently did not involve Saruq, two Jewish arbitrators, Giuseppe Amico and Moise Cardiel, issued a decision in a dispute between Giovanni Vai and Joseph son of Aaron di Segura, on the price of Black Sea alum (*allumi di mar mazzor*), which Vai held as security for Segura's debt, but also involving in some way a transaction of jewels.[121] On 9 January Joseph Segura declared that he was willing that a debt of Francesco Barbaro's, amounting to 800 ducats, which had been transferred to his credit by the arbitrators, be given to Giacomo Ragazzoni, for cloth given to the *Çavuş*.[122] In another document of 14 January Joseph Segura also agreed that the alum, which had been sent to Francesco Bonaldo in Venice in six ships, the *Querina*, the *Viviana*, the ship of the Rais Gafer [*sic*], the *Gradeniga*, the *Scuda* and the *Bonalda*, and which had not been sold, should be consigned to the *Çavuş* Kubad.[123] On 31 January Segura testified that he had received from Hayyim Saruq 34 emeralds, evaluated by experts at 9,000 ducats, as part-payment of the sum decreed by the arbitrators. Like the previous payment on this account, this too was immediately transferred to Kubad, towards Segura's debt to the Sultan.[124]

It is worth noting that the same Alvise Grimani, who was nominated as a special commissioner to solve the complexities of Saruq's bankruptcy, is encountered soon afterwards as one of the most vociferous supporters of the decree to expel the Jews from Venice.[125] His role may be another indication of the connection between the animosity which had grown between Jews and Venetians in the sphere of interna-

---

[120] ASV, LST, filza 2, No [blue] 232, with a translation in No 231, summarized in IB, 416/6.

[121] ASV, LST, filza 2, No [blue] 225 (4 Jan. 1567 *m.v.*), summarized in IB, No 416/8.

[122] ASV, LST, filza 2, No [blue] 217, summarized in IB, No 416/9 (9 Jan. 1567 *m.v.*).

[123] ASV, LST, filza 2, No [blue] 236, with a translation in No 235, summarized in IB, No 416/14 (11 Jan 1567 *m.v.*).

[124] ASV, LST, filza 2, Nos [blue] 240, 216 [the latter being the *verso* of the same document], with translations on Nos 187, 239; summarized in IB, Nos 416/14-15 (Kubad's receipt, 2 Feb. 1567 *m.v.*).

[125] For Grimani's involvement in this act, see Valerio, *Dell'utilità*, pp. 357-59, cited by Ravid, "The Socioeconomic Background", pp. 43-44.

tional trade and the anti-Jewish measures of 1571.

***

In their negotiations with the Ottomans, the Signory, the *Collegio* and the Senate were always eager to emphasize Venice's image as an orderly state, whose different magistracies perform their particular functions according to established, unbreakable, laws and customs. But it was not always possible to obtain the wished-for result of an "affair of state" (*causa di stato*) by these means. Flexibility was often needed, secret and quick moves had to be made, measures which were not consistent with Venetian law had to be taken in cases of great importance to the state. We know that this was where the Council of Ten took over. While the Saruq affair was being dealt with by the Signory, the *Collegio*, the Senate, and the various magistracies which became involved in the intricacies of that bankruptcy, the Council of Ten closely followed, and intervened when necessary. For example, it intercepted letters addressed to Joseph Segura during his detention, and took precautionary measures before passing these letters, and other items of information, to the Senate, whose members were personally sworn to secrecy.[126]

On 22 November, after the *Çavuş* had successfully brought Saruq and Segura to a preliminary agreement, the Council of Ten heard a report on the matter by Alvise Grimani, the patrician who had been appointed a special commissioner for this case. Grimani praised Kubad's conduct, especially his willingness to endorse the accounts of Saruq and Segura in order to authenticate them. It was plain to Grimani that Kubad expected to be remunerated for his efforts. This was the kind of delicate operation at which the Council of Ten excelled. The Ten authorized Grimani to promise Kubad that if he continued in his efforts to reach a final settlement he would receive 1,000 ducats, and 1,000 more in Constantinople once the affair was concluded.[127] The Council was well aware that the final decision depended on the Porte. A proposal to authorize the *Bailo* to spend up to 10,000 ducats to bribe the Grand Vizier if it were not possible to persuade him by arguments, was at

---

[126] ASV, Cons. X, Secreti, reg. 8, f. 95-95v (9 and 27 Aug. 1567).

[127] *Ibid.*, f. 99v (22 Nov. 1567). The *Bailo* was informed on this promise on 13 Feb 1568, see *ibid.*, f. 104v (13 Feb. 1567 *m.v.*).

first suspended,[128] but later the Council authorized the *Bailo* to pay up to 2,000 ducats (later raised to 5,000) to the Ottoman statesman.[129] Ambassador Zane was authorized to spend personally as much as 30,000 ducats on bribes in order to accomplish his mission in Istanbul.[130] Evidently the Signory was not satisfied by the unofficial repeal, but wanted to obtain a formal *firman*, or a new *hüccet* to that effect.[131] On 13 of February 1568 the Ten wrote to the *Bailo* that Kubad had promised to see to the abolition of the *hüccet*. If he succeeded, Kubad was to give him a signal by touching Soranzo's hand with his small finger—after which he would be entitled to another 1,000 ducats. Additional 'gifts' were to be distributed to the Pasha and other dignitaries.[132]

Contrary to Venetian law, which generally forbade official envoys to engage in private business, Ottoman diplomatic envoys were allowed to engage in commerce during their missions.[133] Kubad was no exception. On 15 January 1568 the Council of Ten discussed a somewhat embarrassing situation resulting from his activities. During his stay in Venice Kubad had purchased cloth from local merchants, but was unable to pay for the entire quantity, and remained owing some 5,000 ducats. The Council considered the possibility of asking Francesco Bonaldo, one of the merchants who were in touch with the Segura, to try to persuade the merchants to give Kubad up to six months credit, with himself as a guarantor, and also persuade the Segura and Kubad to consider Hayyim Saruq's vessels and jewels, the collateral for Saruq's entire debts, as security for this payment. Though it was finally rejected, this complicated proposition illustrates the complicated nature of the affairs which arose from Hayyim Saruq's bankruptcy.

Kubad was still in Venice on 17 January 1568. Apparently he was

---

[128] *Ibid.*, f. 95 (20 Aug. 1567). About a month earlier, the *Bailo* was instructed to give 300-400 ducats to the Ottoman chief interpreter, *ibid.*, f. 92 (19 July 1567).

[129] *Ibid.*, f. 100v (10 Dec. 1567); *ibid.*, f. 105 (13 Feb. 1567 *m.v.*).

[130] *Ibid.*, f. 96 (2 Oct. 1567); *ibid.*, f. 96v (7 Oct. 1567).

[131] This is explicitly stated in the Council of X's letter to the *Bailo* on 13 February 1568, *ibid.*, f. 104v (13 Feb. 1567 *m.v.*).

[132] *Ibid.*, f. 104v (13 Feb. 1567 *m.v.*). In the following year Kubad had to remind the Signory on at least two occasions to pay him the promised additional 1,000 ducats, see *ibid.*, f. 142v (8 Feb. 1568 *m.v.*) Barbaro's Letter-book, I, f. 8v (15 Oct. 1568);

[133] For the history of Ottoman missions to Venice during this period, see Pedani, *In nome del Gran Signore, op. cit.*

delayed by one final matter related to the Saruq-Segura dispute, namely Saruq's jewels, which had been in the hands of the Jew Moyse [Moses] Cardiel and Gian Vais, or Vai (described as a Flemish merchant), and were seized by the two special commissioners, Grimani and Barbaro.[134] But this matter too was solved, and on 12 February 1568, the Signory wrote to the *Bailo* that Kubad had left Venice that day on his way back to Istanbul, bearing an official letter to the Sultan and accompanied by Joseph di Segura, among others. Segura and Kubad had received 10,200 ducats in cash from Saruq, as well as 34 pieces of jewels, estimated at 9,000 ducats—a total of 19,200 ducats.[135] The remainder would presumably be paid later. The Signory's letter to the Sultan included a formal request to punish Aaron di Segura and his dependents.[136] Ḥayyim Saruq remained imprisoned in Venice pending a full discharge of his financial liabilities.

At least part of the capital given to Segura must have derived from the goods which had previously been sequestrated by Venetian courts in order to secure the payment of Saruq's debts. The exact procedure by which these sequestrations were repealed is not clear, but after the settlement reached by the arbitration the papal nuncio remarked in his letter to Rome that many merchants on whose behalf the goods had been sequestrated, and who were not paid off, would suffer losses from this settlement.[137] The fact that the Papal nuncio mentioned this in his report shows the impact of the affair on the Venetian business world.

After receiving the Signory's letters with the details of the settlement the *Bailo* reported on the matter to the Grand Vizier. In a long letter to the Senate, written on 1 January 1568, he described his meeting with the Pasha in great detail. Commenting on the machinations of the Segura family, the *Bailo* expressed himself in aggressive terms, saying that "Jews were the most perverse people one could find, and that Muslims, confronted with such falsehoods, would not listen to them at all."[138]

Some minor problems which were somehow connected to this affair kept cropping up in the correspondence between Venice and Istanbul

---

[134] ASV, Sen., Delib. CP, reg. 3, f. 107 (4 Feb. 1567 *m.v.*).

[135] *Ibid.*, f. 111v (12 Feb. 1567 *m.v.*).

[136] ASV, LST, filza 2, f. 182, summarized in IB, No 417 (4 Feb. 1567 *m.v.*).

[137] *Nunziature di Venezia*, vol. 8, p. 310 (29 Nov. 1567).

[138] ASV, Sen., Disp. CP, filza 2, No 86 (1 Jan. 1567 *m.v.*).

in the short time which remained until the outbreak of the war over Cyprus in 1570. The same names came up again—Zuan Vais, Francesco Bonaldi, and of course, the Segura.[139] And in the meantime Hayyim Saruq remained in prison. In October 1568, his creditors, probably after reaching an agreement with him, asked the sequestration of goods sent to Saruq from Istanbul to be repealed, and the Senate authorized Alvise Grimani to look into it, as well as to Saruq's appeal to be released.[140] But Saruq must have remained in custody, because he presented another petition on 5 July the following year. This time, however, the Senate consented to release him from prison subject to the conditions agreed between him and his creditors in Venice.[141] The following is the full text of his appeal, and the appended statement of guarantees:[142]

Serene Prince, Illustrious Signory,
I, the miserable and most unfortunate Hayyim Saruq, a Jew, have been buried alive in prison these 22 months, and reduced to such misery and so deprived of succour that I would prefer death as my last refuge than to see myself with all my family—mother, wife and children—destined to die of hunger. If this should happen, in the absence of any remedy, there would be no avoiding enormous damage and loss to my own and to your affairs. Here I am afflicted by so many troubles, not knowing where to turn for help, except to prostrate myself at the feet of you Serenity, humbly supplicating for fear of God and your natural clemency and goodness, that you should take pity on my misery, knowing full well how honestly I always traded in your city, and how, to my misfortune, I have fallen prey to so many tribulations, and especially how I have acted to show my records and documents in order to prove that the claim for 110,000 ducats had been an obvious scheme (*garbuglio manifesto*).
        Desiring to find a way to save my property, which is declining towards

---

[139] See, for instance, Barbaro's Letter-book, I, 44v-45 (11 Dec. 1568); *ibid.*, 47-47v (23 Dec. 1568); *ibid.*, 92v (30 Apr. 1569); *ibid.*, f. 210 (15 Oct. 1569); *ibid.*, ff. 227-227v (11 Nov. 1569); *ibid.*, f. 320 (10 Feb. 1569 *m.v.*); ASV, Sen., Delib. CP, reg. 4, f. 25v (27 Aug. 1569); *ibid.*, f. 30v (4 Feb. 1569 *m.v.*).

[140] ASV, Sen., Delib. CP, reg. 3, ff. 134v-135 (18 Oct. 1568).

[141] Ibid., reg 4. f. 21 (5 July 1569).

[142] *Ibid.*, ff. 21-22v (5-7 July 1569); see also the guarantors' attestations in filza 3, 12 July 1569, No "3a" (attached to documents pertaining to the decision of 5 July 1569).

total ruin—especially the wool,[143] which has remained for so long in the warehouses and a great part of which is rotten, spoiled and continues to deteriorate—I have addressed the grand gentlemen Messer Thomaso Vivaldi, Messer Camillo Cusano and Messer Bernado Rotollo, Heads of the creditors of Paulo Cicero dal Compasso, whom I owe approximately 17,000 ducats, and who have received nothing on account of my debt, unlike my other creditors, to whom the Heads distributed my goods, since the rest of my goods, sequestrated in their hands at the request of the said Vivaldi, Cusano and Rotollo, have not been distributed, because of the impediments of Constantinople, and I myself have been imprisoned as a surety for the payment of the rest subject to the arbitration, as your Sublime Highness must have intended. Being touched by my calamity, and understanding that unless a swift remedy is found, everything will end without their being able to retrieve any part of what they are entitled to receive from me, they have been so good as to agree to stand surety for the payment of the rest of my debt resulting from the said arbitration, doing it in the manner and form which your highness would prefer, but on condition that all my goods, sequestrated at their request, should be released and consigned to them without impediment, including wool, rock alum, and other goods which have been in possession of my creditors' Heads at the time of the sequestration; all that will remain in their possession as collateral for their surety, until a mandate arrives from Constantinople declaring me totally free, or until I have completed paying off my debt resulting from the arbitration.

I also beg your Sublime Highness to release me in the meantime from the prison in which I am being held, subject to the condition that I remain obliged to appear in palace court (*che non possi partirmi di corte di palazzo*) until the arrival of the mandate from Constantinople, as stated before.

And since the most excellent Senate, in response to a request by the Illustrious Seigneur the Grand Turk, has decreed that the ten gentlemen appointed as judges should not only decide on the difficulties between Joseph, son of Aaron di Segura and myself, but also between the other merchants and myself, now, in order to facilitate my affairs further, if your Sublime Highness would please to appoint three or five judges, with the same authority as the said ten judges, who would expedite all my difficulties, so as to enable me to dissolve my business, for I have many claims against

---

[143] The word in the record is *lame*, but according to what follows is must be a scribe's error for *lane*.

merchants and other persons who have been involved in my affairs. And I agree that any part of my goods which is recovered will be deposited in a bank as security for the implementation of the sentence, in addition to the security described above. For myself, all I ask for is as much as would enable me to live with my poor family and cover the expenses necessary to recover my position. And to the good grace of your Sublime Highness I humbly commend myself.

Guarantors (*piezi*) of Ḥayyim Saruq
In the name of God, on 6 July 1569 in Venice,
We, Thomaso Vivaldo and Bernardino Rotulo, as Heads of the creditors of ser Paulo Cicero dal Compasso, constitute ourselves as guarantors and principal disbursers of Ḥayyim Saruq, the Jew, for the sum of 5,300 ducats, being the balance of the arbitration sentence between him and Joseph di Segura, and similarly that the said Ḥayyim will remain obliged to appear in the palace court (*non partirà della corte del palazzo*), subject to all the conditions and forms included in the appeal presented by the said Ḥayyim to the Most Serene Signory, and in the Senate's deliberation on this subject of the 5th day of the present month.

I, the said Bernardino Rottulo, have written the present record in my own hand, to which the said messer Thomaso Vivaldo will append his signature in the presence of messer Piero Galese and messer Bernardo Salandi, who will sign as witnesses.

I, Thomaso Vivaldo, affirm and promise what is written above
I, Piero Galese, was present when the above was written.
I, Bernardo Salandi, was present when the above was written.

And we, Thomaso Vivaldo and Bernardino Rottulo, Heads, as above, have received from the magnificent messer Zuan Thura, secretary, the keys to two warehouses at Ca Capello, in San Francesco della Vigna, in one of which are stored 68 sacks of clipped coarse wool (*lana grossa succida*) and 16 sacks of clipped fine wool (*lana fina succida*); and in the other are stored 14 sacks of clipped coarse wool and 17 sacks of coarse low-quality wool (*pelada grossa*)[144], and 3 sacks of fine clipped [wool] (*fina succida*), altogether 118 sacks of approximately 60 *miara*. We have

---

[144] *Pelada* signified low quality wool taken from the hides of dead muttons, see P. Racine, "A propos d'une matière première de l'industrie textile placentine: la *carzatura*", in *La lana come materia prima. I fenomeni della sua produzione e circolazione nei secoli XIII-XVII*, Florence, 1974, p. 178.

also received from the above the keys to another warehouse in Ca Rhenier at San Canciano, in which are stored 36 sacks of fine low-quality wool (*lana pelada fina*), one [sack] of fine clipped wool (*fina succida*)[145], and 2 of coarse low-quality wool (*pelada grossa*), altogether in this warehouse 39 sacks of approximately 13 *miara*. We have also received the keys to a warehouse in Ca Molin at San Zuliano, in which there is fine rock alum (*alumi di rocha minuti*), supposed to be about 150 *miara*. This, in accordance with the above-mentioned appeal.

In confirmation of this, I, the said Bernardino, have written by my own hand, and the said messer Thomaso will undersign, as above, in the presence of the same witnesses on this day 7 July 1569 in Venice.

I, Thomaso Vivaldo, affirm what is written above.

I, the said Piero Galese, was present when the above was written.

I, Bernardo Salandi, was witness to the above.

And so, Hayyim Saruq finally regained his liberty.[146] He was able to rejoin his mother, wife and children, and try to consolidate his economic situation. But just as the prospects seemed to look up for Saruq, the political circumstances were growing increasingly difficult for trading relations between Venice and the Ottoman Empire. Saruq's fate during and after the Cyprus war will be discussed in the following chapter.

---

[145] For examples of the use of the expression *succida*, cf. M. Borgherini, *L'arte della lana in Padova durante il governo della Repubblica di Venezia, 1405-1797*, Venice, 1964, pp. 116, 117, 120, 122, 123.

[146] An order to free Saruq from prison was issued by the Collegio on 8 July 1569, following his payment to the creditors of Paolo Cicero; see ASV, Collegio, Notatorio, reg. 38, c. 41. I am grateful to Dr. Maria Pia Pedani Fabris for this reference.

CHAPTER SEVEN

TRADE, ESPIONAGE AND INQUISITION:
ḤAYYIM SARUQ'S RESURGENCE

The *Çavuş* Kubad, who played a central role in solving the complications stemming from Ḥayyim Saruq's bankruptcy, returned to Venice on 28 March 1570. This time his mission was of a far greater scope: he brought a formal demand to cede Cyprus to the Ottomans. Since Venice had no intention of renouncing her richest and biggest overseas colony, the war was only a matter of time. On 1 July Ottoman troops landed on the southern shores of Cyprus, initiating a bloody struggle which was ended on 5 August 1571 with the surrender of Famagusta. The glorious naval victory of Venice and its allies at Lepanto, on 7 October that year, though it shattered the myth of the invincible Turk, did not compensate Venice for the loss of the big island. The state of war continued in a minor key until the conclusion of the new peace treaty between the two powers on 7 March 1573.

The impact of the war on the situation of Jews in Venice, and the role of Solomon Ashkenazi in bringing it to a peaceful conclusion has been covered in previous chapters. Here we shall continue to follow the affairs of Ḥayyim Saruq during the war and after. As before, Saruq's Jewishness, his being an Ottoman subject, and his involvement in international trade, were the key elements in the intricate relationships which accrued around him.

There is no reason to doubt that Ḥayyim Saruq, and probably his family too, shared the fate of the other Jewish merchants during the first stages of the war. If he was released in May 1571, like the other Ottoman merchants, he certainly remained in Venice for some time, for in November of that year, soon after the Venetian victory at Lepanto and a little before the decree of expulsion, he reappears in the Venetian sources in a new guise: this time Saruq was a Venetian secret agent.

The Venetians made cynical use of the image of the treacherous Jew. In religious sermons, in political harangues, in anti-Jewish literature and in formal acts of restrictions and expulsions, the Jew was depicted not as one of the foreigners in the city which hosted various ethnic and religious minorities, but as the enemy of Christianity, a fifth column in the midst of Venetian society. But at the same time, Venice, or rather the Venetian oligarchs, had no qualms about using Jews, among others, either as confidential middlemen in the secret negotiations which were conducted during the war, or sending them as secret agents into Ottoman territories to report back on the situation of the enemy. Jews, like Armenians, Greeks, Slavs, as well as bandits of various extractions, were apparently considered to be ideal candidates for such missions.[1]

In March 1570, on the eve of war, the Council of Ten hastened to reinforce its network in Ottoman territories. It revoked bans and promised safe conducts to many bandits in Dalmatia who were disposed to serve as "explorers". On 2 June it sent the priest Francesco Lupato to Erdel, in Transilvania, from where he was to report in a secret cipher. Ragusa was an important information centre, and here Benedetto Bolizza, a bandit from Ancona, the Jew David Passi, and Triffon Zaguri, a merchant gentleman from Cattaro, were placed as secret agents. From Venice were sent into Ottoman territories the Cretan Marco da Candia, Giovanni Antonio Barata, a bandit from Seville, the Jew Daniel Rodriga and, as will be revealed, Hayyim Saruq. Other agents were sent from Corfu. On 17 November 1570 the Council of Ten authorized the *Collegio*, in collaboration with the Heads of the Ten, to recruit "those persons" (*quelle persone*) as secret agents to be sent as required to Constantinople and other places. The *Collegio* was authorized to spend "as much as needed" (*quanto sarà bisogno*) on this project, an unusual phrase reflecting the urgency of the situation.[2]

Saruq's deployment as a secret agent was therefore not exceptional, and should be seen in the larger framework of Venetian endeavours to have an ample and diverse network of information on the enemy. Nevertheless, considered diachronically, as one stage in Saruq's long relationship with the Venetian Republic, his mission assumes a different significance. It is hard to believe that Saruq volunteered for this dangerous assignment of his own will. In view of his past record, however, it was probably not difficult for the Venetian Council of Ten to pressure him into this adventure.

---

[1] P. Preto, *I servizi segreti di Venezia*, Milan, 1994, p. 251. Ironically, it was another Jew, David Passi, who had warned Venice in 1569 of the imminent Ottoman attack: *ibid.*, p. 250.

[2] ASV, Cons. X, Secreti, reg. 9, f. 102.

The decision to employ Saruq in this capacity appears in the records of the Council of Ten on 23 November 1571. It is a short decree, approved unopposed, to send Hayyim Saruq to Constantinople, in order to collect information on "the affairs, the plans and the military equipment of the Turks" (*le cose et li dissegni et apparati de Turchi*), on which he was expected to report in coded letters, secretly dispatched to the Heads of the Council of Ten. A sum of 500 ducats was allotted him to cover his expenses in Constantinople and for the upkeep of his family in Venice for a period of one year.[3] A copy of the secret code which Saruq was to use has fortunately been preserved among the papers of the Council of Ten, and it is a document of great interest.[4]

The secret code is a booklet of 10.5x25.5 cm. containing 19 pages. On the left pages are listed, in alphabetical order, key words which the secret agent was expected to use, such as the Arsenal of Constantinople, Alexandria, Aleppo, Arabs, Cyprus, Candia, Constantinople, Damascus, Governor of the Morea, Governor of Bosnia, the names of various Pashas and functionaries, names of months, types of ships, arms, types of warriors, etc. The code words, often taken from the Jewish lexicon, appear on the opposite pages. The Council of Ten had stated explicitly that the secret code would be supplied by Saruq himself (*quella zifra che esso darà*). Saruq was probably given the list of terms which had to be coded, and it was left to him to provide their respective codes. According to a note at the end of the booklet, Saruq's letters were to be addressed to three person in Venice—his wife Letitia, Caliman de Grassia and Isaac Naso. Were these persons actually involved in Saruq's secret mission? It is doubtful that the Council of Ten approved such an arrangement. The letters were probably expected to be intercepted by official agents before reaching their nominal addressees.

The names and terms chosen by Saruq as his code are extremely interesting. Many are personal names, all of male Jews, often preceded by the honourary title rabbi—*e.g.*, Rabbi Abraham Levi, Rabbi Samuel Matalon, Rabbi David Navara, Rabbi David Brudo, Rabbi Asher Cohen,

---

[3] Ibid., f.189v.

[4] ASV, Cons. X, Secreti, filza 15. For a brief reference to this document, see Preto, *I servizi segreti*, p. 269 and n. 71. The full text is published in the Appendix.

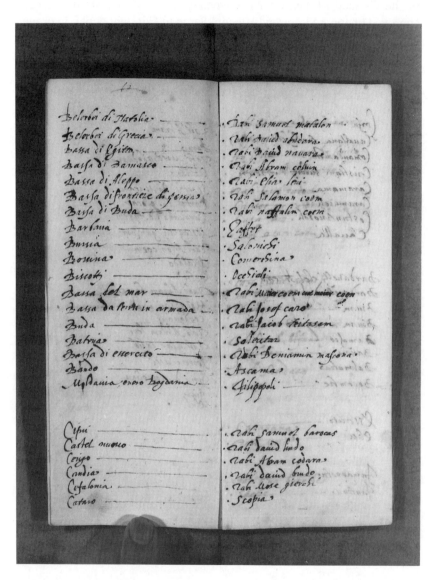

2. Two pages of Hayyim Saruq's secret code-book, 1571
[paper, 10.5x25.5cm.]

officials of the Venetian Ghetto[5], while other appear to have been fictitious, though based on common names in the *Levantini* community in Venice and among Jews in the Ottoman Empire. Some code words combined personal names with terms denoting family relations, such as the brother of..., the son-in-law of... Occasionally the name of a prominent known rabbi occurs, for example Rabbi Joseph Caro, whose book *Ḥeleq Yoreh De'ah*, would be published in Venice six years later under Saruq's patronage.[6] Saruq also included individuals with his own family name. Rabbi Mose [Moses] Saruq, whose name stood for the port city of Modon, is unknown to me, but the name of Isaac Saruq ('the Dardanelles'), might have been that of the Egyptian Jew mentioned above as involved in the copying of a Hebrew book in 1564/5.[7]

The code words also included numerous commercial terms, particularly of goods exchanged between Venice and the East: various kinds of pepper, eyeglasses, window glass, small church bells (*campanelle*), wool, woollen threads and woollen cloth from different production centres, cotton, various kinds of paper, kinds of leather (including cordovans), tin, camlets, kinds of silk, turquoise, rubies (*rubinetti*), cloves (*garofali*), cochineal, *sbiacca* (white dye)[8], drugs (*droghe*), and more generic terms, such as merchandise, money (*danari*), company, agents (*fatori*), affair (*negotio*), goods (*robe*), bankruptcies, caravan. Saruq was primarily a merchant, and commerce was the obvious cover of his secret mission. As a matter of fact, the use of commercial terms as a secret code had been a tradition in the Venetian world since at least the fourteenth century, and during the war of Cyprus it became increasingly common.[9] Since the coded letters had to appear as authentic as possible, these commercial terms must have been typical in the milieu of the *Levantini* Jewish merchants.

---

[5] *E.g.* Rabbi Chia, or Chya Barochas (a code name for 'Famagosta'), who, on 20 Dec. 1563 had sold Saruq a credit, amounting to over 18,731 *scudi* (though at a rate of 35%), "per il gran partito del re di Francia a Lione, nelle mani di Michiel, Arnolfini e Bonvisi": ASV, AN, busta 8250/VI (not. Z.B. Monte), cc. 49-49v; Rabbi David Navara, a code name for 'Pasha of Egypt', can be identified as one of the *Dayyanim* whose names figure at the margin of the contract between Saruq and Joseph di Segura (see the Appendix).

[6] *Supra*, p. 95.

[7] *Supra*, p. 96, n. 3.

[8] Boerio, *Dizionario*, pp. 78, 608.

[9] Preto, *I servizi segreti*, pp. 268-269.

Judeo-Spanish and Hebrew phrases also appear among Saruq's code words. For example, an expression in Judeo-Spanish, '*Alla guerta* [?] *a comer*', was the code for 'Divam a cavallo', or 'mounted *Divan*', probably referring to the audience held during a military campaign. Some Hebrew words are also used: the Hebrew word for 'Egypt' (*Mitsraim*), occurs twice, once as a code word for 'Yemen' (*Gemen*) and once, as 'spices from Egypt' (*Spetiarie di Mitsraim*), standing for 'people from Egypt' (*Gente di Egitto*); the term *Ascama* (Agreement), normally describing a decree approved by Jewish community, stood for 'Bando', *i.e.*, ban, or banishment. Noteworthy is also the interchangeability of the letters *m* and *n* at the end of many words, a very common phenomenon in Venetian sources of that period, including the mention of Jewish names.[10]

Somewhat puzzling is the systematic use of the months of the Hebrew calendar corresponding to those of the Christian calendar, as well as the Hebrew year, as a codes for the corresponding Christian year (1571 = "5332, starting in September").[11] Was it assumed that the Ottomans would not recognize the Hebrew months and years? This is highly unlikely. Another possibility is that the letters were expected to be written in Hebrew. In fact, correspondence of Jewish merchants was routinely conducted in Hebrew. Of course, this would mean that someone would have had to translate the coded letters for the Council of Ten, but that could have been easily done.[12] A Jewish merchant was expected to write in Hebrew and use the Jewish calendar. However, since the Jewish months, being lunar, did not correspond to the Christian ones, it was necessary to specify in the code book which Christian months were denoted by the Hebrew months.[13]

---

[10] *E.g.*, B. Arbel, "A List of Able-Bodied Jews at Canea, Crete (1536)", in *Studies in honour of D. Carpi*, forthcoming.

[11] See the Appendix, p. 213. The correspondence between the Christian year 1571 and the Jewish year 5332 was valid only for the months Sept.-Dec. 1571. Since the decision to employ Saruq was taken in late Nov. 1571, one may wonder whether the compilers of the code simply forgot to include another entry for 1572.

[12] On the translation of a Hebrew letter for the Council of Ten in this period, see above, p. 63.

[13] Preto is therefore probably mistaken in stating that Saruq was supposed to travel disguised as an Albanian. There would be no point in an Albanian using Jewish names and terms in his correspondence. His error probably stems from another cipher which has been preserved together with Saruq's code-book, and was intended for an Albanian

Now and then one gets the impression that Saruq was deliberately humorous, as in the choice of 'alms for the poor' (*Limosina per poveretti*) as the code for the term 'tribute', or 'rabbi' (*raf*, or *rab*) for 'the Pope'.

***

Though it is very likely that Saruq carried out his mission as a Venetian secret agent, none of his coded letters has survived, nor are there any later references to this chapter in his life.[14] We therefore cannot say whether he contributed anything to the Venetian war efforts, or to other Venetian interests, during those years.

But in the meantime, in spite of the war, or probably because of it, Saruq's creditors in the Ottoman capital did not remain idle. It appears that the Segura regarded the military conflict between the two powers as an opportunity to extort further concessions from the Venetians on account of their old claims against Hayyim Saruq. In the circumstances, the Segura could not attack Saruq directly, but the Venetians who stayed in the Ottoman Empire during the war were relatively easy prey. On 19 July 1570, the *Bailo* reported that the Segura protested at the public *Divan* that they were not yet satisfied.[15] In his ciphered letter written in the beginning of the following month, Barbaro described his impressions of the public *Divan* which he had attended that morning, when "the Jews" appeared before the *Kâdîasker* (Chief Judge), accompanied by the *Çavuş* Kubad, and with the Grand Vizier "pretending not to listen". The Jews (*i.e.*, the Segura) simply repeated the demand which they had raised before the war, claiming that they were entitled to receive 110,000 ducats which have been held up in Venice. Asked by the *Kâdîasker* to give his own version, Barbaro gave a detailed report on the whole affair, adding that the Grand Vizier and Kubad could confirm

---

has been preserved together with Saruq's code-book, and was intended for an Albanian agent. *Cf.* Preto, *I servizi segreti*, p. 250.

[14] A proposal to suspend his mission put to the ballot on 4 December 1571 was not passed; see ASV, Cons. X, Secreti, reg. 9, f. 196v. On the other hand, on 30 December Saruq signed a receipt for the 500 ducats given to him for his mission: *ibid.*, filza, 15.

[15] Barbaro's Letter-book, II, f. 48v.

his story. But at that moment Kubad preferred to remain silent.[16] On 10 August Barbaro again wrote to Venice about the sequel to the affair. In the course of a private consultation with Kubad, the *Çavuş* advised Barbaro to do nothing, since the Grand Vizier had already instructed the *Kâdîasker* to abstain from signing any document in favour of the Segura. But Barbaro was worried, and prepared a formal complaint, which he intended to hand over to Sokollu.[17] All of Barbaro's letters of those days reflect his fears of Jewish pressure on the Porte: "...These wretched Jews... are devils, ... they have enough money and every day they present new petitions to the Sultan," he wrote on 17 August.[18]

Barbaro's fears were almost realized in September, when the Segura succeeded in obtaining a sentence recognizing their claim for 90,000 ducats from the Signory. According to the *Bailo*'s letter, through the intervention of "a few *Sultane*" (*i.e.*, influential women in the Harem), they also obtained a Sultanic order permitting them to compensate themselves by seizing property belonging to Venetian noblemen. The execution of the order was entrusted to the Kadi of Istanbul and the *Çavuş* Kubad, who, according to the *Bailo*, immediately started to harass the Venetian merchants. They detained the clerks of Venetian ships, seized their cargo manifests, and compared them with the customs declarations in search of goods belonging to Venetian noblemen. Barbaro's attempts to stop them were of no avail. "...At present, reasonable arguments do not count," (*a questo tempo non hanno luogo le ragioni*), he wrote. The Grand Vizier was reluctant to intervene, since the decision of the *Kâdîasker* was corroborated by the Sultan's order. Moreover, the latter had a personal interest in recovering the debts owed by the Segura to his treasury. Consequently, wrote Barbaro, "those mad devils, now that darkness rules, and that we are greatly hated as the Sultan's enemies, have become most arrogant and fearless." Among the Venetian patricians who suffered most was Marco Sanuto, from whose warehouse a great quantity of indigo was taken and offered for sale at public auction. Barbaro was furious. Having succeeded in protecting the life and property of Venetian subjects till then, he had to witness the ruin of his efforts by those "mischievous Jews" (*da questi tristi hebrei*). Moreover, the measures taken against Venetian merchants

---

[16] ASV, Sen., Disp. CP, filza 5, f. 188.

[17] *Ibid.*, f. 192 (10 Aug. 1570)

[18] *Ibid.*, f. 200 (17 Aug. 1570).

were not limited to Istanbul, but were to be implemented also in Syria and Alexandria. In his efforts to stop these moves, the *Bailo* resorted to threats, warning the Jews that after the war "the entire Hebrew nation" would suffer ruin. He also tried to advance his cause through the intervention of the *Sultane*. As a result, some Jews complained to the Grand Vizier that the whole affair was nothing but "a mischief done by the people of Aaron di Segura" (*una ribaldaria di quei di Aaron di Segura*), and that the entire Hebrew nation would pay dearly because of them. Joseph Nassí was also called upon to intervene, but he took advantage of the crisis to bring up his complaints about the treatment of his commercial agents in Venetian territories. But when the Venetian merchants themselves appeared in the *Divan*, the Vizier seemed more disposed to intervene, telling the *Kâdîaskers* that their verdict had been unsound, and that it was necessary to have better information. The *Kâdîaskers* protested that their decision had been based on testimonies, including that of Kubad, but the dragoman Ibrāhīm Bey intervened, saying that the testimonies were false, as he knew all too well, having dealt with the entire matter together with Kubad. After further deliberation, in which Ibrāhīm and Sokollu clarified the details of the previous dispute between Segura and Saruq, it was concluded, as Barbaro put it, "in order to be able to go on squeezing the Venetians" (*per mantener l'occasione di mangiare*), that the sentence of the *Kâdîaskers* would not be applied to a sum of 90,000 ducats, but only 25,000 ducats. Since Venice had forced the Jews to accept some of it, amounting to 9,000 ducats, in the form of jewels, and since the true value of the jewels was much less, the *Bailo* was asked to take them back and pay the Sultanic treasury (to which the Jews were still in debt) the sum of 9,000 ducats. The jewels, contained in a sealed box, were brought to Barbaro by Ibrāhīm Bey and Kubad, who tried to persuade him that the last arrangement reached in the *Divan* was the best one possible under those circumstances. According to them, if the *Bailo* rejected it, the Ottomans would carry out the original sentence of the *Kâdîaskers*. "...Nothing could be done against a decision taken in the public Divan," they added. But the *Bailo* was resolute in his refusal, saying that he would not hesitate to apply to the Sultan through the Grand Vizier, and that it was unthinkable that the Sultan's decision to leave the Venetian property intact could be so crudely reversed by those troublesome Jews.[19]

---

[19] *Ibid.*, ff. 225-228 (13 Sept. 1570).

During the following weeks the Segura tried to push forward the
public auction of the goods which had been sequestrated from the
Venetian patrician merchants, while Barbaro of course sought to prevent
this eventuality. Under these circumstances the *Bailo*'s position became
increasingly difficult from day to day. In addition to the Segura, a Greek
magnate, Cantacuzenus, also brought pecuniary claims against him,
and caused the Venetian dragoman to be arrested. Moreover, when
the news of the detention of the Ottoman merchants in Venice reached
Istanbul, the demand was made to arrest all Venetians in the East, which
exacerbated Barbaro's troubles. We may also add the sad spectacle
of the Venetians who had been taken into slavery in Cyprus, and
apparently paraded in a way that would shock Barbaro, and the news
about a number of deaths in his family at home—including his father,
his son and his brother-in-law—which must have rendered his stay
in Istanbul quite unbearable.[20] Nevertheless, the new initiative which
led to the release of the Ottoman merchants in Venice, and to secret
negotiations on a peace settlement probably caused a temporary suspen-
sion of the Segura affair. But the Segura were only waiting for another
opportunity to renew their claims. The fact that peace was not swiftly
achieved encouraged them to renew their assault on Barbaro and the
Venetians in the East. On 15 February 1572 Barbaro again reported
that "those Aaron di Segura people" had presented a request to the
Sultan to the effect that the *Bailo* and all Venetian merchants should
be imprisoned, and all their goods confiscated, in order to cover the
Segura credits. It seems that an order to that effect was issued at Edirne,
and similar orders were also prepared for Syria and Alexandria. Only
prompt action by "the *Bailo*'s friend" (probably Dr. Solomon Ashkenazi)
caused these orders to be held in abeyance.[21]

***

Significantly, one of the first issues raised after the signing of the peace
accord on 7 March 1573, was the still unpaid debt of Ḥayyim Saruq
to the Segura of Constantinople. The settlement of the dispute on the

[20] On his personal afflictions, see *ibid.*, ff. 221v-223 (2 Sept. 1570). For the *Bailo*'s
report about the Cypriot captives in Istanbul, *ibid.*, ff. 239 (25 Sept. 1570), 311 (30
Dec. 1570).
[21] Barbaro's Letter-book, II, f. 248v.

eve of the war had not left Saruq enough time to pay off the remainder of it. We have seen that on the eve of war he managed to get out of jail, and to provide securities for his financial obligations. We have also seen how energetically the Segura of Istanbul used the war to extract better terms from the Venetians who were trapped in the Ottoman Empire. As soon as the peace treaty was signed, the indefatigable Segura renewed their efforts. On 11 July 1573 the issue of Saruq's debt was already mentioned in the Senate's letter to the *Bailo*.[22] Three days later the *Bailo* wrote to Venice that the Segura seemed to have in their possession a copy of the old order, which they had obtained two years before, to detain Venetian ships in order to compensate themselves for their claimed credits. Barbaro had to work hard to prevent the Venetian trade in Syria and Egypt from being harassed.[23] A month later, on 17 August, the Venetian Senate discussed the *garbuglio* caused by the Segura, referring to actions against Venetian merchants in Egypt and Syria on account of Hayyim Saruq's debt.[24] The Signory was worried about the reemergence of this everlasting litigation at a time when it was trying to heal the wounds of war. On 7 September 1573 the Senate approved a decree which was apparently based on a petition presented by Saruq, in which he declared his willingness to settle the affair, offering new guarantees, and expecting to collect some of his own old credits in Venice.[25] In a detailed message to the *Bailo,* approved on 20 October 1573, the affair was summarized again, with a description of the measures taken by the Senate to prevent a renewed crisis. Since the old securities given by Saruq before the war were considered insufficient, arrangements were made for them to be renewed. Saruq promised to send at once an agent to Constantinople to settle the remainder of his debt, amounting to 5,300 ducats. The Senate also instructed the *Bailo* to obtain a formal annulment of the famous *hüccet*, which, the Senate believed, was probably at the bottom of the new

---

[22] ASV, Sen., Delib. CP, reg. 4, f. 55.

[23] Barbaro's Letter-book, II, 481v.

[24] ASV, Sen., Delib. CP, reg. 4, f. 58 (17 Aug. 1573). It seems that the Senate was referring in this case to the measures reported in Marcantonio Barbaro's letter of February 1572. Apparently, the orders to arrest Venetian merchants in Syria and Egypt and confiscate their goods were not altogether abrogated.

[25] ASV, Sen., Terra, reg. 49, ff. 184v-185. I am grateful to Prof. Benjamin Ravid for this reference.

difficulties of Venetian trade in the Levant.[26] It is interesting to observe the extent the Segura's ability to involve the Ottoman authorities in their efforts to reverse the pre-war settlement depended on the political atmosphere between Venice and Istanbul. Though they never entirely abandoned the attempt to squeeze additional benefits from the old bankruptcy affair, after the peace treaty of 1573 they were much less effective. They no longer figure so frequently in the correspondence of the *Baili*, and even Ḥayyim Saruq himself was not apparently much affected by their later efforts.

***

As Saruq's bankruptcy demonstrates, sixteenth-century Venetians had to take into account the great influence of Jewish businessmen at the Ottoman court. Such also was the case of Girolamo Priuli, a senior patrician who was elected *Bailo* in Constantinople in January 1575, while he was serving as *Podestà* of Brescia. It should be remembered that though it was one of the most difficult posts in the Venetian state, the office of *Bailo* was also one of the most prestigious, and normally reserved for a restricted group of the greatest patricians. But Priuli asked to be relieved of the obligation to accept the office, and the Senate granted his request. Priuli's reasons were spelled out in his petition of 27 January 1575.[27] He stated that this mission was liable to cause him and the public interest considerable harm. It could lead to a repetition of the embarrassing Cavalli affair of the 1560s. This had to do with the bankruptcy of his father, the famous banker Antonio

---

[26] ASV, Sen., Delib. CP, reg. 4, ff. 64v-65 (20 Oct. 1573). This decree erroneously mentions the sum of 979 ducats and 1 *grosso*, as the debt established by the arbitrators in 1569. The correct sum was 25,979 and 1 *grosso*, of which Saruq remained owing 5,300 ducats; see above, p. 135. In January 1579 Ḥayyim Segura, son of the late Aaron, tried to create a new *garbuglio* in Constantinople, which caused the Senate to recapitulate the whole affair. Concluding its report, the Senate noted that: "quello che deve havere sopra tutte le cose posto fine a questa materia et chiusa la bocca alli hebrei compitamente, è la restitutione dell'amontar delle robbe, fatta dopo la conclusione della pace al q. M^co messer Marco Sanudo, lequali in tempo della guerra erano state fraudolevolmente ottenute dagli hebrei, et da loro vendute, come il tutto viene, dechiarito nella lettera al Clarissimo Bailo", ASV, Sen., Delib. CP, reg. 5, ff. 116-117v. Thus it appears that the Senate considered the affair closed.

[27] ASV, Sen., Delib. CP, filza 3 (27 Jan. 1574 *m.v.*).

Priuli, in 1551. Unable to meet his obligations to all his clients, he was forced to shut down his bank, and remained in debt to the amount of 300,000 ducats. Among the clients who were affected by this bankruptcy were some "Levantine Jews, Turks and *Marrani*", who between them stood to lose about 60-70,000 ducats. The Signory, appealed to by the creditors, decreed that Priuli had to honour his obligations within a year. According to his own petition, Girolamo, though not guilty of the bankruptcy, was also responsible for the execution of the decree. The father, unable to obey the decree, fled, and the son, though confident of his own innocence, retired to a monastery. Antonio Priuli later returned to Venice and obtained a new settlement, to pay his debts within three years, which he did. However, in his absence and before the final settlement, Jews, *Marrani* and Turks who had to get away (probably on the eve of the war) sold their credits—altogether some 20,000 ducats—to private individuals at 60% and 70% of their value. Priuli assumed that among those claimants against him was also "the very same Aaron di Segura, his dependents, and similar persons." They could be expected to act as they had done before, by exerting pressure on him through the Ottoman authorities. If he were retained on account of his debts, it would have ruined him and caused dishonour and damage to Venice. Moreover, Priuli indicated that at the time of his father's bankruptcy, he himself was indebted for a sum of 30,000 *scudi* to "that Mendes lady who later gave her daughter in marriage to Zuan Miches." The money was in Lyons, in the form of a bill of exchange, and was partly sequestrated by the bank's creditors. After a long and costly judicial process it was recovered and paid to the said Mendes lady. Yet, Zuan Miches (*i.e.*, Don Joseph Nassí) made additional claims, for expenses, damage and interest caused by the late repayment. Miches, as it was well known, was "Head and Master of all Jews and *Marrani*" (*capo e guida de tutti hebrei et marrani*), and would also use the help of the Ottoman authorities to obtain his demands. Priuli finally observed that he had four sons, one of whom he wished to train as a merchant by sending him overseas (*facendo navegar*). But he could never send anyone "to Syria, Constantinople or the Levant", considering the above-mentioned constraints.

It could of course be argued that all this was merely an excuse for a patrician who did not wish to take on the prestigious but dangerous office of *Bailo*.[28] But the fact that his petition was approved without much difficulty may indicate that his story was based on facts which the Senate could not ignore. Furthermore, according to Brian Pullan, the collapse of the Priuli bank was directly linked to the decree of expulsion issued against the *Marranos* in Venice in 1550.[29] Girolamo Priuli's case strengthens the impression created by Saruq's case, that Venetian magistrates and Venetian merchants who were interested in the Levant trade had to take into account the central position of Jewish traders and businessmen in the eastern Mediterranean, and the support they enjoyed from the central organs of the Ottoman Empire.

***

Sixteenth-century Europe was marked by religious strife, restrictions on religious grounds and persecution. In this respect Venice was somewhat exceptional. On the one hand, it always stressed its attachment to the Catholic faith and brandished its religiosity on every occasion. Foreign visitors were impressed by the number of churches and other religious and ecclesiastical institutions in the city. But although it was not free from the general tendency to intolerance, sixteenth-century Venice was also the only territory in Western Europe where Catholics, Greek Orthodox, Jews, Protestants and Muslims could live side by side, at least in peacetime. The Church did not like this state of affairs. In his letter of 27 November 1574 the Papal nuncio in Venice noted: "In Venice there are four fountains of torpid water, namely the Germans of the *Fontico*, the Greeks, the Jews and the Turks, all of them enemies of Christendom."[30] But the Church had to acquiesce with this peculiar example of relative tolerance in an age characterized by mounting religious conflict. Though it accepted the institution of the Papal Inquisition in Venice, the Republic did not give it free hand to act

---

[28] On the avoidance of election to offices by Venetian patricians, see D. Queller, "The Civic Irresponsibility of the Venetian Nobility" in *Economy, Society and Government in Medieval Italy*, eds. D. Herlihy, R. Lopez and V. Slessarev, Kent OH, 1969, pp. 223-35 (special issue of *Explorations in Economic History, 7 (1969-70)*; idem, *The Venetian Patriciate: Reality versus Myth*, Urbana-Chicago, 1986.

[29] Pullan, "A Ship with Two Rudders", p. 42.

[30] *Nunziature di Venezia*, vol. 9, p. 283.

without participation of lay representatives of the Council of Ten.[31] Protestants of course, were viewed as the main threat to the Catholic Church during the Sixteenth century, but recent research has further revealed the interest of the Venetian Holy Office in Jews, *Marranos*, and Christian Judaizers.[32] The ambiguous identity of the *Marranos*, the relative freedom of movement of the *Levantini* (some of whom were also suspected as former *Marranos*), and the frequent contacts between Jews and Christians, in spite of the official policy of segregation, often led to intervention by the Inquisition.

It is significant that Hayyim Saruq, too, was subjected on at least three occasions to the activities of this institution. Apart from demonstrating the vulnerability of Jewish merchants in sixteenth-century Venice, and recording Saruq's words and opinions on religious matters and on the world in which he lived, the documents of the Holy Office also provide us with precious biographical data on our protagonist.

The first appearance of Saruq's name to be found in the documents of the Holy office was in the case of Battista de' Leoni, the son of a Venetian schoolmaster, who was suspected of holding some shocking opinions, acquired, apparently, while working as a bookkeeper for Hayyim Saruq in the Ghetto Vecchio for about six or seven months about 1566.[33] De' Leoni denied all the accusations brought against him, maintaining that his relations with his Jewish employer were purely a matter of business. Saruq himself was not called to testify at this trial. But it is significant that Saruq employed a Christian bookkeeper in the Ghetto is revealing by itself.

Saruq's next appearance in the documents of the Venetian Holy Office in the trial of Gaspar Ribeiro, a rich merchant who lived outside the Ghetto as a Christian and was accused in 1579-80 of Crypto-Judaism. Saruq was summoned for interrogation on 26 January and 3 September 1580. Surprisingly, he is described in the documents of the Holy Office as 'Consul of the Levantine nation'.[34] He described Ribeiro, the

---

[31] P.F. Grendler, *The Roman Inquisition and the Venetian Printing Press, 1540-1605*, Princeton, 1977, p. 46; Pullan, *The Jews of Europe*, p. 6.

[32] See *Processi del S. Uffizio di Venezia contro ebrei e giudaizzanti*, ed. P.C. Ioly Zorattini, Florence, 1980-1994, 11 vols. published so far [hereafter: *Processi*]; Pullan, *The Jews of Europe, op. cit.*.

[33] Pullan, *The Jews of Europe*, p. 160.

[34] Pullan, "A Ship with Two Rudders", p. 37; *idem, The Jews of Europe*, p. 209.

accused, as being his "...mortal enemy, being in legal dispute with him over a sum of about 4,800 ducats."[35] Saruq's description of a *converso*, as "one who steers by two rudders: that is, he is neither Christian nor Jew," was used by Pullan as the title of his article on the Righetto case.[36]

The full text of Saruq's interrogation has recently been published and is of immense value for our purpose.[37] He stated that he was 45-years old, an "agent (*agente*) of the *Levantini*", which occupation which kept him outside the Ghetto until late at night. According to this testimony, he was surprisingly young, considering what we know about his previous activities and status. If true, it would mean that he was only about 21-years old in the early 1560s, when he is first mentioned as an active entrepreneur in Venice, and 27-years old in 1566, at the time of his bankruptcy, when he already figured as the patron of book publishing among Venetian Jews. Even his appearance as 'Consul of the *Levantini*' in 1580, or a little earlier,[38] conflicts with the traditional image of a community 'elder', especially in Venice, which was not a conductive environment for young, or relatively young, leaders. But even if we take Saruq's statement of his age with a pinch of salt, it is unlikely that he deviated greatly from his real age, especially in the circumstances in which he made the statement.

Questioned about a certain Isaac Habibi, a Ferrarese Jew, Saruq stated that he had known this person for 35 years, first in Salonica and later in Venice and Ferrara. This suggests that Saruq originated from Salonica and came to Venice at an early age, probably already in possession of a considerable fortune. Indeed, only great affluence can explain his standing in Venice at such an early age. More data about his family can be gleaned from various other sources, some of which have been cited. His father's name—Solomon—and that of his brother—Isaac—appear in the notarial records cited in the previous

---

[35] Ribeiro, presumably the same person, is mentioned in connection with Hayyim Saruq's bankruptcy. See above, p. 136.

[36] Pullan, "A Ship with Two Rudders", pp. 25-58.

[37] *Processi*, vol. 5, pp. 58-60.

[38] A letter from the *Bailo* to the Heads of the Council of Ten of 13 Oct. 1579 includes a reference to the "Consul of the *Levantini*" to whom correspondence from Constantinople had been sent, but had not reached its destination. Though his name is not mentioned, this letter may also refer to Saruq; see ASV, Capi cons. X, Lett. CP, busta 5, No 104.

chapter. Indirect evidence points to his marriage to a woman from a Paduan Jewish family.[39] The name of his wife—Letitia—is known from the documentation of his bankruptcy, as well as the documents concerning his spying activity. His father-in-law, with whom he also litigated, was Moise [Moses] Alfandari.[40] We also know the names of at least two of his offspring: one of them, Joseph, is said to have engaged in printing Hebrew books in Venice[41], and the circumcision of another, Abraham, was recorded in 1577 in a booklet kept by an Italian rabbi[42]. When, in 1569, he petitioned to be released from prison, he mentioned his mother, wife and children (in the plural). We may, therefore, assume that eventually he had more than two children.

About eight years after his appearance in Ribeiro's trial, it was Saruq's turn to be brought in as a suspect before the Inquisitors. He was accused of blasphemy, following a complaint made by Lascaris de Zorzi, a Greek shipmaster from Constantinople, who clashed with Saruq in the office of the Venetian State Attorneys (*Avogadori di comun*). According to the accuser, when he went to that office on 28 October 1588 to ascertain that Saruq had produced a certain book, he was insulted by that "most wicked Jew" (*scelleratissimo hebreo*). Two Armenian merchants, who testified that they had been present, supported the accusation, stating that Saruq insulted the Greek in Turkish, calling him "a dirty dog of an infidel," and other epithets in Turkish. Saruq was described by one of the Armenians as "a big man with a scar on his face" (*era homo grande che ha un sfrizo nel viso*). But the Inquisitors were apparently not very impressed by these accusations, and Saruq

---

[39] In 1591, in response to Hayyim Saruq's protest, the leaders of the Jewish community at Padua agreed to set the burial expenses of Hayyim Saruq's father-in-law at 10 ducats, see D.Carpi, ed., *Minute Book of the Council of the Jewish Community of Padua 1577-1603*, Jerusalem, 1973, p. 279 [Hebrew].

[40] See above, p. 136. It is not certain, though, whether Moses Alfandari can be identified as the unnamed father-in-law mentioned above in a document of 1591, as Saruq might have been married more than once.

[41] Benayahu, "Further evidence", p. 133, but without specific reference to this statement. We assume that there was no other Hayyim Saruq in Venice at the same period.

[42] R. Bonfil, "New evidence on the life of Rabbi Menahem Azaria of Fano and his Times", in *Chapters in the History of Jewish Society in the Middle Ages and the Modern Era dedicated to Prof. Jacob Katz*, Jerusalem, 1980, p. 125 [Hebrew].

was acquitted without much ado.[43]

We are unable to judge at this stage whether Saruq's repeated involvement in litigations and arbitrations reflects a typical pattern of behaviour in the mercantile milieu. Certainly, the Inquisition could be used as a weapon against business opponents. Even as a Jew, Saruq was not immune from investigation by this institution. Moreover, the Jewish merchants in Venice were associated in many ways with the *Marranos*, which, of course, concerned the Inquisition. If Saruq's testimony in the Ribeiro trial shows little sympathy, much less solidarity, with the suspect, faced with the judges of the Holy Office he must have been concerned above all to preserve his own skin. Although he succeeded in this, his experience illustrates the precariousness of Jewish existence, even in this relatively tolerant region of Christendom.

***

The function of 'Consul of the *Levantini*' in Venice, and the general phenomenon of the appearance in the sixteenth century of Jewish consuls in the eastern Mediterranean, has not yet been sufficiently studied. It seems that Saruq acted as agent for the *Levantini* merchants abroad, or at least for a group of *Levantini* merchants, and also had some control over the correspondence between the Ghetto Vecchio and the East. His position as 'Consul of the *Levantini*' in Venice can be considered both as a recognition of his prominent status in the *Levantini* community (in Venice and in other commercial centres), and as an indication of the considerable income which he could obtain from this office. In fact, judging from contemporary *responsa* literature, the Jewish consuls concentrated in their hands a large share of Jewish business enterprises: received the merchandise, provided for its storage in warehouses, handled letters of credit and instructions from merchants abroad relating to commercial and financial transactions. In return, the consuls were entitled to 2% of the value of merchandise transferred or stored, (probably in relation to length of time, too), and 3% for handling bills of exchange.[44] It is not certain how much of the trade of the *Levantini*

---

[43] *Processi*, vol. 8, pp. 73-76 (12 Nov. 1588).

[44] Shmuelevitz, *The Jews of the Ottoman Empire*, p. 147. Venice does not figure in Shmuelevitz's list of places in which the existence of Jewish consuls is recorded in the *responsa* literature. In 1589, Daniel Rodriga claimed that the group of Jewish

was concentrated in Saruq's hands, but considering the great value of the commercial transactions carried out by the *Levantini*, handling even a modest portion of it would have brought Saruq considerable income.

It should be noted that a similar title, that of 'Consul of the Ponentine Jews', was obtained by Daniel Rodriga as early as 1573. He later served as Jewish consul at Narenta, the only Ottoman port of importance on the central Adriatic shore.[45] Later he must have held the title of Jewish consul at Ragusa, before taking this position in Venice.[46] Both Rodriga and Saruq not only engaged in international trade in the eastern Mediterranean, but were also employed as Venetian secret agents[47]. They served as consuls, and acted on behalf of various groups of Jewish merchants at more or less the same time. Yet there seems to have been a difference in their conduct, at least as reflected in official Venetian sources. Saruq generally appears as a lone wolf, even when he was acting for a group of other merchants, whereas Rodriga seems to have been an initiator and organizer of great public projects, some of which, such as the establishment of Spalato as the main Venetian trading post in Dalmatia, or the settlement of the *Ponentini* in Venice, were impressive achievements in which he played a central role.[48]

During the later Middle Ages, the title of consul, with its classical connotations, referred to functions denoting social and political prominence among the merchants in the Italian communes, in their urban institutions, and later in the commercial networks of these cities overseas.[49] The appearance in the sixteenth century of Jews bearing titles which had previously been held exclusively by Christians, and especially the official recognition of these titles by Venice and Ragusa, is worthy of attention, and may be viewed as another manifestation

---

merchants whom he represented was willing to pay him as their consul a stipend of 500 ducats a year and the payment of 1 *grosso* for every bale of merchandise, see Ravid, "Daniel Rodriga and the First Decade of the Jewish Merchants", p. 206.

[45] Paci, *La 'scala' di Spalato*, pp. 50-51.

[46] *Ibid.*, pp. 49-50; Ravid, "An Autobiographical Memorandum", pp. 196, 209; *idem*, "The First Charter", pp. 198, 213. In 1607, Joshua Ferro held the same title: Ravid, "The Third Charter", p. 99.

[47] On Rodriga's employment as secret agent, see Preto, *I servizi segreti*, p. 250.

[48] See above, p. 7 and n. 22.

[49] P. Racine, "Les débuts des consulats italiens outre-mer", in M. Balard, ed., *Etat et colonisation au Moyen Age et à la Renaissance*, Lyons, 1989, pp. 267-276.

of the increasing importance of Jews in the international trade in the eastern Mediterranean.

***

The name of Ḥayyim Saruq continues to crop up in Venetian documents of the 1580s and 1590s, always in connection with his mercantile activities. During these years too he seems to have been continuously entangled in judicial disputes. In addition to the Segura, and various creditors in Venice mentioned earlier, a new dispute concerned another colourful Jewish figure, David Passi. Passi was also a 'Levantine' merchant, who first appears in Venetian sources as a Jewish merchant at Ragusa, warning the Venetian authorities of the imminent Turkish attack on Venetian Cyprus. During the war he was an active Venetian agent. After the peace accord he seems to have spent a few years in the Ghetto Vecchio, where he is said to have kept a salon also attended by Venetian patricians.[50] He later moved to Istanbul, where he attained a prominent position at the Ottoman court from about 1585 until his fall from grace in the early 1590s. During this short period his name recurred in the international diplomatic correspondence as a highly influential person, described as rivalling even the Grand Vizier.[51] From our viewpoint, it should be emphasized that the source of Passi's power was in his trade in the Balkans, as well as the special relations which he had formed with the Venetian Republic.

Passi's dispute with Saruq does not seem to have left many traces in the archives, but it can be partially reconstructed by means of two petitions, one presented by Saruq in 1590, and the other by Passi about

---

[50] In 1579-80, a certain Antonio Saldanha was accused before the Venetian Inquisition that as a Franciscan friar, he lived a few month in David Passi's house in the *Ghetto* and participated in prayers in the Synagogue: *Processi*, vol. 4, p. 151; in 1575, Felipa Jorge, accused of Judaizing, was also said to have lived in David Passi's house in the *Ghetto*: *ibid.*, p. 151. Passi is also mentioned in 1575 in a letter in Portuguese, which was presented to the same court: *ibid.*, vol. 4, pp. 237-40 and App. I, 190. See also Pullan, *The Jews of Europe*, pp. 104, 172.

[51] Preto, *I servizi segreti*, pp. 100, 104, 120, 240, 295; S. Faroqhi, "Ein Günstling des osmanischen Sultan Murad III: David Passi", *Der Islam* 47 (1971), pp. 290-297; Baron, *A Social and Religious History*, vol. 18, pp. 134-41.

eight years earlier.[52] Saruq's petition, which included a summary of the previous developments of this affair, shows that the repercussions of his 1566 bankruptcy were still affecting his life some 24 years later. It should be remembered that when he appealed to be released in 1569, Saruq asked that three or five special commissioners be assigned to deal with the collection of his credits and the payments of his debts. Later documentation shows that this was done and that five noblemen, who were then serving as Financial Commissioners of the Reclaimed Lands (*Provveditori sopra i conti dei beni inculti*), were appointed to administer his estate, with ample authority from the Senate.[53] According to Saruq, while these magistrates were still active, David Passi, described as "a Jew and a certain persecutor of mine" (*hebreo e certo mio persecutore*), sued him before the court of *Consoli dei mercanti* (which also dealt with insolvent debtors). Passi demanded from Saruq 800 ducats on account of a bill (*scritto*) of 20 March 1565, payable to a certain Abraham Francese, a Ferrarese Jew.[54] Saruq was jailed for a short while, but was soon released at the behest of the five commissioners. According to Passi, who referred to this incident in his petition, Saruq's detention by the *Consoli* and his later release took place in 1579. To follow the developments of this conflict we must now turn to Passi's petition.

In a letter addressed to the Heads of the Council of Ten, Passi presented himself as acting on behalf of the 'Most Serene Queen Mother of the Grand Seigneur' (*la Serenissima Regina Madre del Gran Signore*), the highly influential Nūr Bānū, mother of the reigning Sultan, Murad III.[55] Among other things, he was asked by the Sultan's mother to see to it that her personal physician and protégé, Dr. Rabbi Emmanuel Brudo, was finally paid the sum of 2,593 ducats, which Hayyim Saruq owed him after a commercial transaction involving precious red cloth (*cremesin*). Passi stated that the 'Queen Mother' was well informed

---

[52] For Saruq's petition, see ASV, Senato, Terra, filza 117, under 6 Oct. 1590 (I am indebted to Prof, Benjamin Ravid for sending me a photocopy of this document); for Passi's petition, see ASV, Capi X, Lett. CP, busta 6, No 22 (4 Jan. 1581 *m.v.*).

[53] For the renewal of this mandate on 7 Sept. 1573, see ASV, Senato, Terra, reg. 49, ff. 184v-185. It was normal procedure in Venice to appoint magistrates to deal with matters which had nothing to do with the original task to which they were assigned.

[54] This could also be seen as an indication that Passi was in Venice in 1579.

[55] On this personality, see B. Arbel, "Nūr Bānū (c. 1530-1583): a Venetian Sultana?", *Turcica*, 24 (1992), pp. 241-59.

about Saruq's financial situation, which must have been good, since he was able to pay off even larger debts. Moreover, Passi alleged that Saruq was making a profit of 2,000 ducats a year at the expense of Venetian customs revenues by trickery and false claims, as he proposed to prove. In 1579 Saruq had been arrested by order of the *Consoli dei mercanti*, but was soon released. Passi wrote that although he was personally interested in obtaining the said sum, he would not have bothered the Signory if he had not been urged to do so by the Sultan's mother and other prominent persons at the Porte.[56]

Unable, apparently, to obtain redress by judicial procedure, Passi began to pressure Venice by means of his connection with one of the most influential figures at the Porte, the Sultan's mother, and by trying to ruin Saruq with the offer to produce evidence before the Council of Ten about what he described as Saruq's fraudulent conduct. Although Venice tried hard to please the Sultan's mother on every occasion, I have been unable to find any document to show that the Ten took these accusations seriously, or even that Emmanuel Brudo's claim received any special treatment. Passi's reference to Saruq's profit from Venice's customs revenues may be connected with the *Haskama* quoted at the beginning of Chapter Six.[57] In fact, fraudulent or not, the affair related to the reduction of the customs tariffs, which entitled Saruq to payments from the *Levantini*, should probably be assigned to this period of the late 1570s and early 1580s, and not to the 1550s, as suggested.[58]

Turning back to Saruq's petition of 1592, we find that Passi's vindictiveness was not dismissed. Saruq's petition refers to events which must have happened not long before the Senate's action on his appeal, *i.e.*, about the beginning of October 1590. According to Saruq, Passi had taken advantage of the fact that the five special commissioners, who had administered his estate, had died in the meantime, to renew his attacks on him, this time through the court of *Giudici del proprio*, a magistracy with a very broad mandate, including the settlement of dowries after the dissolution of marriages.[59]

This was the issue behind Passi's renewed attack. The sons of

---

[56] ASV, Capi Cons. X, Lett. CP, busta 6, No 22 (4 Jan. 1581 *m.v.*).

[57] See above, pp. 96-97.

[58] See above, p. 98.

[59] Tiepolo, "Archivio di Stato di Venezia", p. 988.

Abraham Francese now demanded, on the basis of the same bill which had been used before, to be recognized as heirs to their late mother's dowry. This time Saruq was less fortunate, and the judges ordered him to pay 1,200 *scudi* [equivalent to 1,200 gold ducats], which must have included costs and interest on top of the 800 ducats demanded in 1579. Saruq asked the Signory, "to avoid starting him again on a path of new worries and hardships, and to prevent damage to public interest," by nominating new commissioners in place of the deceased ones, with similar authority, and thus enable him to defend himself from his "old and too cruel persecutors" (*li mei antichi e troppo crudelli persecutori*). This time, the Senate refused to resort to the emergency procedures which had been adopted during the pre-war diplomatic crisis, and transferred the case to the Court of *Cinque savi alla mercanzia*, which normally dealt with disputes involving the *Levantini*, as demanded by Simon Francese, Aloise Abegnigni and other persons interested in this case.

There is no doubt that Passi nursed a personal grudge against Saruq, but in all these attempts he made no pecuniary claims of his own, but acted in the name of other claimants, either members of his own family, or other Jews connected or related to Saruq's old rivals, who felt that they had been affected by the repercussions of his bankruptcy, some 24 years earlier. Significantly, all these disputes among Jewish litigants, including matters of dowries and inheritance, which were normally brought before rabbinical authorities, took place before Venetian courts.

Did Saruq's continuous litigations make his an exceptional case, or was it typical among Jewish, and probably also non-Jewish merchants in his milieu? At this stage it is hard to tell. The records for this period of the *Cinque savi*, the *Giudici del proprio* and the *Consoli dei mercanti* are very fragmentary and insufficient for a broad or quantitative research. Nor do they allow us to follow the later developments of the dispute between Saruq and Passi. Not being related to a political crisis, Saruq's litigation with Abraham Francese and David Passi left fewer traces in the decisions of the Republic's central organs of government, which are much better documented for this period. It is possible, however, that David Passi's fall from his high position at the Porte, preceded in 1591 by growing suspicions in Venice as to his secret activities in the service of Spain and of the Ottomans, also affected the attitude of the Venetian authorities to his requests.[60]

Saruq, however, did not disappear from the Venetian scene. We encounter him again in 1594 and 1595, involved in the maritime insurance business. In 1594 he figured among the insurers of a ship detained in an island near Ragusa on its way from Constantinople to Venice, and in 1595 among the insurers of the ship *Martinenga*, which foundered on its way from Constantinople to Venice.[61] The latest record concerning Saruq which has so far been uncovered appears to refer to his letter to the Cairene Jewish community, sent presumably about 1600, and mentioned in Rabbi Ḥayyim Caphusi's letter.[62]

It is certain that the Venetian archives, and probably other archives too, contain additional material on this fascinating personage. The material which has been discussed in the two chapters in which he is the chief protagonist reveals not only an extraordinary personal story of a sixteenth-century Jewish merchant, but also illustrates the spectacular rise of Jewish trade in the eastern Mediterranean during the sixteenth century, which became an important factor in Venetian and Ottoman economy, and an influential factor in the relations between the two powers.

---

[60] Preto, *I servizi segreti*, pp. 104, 295.

[61] Tenenti, *Naufrages*, pp. 116, 167-168.

[62] See above, p. 96.

CHAPTER EIGHT

JEWISH SHIPOWNERS IN THE EARLY MODERN EASTERN MEDITERRANEAN

> ...But now how stands the wind?
> Into what corner peers my Halcions bill?
> Ha, to the East? Yes: See how stands the Vanes?
> East and by-South: why then I hope my ships
> I sent for Egypt and the bordering iles
> Are gotten up by Nilus winding banks:
> Mine Argosie from Alexandria,
> Loaden with Spice and Silkes, now under saile,
> Are smoothly gliding downe by Candie shoare
> To Malta, through our Mediterranean sea...[1]

Following the involvement of Ḥayyim Saruq and Solomon Ashkenazi in commercial shipping led me to a new investigation. Were they only an unusual episode in the sixteenth-century Mediterranean, or did they represent a phenomenon of wider historical significance? The present chapter is an attempt to answer this question.

International trade and shipping have always been so closely related, that historians do not always clearly distinguish between them. But although it is hard to imagine international trade, particularly in the Mediterranean basin, which is not maritime, the two activities fields are not identical. From the vantage point of Jewish history, the distinction is even more important, as will shortly be elucidated.

It is hardly necessary to spell out the advantages of ship-owning for anyone engaged in international maritime trade. The merchant was very much dependent on the owners of the vessels which transported his goods. Profits from international trading depended to a large extent on the timing of purchase and loading in the port of origin, on the

---

[1] Christopher Marlowe, "The Jew of Malta", Act I, in *The Complete Works*, ed. F. Bowers, vol. 1, Cambridge, 1973, p. 265.

speed of transport to the port of destination, on freight charges, safety on board, general conditions on board, and on the reliability of shipowners and crews. For the merchant to be in full control of the ship, enabled him to operate along the safest and most profitable routes, to adjust the navigation schedule to changing market conditions, to save the freight charges and to profit from the freight charges paid by other merchants and passengers. On the other hand, owning and operating a ship also required a substantial investment to build or acquire a ship, and for its maintenance, the wages of the crew, wear and tear, insurance expenses, etc. In addition, and in spite of maritime insurance, there were great risks involved.

The appearance of Jewish shipowners not only indicated that they had the necessary capital and organizational capacity, it was also a sign of a change in their legal and social status. For them to have penetrated into that sphere revealed the weakening of the walls around the command posts of economic activity. Shipowners and captains filled authoritative functions in their societies, wielding power and having considerable responsibility over many other people. Thus, for instance, in 1629 French law recognized that shipping and international trade were occupations which did not entail the loss of noble status.[2] We must also remember that the maritime trade of the Mediterranean played a central role in the economic development of the surrounding countries, and the presence of Jews in its commanding positions meant that they were playing a central role in the economic and social development of the Mediterranean world.

Was the sixteenth century a turning-point in this regard? The search for evidence of ship-owning Jews during the Middle Ages has produced little. Historians often mention the *navicularii*, a corporation of Jewish shipowners who were active in Alexandria in late Antiquity.[3] But it is not known if this was an exceptional case, or an expression of a wider social and economic phenomenon in the early centuries of the

---

[2] H. Kamen, *European Society 1500-1700*, London, 1971, p. 99.

[3] S.W. Baron, *A Social and Religious History of the Jews*, vol. 4, New York-London, 1965, p. 183; S. Tolkovsky, *Jewish Seamen*, Tel Aviv 1970, p. 52 [Hebrew], citing Juster, *Les Juifs dans l'Empire Romain*. On Jewish maritime activities in ancient times, see also R. Patai, *Jewish Seafaring in Ancient Times. A Contribution to the History of Palestinian Culture*, Jerusalem, 1938 [Hebrew], and a shorter English version in R. Patai, "Jewish Seafaring in Ancient Times", *Jewish Quarterly Review*, 32 (1941-42), pp. 1-26.

Christian Era. At any rate, in the following centuries there seems to have been little association between Jews and shipping. A scholar who gleaned all the maritime expressions in the Talmud stated that their rarity indicates that this activity was marginal in comparison with other kind of economic occupation.[4] The so-called *al-Radhaniyya* have also attracted considerable attention among historians of the High Middle Ages. Those who accepted the testimony of Ibn Khurradadhbah attributed to these Jewish merchants an important role in the international trade between the worlds of Christianity and Islam, and beyond it, during the ninth century; others question their very existence.[5] It should be noted, however, that Ibn Khurradadhbah says nothing about the *al-Radhaniyya* as shipowners.[6]

It is possible that a certain maritime tradition persisted among some Jewish communities in the western Mediterranean during the early Middle Ages, and in a few regions even a little later. In one case, made known by the intervention of Pope Gregory the Great (590-604), a Sicilian Jew, Nostamnus, or Tamnus, was deprived of his ship by the Papal *defensor* in Gaul.[7] Another piece of evidence appears in the ninth-century chronicle of St. Gallen, describing Norman vessels

---

[4] D. Sperber, *Nautica talmudica*, Ramat Gan, 1986, p. 119.

[5] L. Rabinowitz, *Jewish Merchant Adventurers. A Study of the Radanites*, London, 1948; R.S. Lopez and I.W.Raymond, *Medieval Trade in the Mediterranean World*, (New York n.d.), pp. 31-33; S.D. Goitein, *Jews and Arabs. Their Contacts Through the Ages*, New York, 1955, pp. 105-107; C. Cahen, "Y a-t-il eu des Rahdânites?", *Revue des Etudes Juives*, 3 (1964), pp. 499-505; M. Gil, "The Rādhānite Merchants and the Land of Rādhān", *Journal of the Economic and Social History of the Orient*, 17 (1974), pp. 299-328.

[6] Rabinowitz, who dedicated a book to the Radanites, briefly discussed the question of "Jewish ships" during that period. Beside the scanty evidence cited above, he also claims that "the unusually large number of *Responsa* dealing with the question of the permissibilty of sailing on the Sabbath shows how acute this question had become": Rabinowitz, *Jewish Merchant Adventurers*, p. 107. But the rabbinical literature referred to, including the three examples cited by Rabinowitz, says nothing about Jewish shipowners, but only deals with questions pertaining to sea voyages.

[7] *Monumenta Germaniae Historica. Epistolae*, II, ed. C. Hartmann, 2nd Edition, Berlin, 1957, p. 68, cited in Baron, *Social and Religious History*, vol. 4, p. 330, n. 42 ; for the same document, see also *Regesta pontificum romanorum ab condita ecclesia ad annum post christum natum MCXCVIII*, ed. P. Jaffé, 2nd edition revised by G. Wattenbach, vol. 1, Leipzig, 1885, p. 184, No 1564 (1214), cited in H. Pirenne, *Mohammed and Charlemagne*, London, 1968, p. 85.

172   CHAPTER EIGHT

approaching the coast of Galia Narbonensis, which were at first wrongly identified as ships belonging to Jews, Africans or Britons.[8] Sporadic references to Jewish shipowners in twelfth-century Salerno,[9] twelfth-century Barcelona, and thirteenth-century Marseilles, have been made by historians.[10]

In the eastern Mediterranean maritime tradition could have persisted among Jews here and there, but in this area too the evidence suggests that it was of marginal significance. Observing the Sabbath seems to have been a serious obstacle for active Jewish participation in shipping. A letter of Synesius, one of the Fathers of the Church (c.370-414) described a crossing from Alexandria to Kyrenia about 404 AD on a ship whose captain was a Jew. At the start of the Sabbath the captain left his post and the ship was without command when a storm threatened to wreck it. The entreaties of the passengers to the captain to return to his post were of no avail, and only at the last moment, when it seemed that the ship was doomed, was he persuaded that the percept of *piqquah nefesh* (danger to life) permitted his return to the rudder and he saved the vessel and its passengers.[11]

Though occasionally mentioned in the sources, Jewish shipowning does not seem to have been common or continuous. S.D. Goitein, who in a masterly study revealed the role of North African Jews in Mediterranean economy between the eleventh and the thirteenth centuries, emphasized the paucity of evidence of Jewish involvement in Mediterranean shipping.[12] A similar conclusion rises from the examination of

---

[8] Baron, *Social and Religious History*, vol. 4, p. 183.

[9] Solomon of Salerno, a rich Jewish shipowner is mentioned in the records of the Genoese notary Giovanni Scriba; see E.H. Byrne, *Genoese Shipping in the Twelfth and Thirteenth Centuries*, Cambridge, Mass., 1930, p. 12.

[10] Baron, *Social and Religious History*, vol 4, p. 183. In the latter two cases (Barcelona and Marseilles), I believe that the evidence demands further examination. Historians of medieval Marseilles have been unable to find evidence of Jewish shipowners in that town; see R. Pernoud, *Histoire du commerce de Marseille. Vol 1: Le Moyen Age jusqu'en 1291*, Paris, 1949, pp. 290-293; E. Baratier and F. Reynaud, *Histoire du commerce de Marseille, vol. 2: de 1291 à 1480*, Paris, 1951, p. 95 and n. 1.

[11] Goitein, *Jews and Arabs*, pp. 108-109; Tolkovsky, *Jewish Seamen*, pp. 52-53.

[12] S.D. Goitein, *A Mediterranean Society*, vol. 1: Economic Foundations, Berkeley-Los Angeles, 1967, pp. 309-311; *idem, Jews and Arabs*, p. 109. See also Baron, *Social and Religious History*, vol. 4, p. 183. In the twelfth century Benjamin of Tudela

eleventh-century *Geniza* letters written in Arabic, recently studied by Aodeh. There is no mention in them of ships owned by Jews, and the writers often have difficulty in distinguishing between the various types of vessels.[13] Goitein suggested that the increasingly strict observance of the Sabbath caused Jews to keep away from the shipping business, especially on long routes, and even with a non-Jewish crew.[14]

The ownership of a vessel was often divided among several partners. This device enabled Jews to invest in shipping without being directly identified as shipowners. Notarial documents from Marseilles indicate that during the late fourteenth and early fifteenth centuries Jews partici- pated as junior partners in the ownership of commercial vessels.[15] Ashtor discovered similar instances from the central Mediterranean: one concerns an association between a Jew and a Greek in Crete in 1352, who owned equal shares in a ship destined to navigate between the ports of the eastern Mediterranean;[16] another refers to a Jew of Trapani, in Sicily, who owned one fourth of a commercial vessel called *L'annunziata*, which in 1440 commuted between Trapani, Tunisia and Naples.[17] The latter case shows that the Jewish involvement had no effect on the ship's very 'Christian' name. We may assume that in such cases the influence of Jewish part owners on decisions concerning the ships' operations must have been limited. In any case, this phenome- non did not reflect a radical change in legal or social status of Jews, since evidently the ships in question were not regarded as 'Jewish'.

Another fairly common system of Jewish involvement in commercial shipping was the hiring or chartering of ships. Great merchants who transported substantial goods overseas sometimes preferred to lease ships for this purpose. Such, for instance, was the case of two Jews

---

mentioned in his travel-book having encountered Jewish shipowners in Tyre: *The Itinerary of Benjamin of Tudela*, ed. and tr. M.N. Adler, London, 1907, p. 20 of the Hebrew text and p. 18 of the English translation.

[13] S. Aodeh, *Eleventh-Century Arabic Letters of Jewish Merchants from the Cairo Geniza*, unpublished Ph. D. dissertation, Tel Aviv University, 1992 [Hebrew], p. xi of the English abstract.

[14] Goitein, *A Mediterranean Society*, vol. 4, p. 183.

[15] Baratier and Reynaud, *Histoire du commerce de Marseille*, p. 95.

[16] E. Ashtor, "New Data for the History of Levantine Jewries in the Fifteenth Century", *Bulletin of the Institute of Jewish Studies*, 3 (1975), p. 74.

[17] *Idem*, "The Jews of Trapani in the Later Middle Ages", *Studi Medievali*, 3rd ser., 25 (1984), p. 25.

from Marseilles, who in 1391 hired a Catalan ship for the route Marseilles - Collioure - San Feliou - Majorca - Valencia - Marseilles.[18] Rabbi Elijah Capsali acted in the same way when he exported Cretan wine to Egypt in 1422.[19] In the first half of the fifteenth century Jews of Trapani chartered ships for their trade with southern Italy and North Africa.[20] Transactions of this kind sometimes involved Jews and gentiles from various Mediterranean cities—for example the chartering of a ship in Messina, in 1417, by a Christian merchant from Barcelona, a Jew from Cagliari in Sardinia, and another Jew from Marseilles who was represented by a Sicilian notary.[21] But this form of involvement in commercial shipping was even less of an indication of a changed status of the Jews, since the ships continued to operate under their owners' names, and the involvement of the Jews in their operation was brief and indirect.

Partial ownership of a commercial vessel, or its chartering for a single voyage, could be helpful to Jewish businessmen without unduly exposing them to legal complications and dangers. It could also be sufficiently in line with religious restrictions on the operation of Jewish-owned ships on long voyages. But from the economic point of view, these arrangements left them dependent on external factors, which was actually in harmony with the general status of Jews in the societies in which they were active.

It has occasionally been argued that the rise of the maritime republics, such as Venice, Genoa and Pisa, and their appropriation of a great part of the international trade in the Mediterranean, drove the Jews out of this activity. In fact, these states tended to conduct a monopolistic policy, seeking to concentrate this lucrative activity in the hands of small oligarchies, and to oust outside competitors, among them Jews. The statutes of Marseilles, for instance, ruled that no more than four

---

[18] Baratier and Reynaud, *Histoire du commerce de Marseille*, vol. 2, pp. 93, 120 n. 3.

[19] Ashtor, "New Data for the History of Levantine Jewries", p. 78.

[20] *Idem*, "The Jews of Trapani", pp. 23-24.

[21] *Idem*, "The Jews in the Mediterranean Trade in the Fifteenth Century", p. 444. For the chartering of a ship at Trapani, in 1422, by two Jews from Mazara, in western Sicily, for grain export, see *ibid.*, p. 442; for the chartering of a vessel in Chios by two other Jews to sail to Smyrna at the end of the fifteenth century, see *idem*, "Levantine Jewries", p. 71.

Jewish merchants could be transported on any one of its ships.[22] Venetian maritime legislation of the fourteenth and fifteenth centuries referred to Jews as rivals to be excluded from the Venetian commercial system.[23] Nevertheless, Jews continued to be involved in international maritime trade even during the later Middle Ages, when the maritime republics were dominant in this field, and sometimes even held important positions in this area. But at that time also they were absent from the world of shipping. Jewish merchants were obliged to use the shipping services of the countries which dominated the maritime trade. Even when not explicitly barred from ship owning, and in spite of their having sufficient capital and business capabilities, other obstacles prevented them from entering this field. No doubt obstacles stemming from Jewish religious laws made them reluctant to engage in this activity, but external factors must also have militated against it. Piracy, for instance, was a grave deterrent. It was omnipresent in the Mediterranean, and Jews were particularly vulnerable to it, since it was often conducted under the guise of religion. Commercial shipping needed military protection against pirates and corsairs, and it was practically impossible to operate a merchant fleet, much less a single ship, without arms, which in itself was a problem for Jews, and without formal and effective state protection. The status of a shipowner was normally associated with a commanding social position vis-à-vis the crews and passengers. Considering that most of the latter were not Jews, and that Jews were generally regarded as inferior in Christian, and to a lesser extent in Muslim, societies, this too created an obstacle.

In summary, even during those times in the Middle Ages when Jews were relatively prominent in the international trade of the Mediterranean world, the evidence of their involvement in shipowning is scanty and sporadic. There is no indication of a continuous maritime tradition among Jewish communities between late Antiquity and the late Middle Ages. Wherever there is evidence of Jewish involvement in commercial shipping, it is usually indirect, discreet and limited.

***

[22] Pernoud, *Histoire du commerce de Marseille*, vol.1, p. 291. Pernoud notes, however, that according to notarial documents this restriction was not strictly observed.

[23] See above, p. 2.

This situation began to change in the sixteenth century. Alongside the limited involvement in shipping, which continued as before, a new phenomenon appeared, which later grew and expanded into other geographical areas: the rise of the Jewish shipowners, who operated their commercial vessels openly and independently.

This important turning-point had to do with the new conditions offered in the sixteenth century to Jewish entrepreneurs in the Ottoman Empire. For the first time in many centuries, a powerful state offered the Jews full protection, including the field of commercial shipping. Unlike the Italian maritime republics, where the ruling circles were directly involved in commercial shipping, the political and social elite of the Ottoman Empire tended to be associated with landed interests. Maritime commerce thus remained largely in foreign hands, or in the hands of minorities from among the Ottoman subjects. The ability of Jews to engage in commercial shipping was not contingent on legal restrictions on the part of the Ottomans, but rather on the disposition of the Jews themselves to disregard to some extent their own religious restrictions and their traditional patterns of economic activity, as well as on their ability to raise the necessary capital and take the necessary precautions against the occupational hazards. The latter issue affected Jews more than other groups, which must have deterred many of them from entering this risky, though remunerative, sector.

We have seen that two of the protagonists of the earlier chapters of this book, Ḥayyim Saruq and Solomon Ashkenazi, engaged in this activity. The earliest evidence about Saruq's ships is a contract which he signed on 1 February 1563 with the shipbuilder Francesco Marangon, of the island of Curzola in Dalmatia, for the building of a *brigantino*. The contract specified the exact measures of the small vessel, which was apparently intended to sail in the Adriatic sea: 44 feet long at the keel; 14 feet at the beam; 4.5 feet in depth; and 2.5 feet above deck. The vessel was supposed to be ready within five months.[24] In spite of the small size of the vessel, the price of 150 ducats, seems rather low, considering that about six months earlier Saruq had paid 200 ducats for half a *brigantino* of 600 *stara* capacity.[25] Saruq, who continued to invest in ships, must have used these vessels to import wool, hides

---

[24] ASV, AN, busta 8250/I, ff. 27-27v; *ibid.*, busta 8251/II, ff. 24v (17 Mar. 1564), 25.

[25] *Ibid.*, busta 8249/IV, ff. 44-44v.

and leather from Ottoman lands to Venice. On 20 March 1563 he acquired a two-year old *brigantino* for 330 ducats[26], and on 7 May of that year, another vessel of the same type of 500 *stara* capacity, for 220 ducats.[27] Do these sums reflect the true value of those vessels? According to another Jewish merchant, in 1567 Saruq's three *brigantini* were said to be worth 1,000 ducats each.[28] Saruq also owned half of the ship *Mazzona*, which was of larger capacity and sailed outside the Adriatic. It was apparently used to import alum from the Aegean to Venice, and probably also carried various goods from Venice to the East.[29] As we have seen, during the Venetian-Ottoman war Solomon Ashkenazi operated a vessel of his own between Constantinople and Crete.

My hypothesis that these findings are not episodic, but reflect a wider phenomenon, can be corroborated by further instances from various locations in the early Modern Mediterranean. Gilles Veinstein has found in the judicial registers of Ottoman Avlona (Valona), dating from 1567-68, evidence of Jewish shipowners, operating their vessels between that Albanian port and Venice.[30] Under Ottoman rule (1539-1687) the small Dalmatian port of Risano in the gulf of Cattaro (Kotor) seems to have been a centre of Jewish shipping in the gulf itself as well as along the Dalmatian and Albanian coasts.[31] Jewish shipowners also appear in Tenenti's study on Venetian maritime insurance in the late sixteenth and early seventeenth century: the ship *Pisana e Mazza*, as its name suggests, was jointly owned by the Jewish Mazza family and the Venetian Pisani. Significantly, the Jewish name appears on equal footing with the Christian. Abraham Lass appears as *patron* of a ship sailing to Zante in 1601; and Adam Arens is mentioned as patron of another ship, called 'The King David' (*Re Davit*), chartered to sail

---

[26] *Ibid.*, busta 8250/II, f. 44.

[27] *Ibid.*, busta 8250/III, ff. 33v-34v. In a statement of 25 May 1563, it appears that the vendor, Nicolo di Elia Pastrovich, owned half this vessel, *ibid.*, ff. 48-48v.

[28] For Saruq's ownership of three *brigantini* in 1567, see above, p. 126.

[29] For his partnership in the *Mazzona*, see above, p. 128. The ship *Mazzona* was reported in 1567 as transporting alum from Phocaea (Foglie nuove) in western Anatolia to Venice; see ASV, Sen Delib. CP, reg. 3, f. 95v (5 Sept. 1567).

[30] G. Veinstein, "Une communauté ottomane: les Juifs d'Avlonya (Valona) dans la deuxième moitié du XVIe siècle", in *Gli Ebrei e Venezia, secoli XIV-XVIII*, ed. G. Cozzi, Milan, 1987, p. 800

[31] Paci, *La 'scala' di Spalato*, p. 89.

to Cyprus in 1608.[32] Rabbi Manuel Habibi, was both owner and captain
of the *Habiba*, which sailed from Constantinople to Venice in 1592.[33]
The *Responsa* of Rabbi Samuel de Medina (d. 1589) mention a ship
owned by Jews which was attacked on its route from Patras to Venice
by Maltese corsairs.[34] It is also interesting to find Jewish shipowners
of Portuguese descent, such as the Rodrigo, active in the kingdom of
Fez. A ship they owned was on its way to Venice in 1592, loaded with
a large quantity of sugar.[35]

The Jews of Venetian Corfu were probably among the earliest
pioneers in this sector. The Cretan Rabbi Elijah Capsali (c. 1483-1555)
mentions in one of his texts a case which had come up before a rabbinical court in 1530, concerning one Daniel of Corfu, son of Shamo,
who was captured by Rhodian corsairs when he was a clerk on a ship
owned by Joseph Nahum.[36] This case is of special interest, not only
because Corfiote Jews were Venetian subjects (though with distinct
privileges), but also because it took place some eleven years before
the establishment of the *Levantini* Jewish merchants in Venice.

It should be remembered that Jewish merchants such as Hayyim
Saruq, though Ottoman subjects, lived for many years in Venice. The
appearance of Jewish shipowners in the midst of Venetian society is
highly significant, considering the traditional association between the
maritime trade and the upper strata of Venetian society. It is true that
in the sixteenth century the Venetian patriciate was less dominant in
this area,[37] but the penetration of Jews living in Venice into what
had previously been the very essence of Venetian prosperity is of no
small consequence.

In 1589, when the Venetian Senate granted a charter to the Jewish
merchants, described as *"Levantini, Spagnoli et altri"*, it stated that
they were allowed "to navigate freely as the Levantine visiting merchants

[32] Tenenti, *Naufrages, corsaires et assurance maritime*, pp. 187 (1596), 305 (1601),
521 (1608). *Cf.* Blumenkranz, "Les Juifs dans le commerce maritime de Venise",
p. 148.

[33] Brulez, *Marchands flamands à Venise*, Nos 340, 342.

[34] Rozen, "Strangers in a Strange Land", p. 136.

[35] Maestro, *L'attività economica*, p. 37.

[36] Rabbi Elijah Capsali, *Beauty and Bands*, ed. M. Benayahu, Tel Aviv, 1990
[Hebrew], p. 19.

[37] U. Tucci, "The Psychology of the Venetian Merchants in the Sixteenth Century",
in *Renaissance Venice*, ed. J. R. Hale, London, 1973, pp. 346-378.

presently do" (*navigar liberamente come fanno al presente li ebrei levantini viandanti*).[38] Did this phrasing denote only the exercise of foreign trade, or did it also signify that the Jews were allowed to own ships, as one historian argued?[39] Even if the former interpreted (to which I incline) is the correct one, the wording of the charter implicitly covered ship-owning, since by that time Levantine merchants were actually operating their own ships.[40]

A systematic search through the Venetian sources for Jewish shipowners is yet to be done. Since we are obliged to rely in this matter chiefly on published material, we have to move on to the late seventeenth century to discover more Jewish shipowners in Venice. A memorandum submitted in 1694 by the Venetian Board of Trade to the Senate, lists five big ships owned by Jews: 'The Merchant of Egypt' (*Mercante d'Egitto*), owned by Aaron Volterra; the 'Judith' (*Giuditta*), owned by Aaron Uziel; the 'Hope & Good Fortune' (*Speranza Bonaventura*), also owned by Volterra; the 'Abraham's Sacrifice' (*Sacrificio d'Abram*), owned by the Perera family; and 'The Merchant of Portugal' (*Mercante di Portogallo*), also owned by Aaron Uziel. Another list, undated but probably from January 1699, indicates that 12 out of the 69 biggest ships of the Venetian merchant navy of the day were owned by Jews. The number of Jewish shipowners was actually smaller, with three ships belonging to Aaron Uziel and three to Aaron Volterra.[41] But these lists only show the situation at two moments and cannot be considered exhaustive. For example, Roth mentions another Jewish shipowner, Abraham Franco, who during the same period supposedly owned no less than six ships.[42] Some of these ships bore names which seem typically Jewish, at least in Venice, where ship names usually

---

[38] Ravid, "The First Charter", p. 220. The Senate did not adopt the phrasing included in Daniel Rodriga's petition, which was at the basis of this legislation, stating that the Jewish settlers would be able to "navigate freely like Venetian citizens", *ibid.*, p. 215.

[39] Paci, *La 'scala' di Spalato*, p. 39.

[40] "Navegare liberamente" should be translated "freely ship [merchandise]". See, for instance Sanuto, *I diarii*, vol. 36, col. 239, citing a Senate's enactment of 1524 using this expression ("navegar ... mercantie") to denote the shipping of merchandise.

[41] G. Luzzatto, "Armatori ebrei a Venezia negli ultimi 250 anni della Repubblica", *La Rassegna Mensile di Israel. Scritti in Memoria di Federico Luzzatto*, Rome, 1962, p. 163.

[42] Roth, *Venice*, p. 178.

bore the family name of the principal owners, names of saints, or expressions of good fortune. To the ship names already mentioned we may add 'The Beautiful Esther' (*La Bella Ester*), 'The Prophet Daniel' (*Profeta Daniel*), and 'The Prophet Jonah' (*Profeta Giona*).[43] It is significant that Jews did not hesitate to give their ships names which exposed their owners' Jewish identity, especially by comparison with the manner of Jewish involvement in this area during the Middle Ages.[44]

The seventeenth-century lists of ships published by Luzzatto also show that although the relative presence of Jewish commercial shipping in Venice was impressive, the actual number of Jews involved was quite small. What is also striking is the fact that these ships were considered at this stage to be Venetian. This was clearly the result of the later renewals of the 1589 charter, in which the Jewish merchants were treated not as Ottoman but as Venetian subjects (though officially on a temporary basis). Were Ottoman Jews at this stage still engaged in commercial shipping? This remains to be investigated. At any rate, even in Venice we have no evidence of continued activity in this field between the years treated in this book and the latter half of the seventeenth century, to which Luzzatto's data pertain. The crisis which Venetian commercial shipping underwent in the early seventeenth century probably affected Jewish shipping too.[45] It did not, however, result in the disappearance of Jewish shipowners from the Mediterranean.

Beginning in the late sixteenth century, Livorno was another centre of Jewish shipping. In the 1540s the Grand Dukes of Tuscany adopted

[43] Luzzatto, "Armatori ebrei", *loc. cit.* Apparently, some Jewish shipowners chose more ambiguous ship names, such as the 'The Merchant of Portugal' (*Mercante di Portogallo*), which discreetly referred to its owner Aaron Uziel, a Jew of Portuguese descent who, according to Roth, had obtained in 1686 a license to trade with East and West: Roth, *Venice*, p. 177.

[44] This custom of calling ships by typically Jewish names is also found in seventeenth and early eighteenth-century London and the Caribbean, as well as in eighteenth-century Algiers, where we find ships named 'The Prophet Samuel', 'Isaac', 'Queen Hester', 'Beautiful Sarah', 'Rachel', 'Abraham', 'King Solomon' etc.; *cf.* W.S.S., "Anglo-Jewish Ships' Names", *The Jewish Historical Society of England. Miscellanies*, Part III (1937), pp. 103-105; Tolkovsky, *Jewish Seamen*, pp. 111-112.

[45] On the difficulties of Venetian shipping in the seventeenth century, see F.C. Lane, "Venetian Shipping During the Commercial Revolution", *op. cit.*; Tenenti, *Piracy and the Decline of Venice*, pp. 89-109.

a policy of attracting Jewish entrepreneurs to this city, which was destined to become one of the principle ports of the Mediterranean world. A series of measures, culminating in the famous *Livornina*, granted Jewish settlers tax exemptions, judicial amnesty, the right to bear arms, and last but not least, protection from the harassments of the Inquisition.[46] Florentine documents from as early as the second half of the sixteenth century mention Jewish shipowners based in Livorno.[47] It is likely that they moved their base of operations from one centre to another to meet the changing economic circumstances.[48] During the seventeenth and eighteenth centuries the Jews of Livorno spread their business connections over the entire Mediterranean world.[49]

The appearance of Jews as *patroni* of some of the named vessels raises the question whether Jews were also professional seamen. But references to Jewish seamen are even scarcer than to shipowners, though one does occasionally encounter these rare creatures in fifteenth and sixteenth-century documents. A Jew of Trapani, Bracha Chasen [*sic*], is mentioned in a notarial document as a mariner in 1440.[50] The famous pirate Sinan, who was active in the Mediterranean in the 1520s and 1530s, and later served Sultan Süleyman in prominent positions, was reputed to have been originally a Jew from Izmir.[51] In Venetian sources of the 1530 he is repeatedly referred to as 'The Jew'.[52] To

---

[46] R. Toaff, *La nazione ebrea a Livorno e Pisa (1591-1700)*, Florence, 1990, pp. 419-35.

[47] F. Braudel and R. Romano, *Navires et cargaisons à l'entrée du port de Livourne, 1547-1611*, Paris, 1951, p. 26, n. 83.

[48] For some examples, including Jewish migration from Venice to Livorno from 1645, see J. Israel, *European Jewry in the Age of Mercantilism*, pp. 49, 66, 114.

[49] A. Milano, *Storia degli ebrei italiani nel Levante*, Florence, 1949, pp. 169-74; S. S. Schwarzfuchs, "La 'Nazione Ebrea' livournaise au Levant", *La Ressegna Mensile di Israel*, ser. III, 50 (1984), pp. 707-724; N. Svoronos, *Le commerce de Salonique au XVIIIe siècle*, Paris, 1956, p. 191; M. Rozen, "Contest and Rivalry in Mediterranean Maritime Commerce in the First Half of the Eighteenth Century: The Jews of Salonica and the European Presence", *Revue des Etudes Juives*, vol. 147 (1988), pp. 309-552.

[50] Ashtor, "The Jews of Trapani", p. 17.

[51] Tolkovsky, *Jewish Seamen*, pp. 101-112.

[52] *E.g.* Sanuto, *I diarii*, vol. 56, cols. 48, 102-3, 122, 179, 181, 208, 236, 238-9, 295, 318, 583, 811 (Mar.-July 1532); *ibid.*, vol. 58, cols. 57, 83, 88, 137, 220, 225, 279, 370-1, 420, 450, 478, 507, 514, 527-8, 578, 585-6, 602, 656-7, 666, 670, 700, 710, 724 (Apr.-Sept. 1533). See also Jones, *Venice and the Porte*, pp. 12-18.

these we may add the above-mentioned Manuel Habibi. But in contrast
to the rise of Jewish entrepreneurs as owners and operators of commercial vessels, Jewish professional seamanship was less significant during
the early modern period. This occupation involved relatively lower
social strata, and among such Jews, the weight of religious tradition
of the family and community, and the restrictions on manual labour
during Saturdays and holy days must have been more effective than
among the affluent entrepreneurs. It should be noted, however, that
it is very difficult to identify the ethnic origin of professional seamen
in the relevant sources.[53]

***

The short passage from the first act of 'The Jew of Malta' by Christopher Marlowe (1564-93), quoted at the beginning of this chapter, seems
to be the earliest depiction of a Jewish shipowner in modern literature.
Barabas of Malta, the rich Jew who sends his ships across the Mediterranean, is no doubt a literary invention, but at the time when this play
was written and was enjoying great success on the English stage, the
figure of the Jewish shipowner was taking on flesh in the Mediterranean
world. The social significance of the appearance of Jewish shipowners
in the early modern Mediterranean is greater than its relative weight
in the world of shipping. Firstly, because a ship is by its very nature
not tied to a particular locality—once launched, and as long as it remains
afloat, it not only transports goods and people, but also proclaims its
identity and that of its owners on a wide geographical scale. When

---

[53] The rules (*Takkanot*) of the Jewish community of Candia (Crete), which record
the communal legislation between the thirteenth and the sixteenth centuries, mentioned
that many members of the congregation avoided the Synagogue on the Sabbath and
holy days, preferring to promenade through the gardens and orchards, or to go "to
the ships" at the seashore (אל חוף הימים אל אניות אבה). The same rule returns
to the subject by forbidding the local Jews to go on holidays to the "shore where the
ships were anchored" (לא ללכת אל חוף האניות); see *Statuta iudaeorum Candia*,
pp. 9-10. Apparently, the Jews preferred to spend their free days looking at the ships
anchored off the coast. The interpretation of this rule as if it referred to "boating"
is therefore erroneous; *cf.* S. Freehof, "A Brief History", in *Encyclopedia of Jews
in Sport*, eds. B. Postal, J. Silver and R. Silver, New York, 1965, p. 8, cited in A.
Hanak, *Physical Education of Jews in the Middle Ages and Early Modern Times*, Tel
Aviv, 1987, p. 6.

this phenomenon ceased to be sporadic and became a more or less permanent feature, it reflected a change in the status of Jews, both within the relevant societies and in the international arena of the maritime trade. No doubt there were ups and downs in this development. Thus, between the Venetian records of the late sixteenth century and those of the late seventeenth there seem to have been periods in which there were no Jewish shipowners around. When Rabbi Simḥa Luzzatto wrote his famous treatise on the Jews of Venice in 1632 he noted that unlike Hamburg, Amsterdam or Rotterdam, there were no Jewish shipowners in his city. His assertion not only indicates that, for some reason, Jewish shipowners disappeared for a while from the Venetian scene; it also suggests that the phenomenon did not vanish, but had moved to places where Jews were in the forefront of economic development. The phenomenon apparently gained momentum from the late seventeenth century on, not only in Venice—where the Treves family, for instance, was a leading shipping firm in the eighteenth century, trading between Venice and America—but also in Trieste, Livorno, Algiers, Tunis, Hamburg, Amsterdam and London, as well as in the New World.[54] During the nineteenth century, a few shipping firms controlled by Jewish entrepreneurs, such as the 'Lloyd Austriaco' or the 'Hamburg-America Line', were leaders in the field.

In the period of commercial capitalism there was a strong link between the domination of trade and the control of commercial shipping. Those who succeeded in combining the two often came to dominate their respective economies. In the pre-industrial era, the rise or decline of a nation's merchant navy was a clear indication of its general prosperity or decline. For the Jews, involvement in this field was conditioned by social, political, economic and cultural transformation, both within Jewish society and in the surrounding environment. Such transformations did not take place in the Middle Ages. A combination of circumstances at the beginning of the modern era in the eastern Mediterranean made some modest beginnings possible. The relative economic freedom enjoyed by Jewish entrepreneurs who were subjects of the Ottoman

---

[54] *E.g.* Rozen, "La vie économique", p. 339 and n. 549; M.J.M. Haddey, *Le livre d'or des Israélites algériens*, Algiers, 1872, esp. pp. 33, 53-56, 67-70; W.S.S., "Anglo-Jewish Ships' Names", pp. 103-105; S.A. Fortune, *Merchants and Jews. The Struggle for British West India Commerce, 1650-1750*, Gainesville, FA, 1984, pp. 131, 146, 148.

Sultan, the dependence of the Ottoman Empire on external elements in international shipping, and the inability of those elements to provide their services on a constant basis, opened the door to Jewish involvement. The influx of Jewish migrants from Spain and Portugal, some of them with the capital and the administrative know-how for shipping operations, combined with the weakening hold of commercial shipping by those who had dominated this field in the past, finally caused a shift in the policy of several Christian states towards Jewish involvement in their own maritime trade. This seems to have formed the basis of a phenomenon which spread to northern Europe and, following the European expansion, to other parts of the globe in later centuries. It is not surprising that the societies which were involved in maritime trade, and which allowed Jews to participate in the field of shipping, were also those in which the general position of Jews was relatively better than in others.

CONCLUSION

The rise of Jewish entrepreneurs to prominent positions in various parts of the Ottoman Empire produced a complex of relationships with Venetian businessmen and with Venice as a state. In the Ottoman provinces of Syria and Egypt, for example, the main problem for the Venetians consisted of the need to deal with local Jewish middlemen in commercial transactions and Jewish customs collectors in the key positions of the maritime trade. A similar situation obtained in Istanbul and the Balkans, but there the Jewish entrepreneurs were also active in international commerce itself, as merchants, as organizers of large commercial and financial networks, as 'consuls', and as shipowners, and had actually become, in a short space of time, the leading actors in the commercial intercourse between Venice and the European parts of the Ottoman Empire. The official invitation extended by Venice in 1541 to the *Levantini* merchants was a direct consequence of their powerful position in this sphere.

Such figures as the two Abraham Castros, Solomon Ashkenazi and Hayyim Saruq might have been exceptional in various ways. But beyond their individual histories, which are highly instructive in themselves, each of them illuminates a broader area. Their disparate relations with Venice enable us to examine Ottoman policies and Venetian attitudes as they developed in the course of the difficult new relationship between Venice and the Jewish merchants of the eastern Mediterranean. They also shed light on the *modus operandi* of the rising Jewish merchants in the early modern period. We should remember that Saruq and the Castros were hardly known in the annals of history until very recently, and that they were certainly not isolated figures in their respective fields. Their various achievements and the patterns of their behaviour can be considered characteristic of their time and place. The two Abraham Castros exemplify in their respective careers the central role played by Jewish customs officials in the sixteenth-century Levant, and the dependence of Venice's maritime trade depended on those figures. Solomon Ashkenazi's rise in Istanbul, and his involvement in the Ottoman relations with Venice, represent not only the important role of this Jewish physician in the Ottoman court and its politics, but also the way that it was used to further the private and public interests of Jewish entrepreneurs. Ashkenazi's activities demonstrate the connection between three issues which preoccupied Venice at the time: her relations with the Ottomans, her trade with the East and the presence of Jews in Venice and her dominions.

Hayyim Saruq's story, which has been uncovered in detail for the first time here, reveals the ample possibilities open in his time to Jewish entrepreneurs in the eastern Mediterranean. Established as a young man in Venice, probably with some initial capital brought over from Salonica, Saruq became part of a great commercial network which was apparently controlled by the Segura family in Istanbul. With his remarkable ability to overcome great difficulties, a marked tendency to litigation (often resolved through arbitration), true capitalistic spirit and evidently also talent, Saruq seems to have become at a relatively early age a central figure among the *Levantini* in Venice. His long residence in Venice, where he also had family, is significant in view of the legal restrictions, and underlines the attraction of Venice for Jewish entrepreneurs of his kind.

Saruq's activities also demonstrate the openness of the economic world in the sixteenth century. His business relations with the Segura of Istanbul represent the link between capital invested in international trade and capital invested in the farming of Ottoman state revenues. Venice's growth into a major industrial centre during the sixteenth century was greatly dependent on this connection, both for the supply of raw materials from the East and for marketing Venetian products, such as cloth and glass, in Istanbul and other Ottoman territories. Saruq's involvement in the shipbuilding industry in Venice's Dalmatian colonies, or in the credit to the French crown, through the *Grand Parti* of Lyons, also illustrates the interdependence of the various economies in that age. The impressive amount of capital involved in Saruq's transactions indicates the scale of these trading activities, but presumably he was not a unique case, neither in the pattern of his trading activities, nor in the amount of capital involved. The actual number of Levantine Jewish merchants and entrepreneurs must have been quite small, constituting a small percentage of their original communities in the Ottoman Empire, but their place in the economy of the sixteenth-century eastern Mediterranean seems to have been considerable.

The long crisis which arose from Saruq's bankruptcy is also revealing of Venetian official attitudes. It is interesting to see how a Jewish merchant, a subject of the Sultan living in Venice, was treated by the Signory. Throughout the affair, from 1566 to 1573, Venice seemed to be protecting Saruq from his brethren in Istanbul, who used their connections at the Porte to further their interests, even if it meant creating a grave diplomatic crisis. But Venice was not really defending Saruq but a principle, namely, that commercial affairs had to be settled by ordinary courts, and that the Republic's representatives abroad were not to be molested on account of the debts of private subjects (in this case not even a Venetian subject!). Even when forced to compromise on this principle, the Signory made a determined effort to ensure that no new principles of public conduct were established.

The place of the *Marranos* in Venice's trade with the East has been barely touched on in this book. Occasional passages in notarial and Inquisition documents refer to Saruq's business dealings with persons belonging to that group. A noteworthy testimony made in 1572 before the court of the Venetian Inquisition, stated that the 300 *Marrano* families that had settled in Venice following their expulsion from the Low Countries in 1549, possessed between them capital valued at over four millions in gold.[1] A part of this capital, at least, must have been invested, directly or indirectly, in the trade between Venice and the Ottoman East.[2]

***

The foregoing chapters have also demonstrated, if further proof was needed, the importance of Venetian documentation for the study of Levantine affairs in general and of Levantine Jews in particular. Venetian source material is not only very rich, it also covers areas which Jewish or Ottoman sources hardly touch on at all. It allowed us, for example, to solve the puzzle of Castro's double identity and to see through the flattering formulas to the rather different picture of these Levantine customs collectors. Similarly, the detailed reconstruction of the discussions in the *Divan*, including the behaviour of the participants, found in the dispatches of the Venetian *Bailo*, offer a unique glimpse behind the façade of official documentation. Venetian notarial documents have

---

[1] Pullan, *The Jews of Europe*, p. 175.

[2] For allegations regarding illicit involvement of *Marranos* in Venice's Levant trade, see Pullan, *The Jews of Europe*, p. 178.

no equal either. Judicial records, though not unique, and patchy for the period examined here, contribute greatly by filling in the areas uncovered by the Ottoman judicial records and Jewish *responsa*. Thus the importance of Istanbul as a centre of Jewish international business, and particularly of the trade between Venice and the Ottoman Empire, as shown in various parts of this book, is hardly reflected in the *responsa* literature. The same may be said of the advent of Jewish shipowning.[3] Exclusive reliance on the *responsa* can also be very misleading, in that they create the false impression that the rabbinical courts and rabbinical authority controlled Jewish economic activity. The repeated prohibitions issued by various rabbis during that period against recourse to *'arka'ot shel goyyim* (gentile courts of law) suggest that the practice was threatening their authority.[4] Ottoman judicial records may contain relevant material, but I know of no study derived from Ottoman judicial archives which produced material pertaining to the rise of Jews in international trade on similar scale as this work.

***

About twenty years ago, Ugo Tucci, an important economic historian of Venice, published an article about the commercial milieu of sixteenth-century Venice, in which he argued that "only the Jews remained excluded from this great consortium of merchants from every nation," and that Jews were "not allowed to trade with the Levant, but had to make use of a Venetian intermediary."[3] He went on to state that:

---

[3] I am grateful to Prof. Minna Rozen for checking this point in the *responsa* material.

[4] For rabbinical prohibitions to have recourse to courts of Gentiles, see Shmuelevitz, *The Jews of the Ottoman Empire*, pp. 68-73. For the frequent recourse of Jews to Ottoman courts, see, for instance, Veinstein, "Une communauté ottomane" *op. cit.*; For the potential and limitations of the *responsa literature* as historical sources, see D. Weinrib, "Problems in the Research of the History of the Jews in Palestine", *Zion*, new series, 2 (1937), pp. 189-215; 3 (1938), pp. 58-83 [Hebrew]; Shmuelevitz, *The Jews of the Ottoman Empire*, pp. 2-9; H. Soloveitchik, *The Use of Responsa as Historical Source*, Jerusalem, 1990 [Hebrew]. For the particular problems regarding trade, Baron, *Social and Religious History*, vol. 18, pp. 235-36.

[3] U. Tucci, "The Psychology of the Venetian Merchant", pp. 365-66. This assertion hardly explains the same historian's observation that in 1580, the Cinque Savi had recognized the benefit and great utility to the customs receipts which ensued from Jewish commerce. Tucci had nothing to say about the development which made such a declaration possible.

...the tolerance from which they benefited at certain moments never weakened the notion, universally felt, of the difference in function and spirit which characterized the Jewish and the Christian ways of doing business, a constitutional difference which was thought to draw the lower aspects of the profession to the one, and to the other modes of behaviour which ennobled it; like Shylock and Antonio in Shakespeare's play, because of the different conception of the activity each pursues, the Jewish merchant and the Venetian, even though breathed the same air they belonged to two worlds which could never meet...[4]

How do these statements stand in the light of the foregoing data? A great part of our discussion concerned the years around the Cyprus war, which was obviously not a 'normal' one in the relations between Venetian society and the Jews. But it is precisely at such times that the deeper attitudes and sentiments, which might be hidden or suppressed in peacetime, surface and are exposed in broad daylight. The Venetian state was ruled by a mercantile oligarchy guided by pragmatic considerations. But Venice was also a Christian state and society, imbued with all the prejudices and psychological and religious weaknesses which were largely directed against the Jews, whenever the occasion arose to express them, especially in relation to the sensitive subject of Venice's role in the world of international trade. The need to deal with at almost every stage of their trading activities in or with the East, accompanied by the repetitive incidents and clashes of interests, inspired anti-Jewish moves when the tension with the Ottoman Empire intensified. Tucci's view, attributing to the Venetians a hostile attitude to Jewish merchants based on 'natural' or 'constitutional' differences, may indeed be a true reflection of the attitude of many Venetians during those years. But in spite of the basic anti-Jewish religious feelings, pragmatic considerations gave rise to practical or economic tolerance. Once convinced that the Jewish traders could not be set aside, and that their stay in Venice could benefit Venetian economy, the Republic followed the maxim 'If you can't beat them, join them.'

This does not mean that the Venetians of that period became philo-Semites. The decision to invite Jewish traders to Venice, and their subsequent integration into the Venetian trading system, occurred during one of the most difficult years of Venetian-Jewish relations, and cannot

---

[4] *Ibid.*.

therefore not be construed as evidence of religious tolerance. The practical tolerance of Jews was imposed on Venice by economic considerations, which proved, in the long run, to be stronger than the traditional religious attitudes, though without changing them in a significant way. If a change of attitude did occur, it followed (only in the chronological sense) the rise of Jews to economic prominence, not the other way round. And if religious tolerance played any part at all, it did so in the Ottoman court of Istanbul, not in sixteenth-century Venice. We must keep in mind that the Jewish merchants who were invited to Venice in 1541 and 1589 were never accepted as full members of Venetian society. Their charters insisted on segregation, on distinctive dress, on the limitation to a fixed period subject to periodical renewals, and on other restrictions. But even if economic tolerance was not necessarily the product of religious tolerance, the opposite process—*i.e.*, religious intolerance infringing upon practical concerns—was possible during periods of great tension, as demonstrated in the period around the Cyprus war.

All that being said, and notwithstanding the Venetian policy of segregation and the separatist tendencies of Jewish society, Tucci's assertion that Jewish merchants and the Venetian and other Christian merchants, though breathing the same air, belonged to "two worlds which could never meet," is greatly exaggerated. Likewise, the notion of a "difference in function and spirit" between Jewish traders and Christian ones, and the distinction between two different "ways of doing business" has little base in historical reality. In fact, to Shylock's famous series of rhetorical questions: "Hath not a Jew eyes? Has not a Jew hands, organs, etc.",[5] one might add, in a similar spirit, another question, more specific to the trading milieu: Were not the trading practices of the Jewish merchant much the same as those of the Christian? If Tucci's description reflects the real attitudes of sixteenth-century Venetians, one must look for them in the realm of Christian tradition, and imagination rather than in the practice of Jewish trade. It was widely accepted among Jews that international trade was ruled by international practices, and could not always be subject to Jewish religious law.[6] We have seen that Jews frequently resorted to Venetian courts of law to settle disputes between them; engaged non-Jews to arbitrate their

---

[5] W. Shakespeare, "The Merchant of Venice", Act III, Scene 1.

[6] Shmuelevitz, *The Jews of the Ottoman Empire*, p. 129.

disputes; used the same financial and commercial instruments as Western merchants; were involved in shipping and public finance. All of which demonstrates that Venetians and Jews operated in the same way, had a common language of communication, and were in constant contact, both on Venetian soil and abroad. A figure such as Saruq is unimaginable without his Venetian, Florentine, Ferrarese and Dalmatian business associates. The Jewish merchants in Venice spent the great part of their day outside the Ghetto, in their warehouses at Rialto, at the Rialto banks, in the offices of the Venetian state, on board Venetian vessels, and in all likelihood (though I can offer no evidence) in the homes of Venetian citizens and patricians. This last seems very plausible in view of presence of the *Marranos*, which blurred to some extent the strong link with Jewish religion, and enabled members of this 'modern' cosmopolitan group to feel at home among Jews and Christians alike.[7] Even inside the Ghetto contacts with non-Jews were not infrequent, as the cases of Hayyim Saruq and David Passi show. The basic nature of international trade is contact between different 'worlds'. This contact can of course assume an external or even hostile nature, as demonstrated in this book. But the necessity inherent in the practice of commerce, to be in constant contact with others of the same occupation makes it a word of intercultural exchange.

***

Yosef Kaplan and Jonathan Israel have each recently illuminated certain aspects of Jewish economic activity in the early Modern period. Kaplan has focused on the Iberian Jewish Diaspora of north-western Europe in the seventeenth century. He argues that the relative ease of movement between the Jewish and the Christian worlds, which characterized the entrepreneurial group of Spanish and especially Portuguese Jews and *Conversos*, weakened their reliance on Jewish religious percepts in the economic sphere. He contends that this was one factor in the 'path' of this group towards modernity.[8] According to Israel, western and

---

[7] Pullan, *The Jews of Europe*, pp. 176-177.

[8] Y. Kaplan, "The Portuguese Community of Amsterdam in the Seventeenth Century", in *Proceedings of the Israel Academy of Sciences*, vol. 7/6 (1986), pp. 177-79 [Hebrew]; *idem*, "The Path of Western Sephardi Jewry to Modernity", *Pe'amim*, 48 (1991), p. 96 [Hebrew].

central European Jewry underwent structural changes in the economic sphere which radically transformed Jewish life and its place in Western society. As he sees it, the turning point was about 1570, a historical moment which was characterized, among other things, by a general change to a more pragmatic Christian attitude to the Jewish presence, partly as an outcome of post-Reformation and post Counter-Reformation intellectual trends. As a result, not only did Jewish communities resettle in areas from which they had been previously expelled, but they also became more directly and significantly involved in the world of international trade and finance.[9] Israel notes that in Ottoman and Mediterranean societies, these new trends could be discerned earlier in the sixteenth century.[10]

Indeed, in the eastern Mediterranean the shift in the patterns of Jewish economic activity can be perceived somewhat earlier than elsewhere, thanks to the favourable conditions offered by the Ottoman regime. The ambiguous religious identity of the *Conversos*, or the *Marranos*, was less significant here, though it was still meaningful in Italy, which was an essential part of Jewish international economy in the Mediterranean. But here, too, recourse to *Halakha* and rabbinical authority, though not abandoned, was often dispensed with. We have noted that the rabbis were forced to àcknowledge the commercial practices which were not ruled by Jewish Law, and which no serious Jewish entrepreneur could circumvent. The case of Hayyim Saruq is noteworthy in this respect. Other than the 1565 agreement, which was undersigned by three *Dayyanim*, and his recourse to the rabbinical authority of Samuel de Medina in the case of the reduction obtained by him on customs duties, the rest of Hayyim Saruq's transactions and disputes which have been uncovered, including those with other Jews, were handled before non-Jewish notaries and courts, or before bodies of arbitrators composed of both Jews and non-Jews. One may, of course, argue that this impression is affected by the source material which has been used for this work, which could cause a certain bias. I can only retort by stating that the sheer quantity of similar material concerning a great many

---

[9] Israel, *European Jewry in the Age of Mercantilism*, pp. 35-52; *idem*, "The Contribution of Spanish Jewry to the Economic Life and Colonization in Europe and the New World", in *The Heritage of Sepharad*, Jerusalem, 1992, pp. 664-65 [Hebrew].

[10] Israel, *European Jewry in the Age of Mercantilism*, pp. 33-34.

merchants, only a tiny part of which has been exposed here, is sufficient evidence for these tendencies. In the sixteenth-century eastern Mediterranean Jews again became a trading nation, not merely as peddlers and small tradesmen, or as merchants accompanying their goods in a trading venture, but on the higher level of international economy as it developed in late medieval and early modern Europe and the Mediterranean world. Changes similar to those which have been described as characterizing certain entrepreneurial groups of northern Europe in the following century, developed somewhat earlier among their counterparts in the Mediterranean world.

***

The spectacular rise of Jewish merchants in the eastern Mediterranean in the sixteenth century was not an irreversible process. It depended on the attitude of Ottoman rulers, who during the 'classical age' of Ottoman history were relatively tolerant, and even encouraged Jewish involvement in the highest echelons of the Empire's economic life. Because of the weight of the Ottoman Empire in the economy of the 'greater Mediterranean', the rise of the Jewish merchants in the East also influenced their role in other parts of the Mediterranean world, particularly in Italy. However, any change in this favourable Ottoman attitude could jeopardize the conditions which had made Jewish economic advance possible. Indeed, in Syria and Egypt during the seventeenth and eighteenth centuries other minority groups, such as Syrian Christians and Armenians, took the lead in areas which had previously been largely in the hands of Jews, such as the administration of customs in the Ottoman Levant.[11] In Istanbul and the Balkans, it was mainly Greek, Serbian and other Orthodox merchants who took the lead in the sphere of commerce.[12] In seventeenth-century Izmir, the rising commercial centre in the Ottoman Empire, Armenians and Westerners dominated international trade, while Jewish activity remained essentially local,

---

[11] Gibb and Bowen, *Islamic Society and the West*, vol. 1, pp. 310-312; In early seventeenth-century Izmir Jewish customs collectors were still dominant: D. Goffman, *Izmir and the Levantine World, 1550-1650*, Seattle and London, 1990, pp. 86-90.

[12] T. Stoianovich, "The Conquering Balkan Orthodox Merchants", *The Journal of Economic History*, 20 (1960), pp. 234-313.

i.e., as customs collectors, middlemen, factors and translators.[13] So it was mainly in central and north-western Europe, as well as in the colonial world, that the process described above continued through 'the age of mercantilism'. There was no reason to expect that Jews would remain prominent in international trade and finance for many centuries, or even decades, in the same region. It is therefore important to note that from the sixteenth century on, the phenomenon did not disappear from the Mediterranean and the western hemisphere, but rather shifted from one region to another, often as a result of the migration of the same Jewish entrepreneurs from one commercial centre to another.

About half a century after the establishment of the Ghetto Vecchio, while Jews became increasingly prominent in international commerce and finance in other regions, in Venice itself circumstances were also changing. The general atmosphere was more lenient. The presence of Jewish merchants was becoming a normal feature of Venice's variegated urban scene. The *condotta* of 1589 is significant in this respect, recognizing the Jewish merchants as Venetian subjects, though formally only on a temporary basis. The *scala* of Spalato, largely based on Jewish mercantile activity, proved to be a success. Moreover, the Ottoman Empire was no more so menacing, and the Jews of Istanbul lost much of their capacity to use their influence at the Porte to gain support for their commercial strategies. All that brought to an end the difficult and stormy chapter treated in this book. In Venice, as in other Mediterranean centres, such as Livorno, Jewish entrepreneurs seem to have retained prominent positions in the Eastern trade, yet the perspective of their activities was gradually reversed. Rather than using their Ottoman identity as a lever for their mercantile operations, they increasingly used their position as subjects of Venice or of other Western States, such as Tuscany or France, in order to conquer markets in the East.[14]

---

[13] Goffman, *Izmir*, pp. 85-90.

[14] Milano, *Storia degli ebrei italiani nel Levante*, pp. 169-174; Schwarzfuchs, "La 'Nazione Ebrea' livournaise", *op.cit.*; M. Rozen, "Contest and Rivalry in Mediterranean Maritime Commerce in the First Half of the Eighteenth Century: The Jews of Salonika and the European Presence", *Revue des Etudes Juives*, 147 (1988), pp. 322-52; *idem*, "Strangers in a Strange Land", pp. 147-154.

APPENDIX

Note concerning the transcription: The original spelling has been preserved. Abbreviations have been extended and capitalization, punctuation and paragraphing, as well as accents and apostrophes, have been introduced when necessary.

I: The report of Giovanni Alvise Bembo, captain of the merchant galleys returning from Alexandria, presented in Venice on 19 February 1531

Relatio viri nobilis ser Ioannis Alovisii Bembo qui fuit capitaneus triremium Alexandriae

È statuito per leze, Serenissimo Principe, che tuti li capitanei de galie da mercado, facta la sua relation nelo Illustrissimo conseglio de pregadi, poner etiam quella in scriptis. Perhò io Zuanalvise Bembo, noviter venuto capitaneo dele galie de Alexandria, per non manchar dal debito mio brevemente ponerò in scriptis quel poco mi occorre.

Prima, cum ogni debito de reverentia, ricordo a Vostra Sublimità, che se mente è di quella, spirada che sia la muda le galie debano partir de Alexandria, faci de haver uno commandamento dal Serenissimo Signor Turco in bona forma, che le galie, spirada che sia la muda, et facti per marcadanti li sui conti, siano lassate liberamente uscir de porto. Item, che el comprar et vender sia libero. Altramente è in libertà de quelli sono al governo de Alexandria tenir dicte galie in porto ad suo beneplacito, né di quello si po uscir senza sua licentia, rispecto al farion, che è bellissima fortezza, et ben munido de artegliarie. Et come le galie intrano in quel porto, dir si po esser in una cortese pregione.

Delì in Alexandria si attrova un zudeo nominato Abraam Castro overo *male[m]*. Questo è inimico capital de la nation, el qual ha ad aficto dal Serenissimo Signor Turco, per quanto ho havuto relation, tuti li datii de Alexandria per ducati 85,000 all'anno, nel qual anno se comprehende una muda de galie che cargerà. Non cargando, è debitor solum de ducati 55,000. Questo zudeo, come giongeno le galie, et chel vede esser poche specie, ita che non possi trazer utilità, opera cum el Signor Bassa del Cayro, cum spender qualche ducato, et non pochi, chel dicto Signor Bassa non lassa né contractar, né trazer quelle poche spetie se attrova in tempo de muda, come el seguido l'anno presente, movendoli diversi garbugli cum danno grandissimo del Serenissimo Signor gran Turco, et ruina dele galie. Contra questo zudeo la Sublimità Vostra potrà far quella provision che alla sapientia di quella parerà.

El partir di questa terra, come el navegar di tuto el viazo, non mi extenderò altramente narrar a Vostra Sublimità, per esser cosa di poco momento. Alla gratia de laqual me ricommando.

Archivio di Stato, Venice, Collegio, Relazioni, B. 61-I, ff. 120v-121

II: The Senate's decision exempting goods originating from and destined to 'Upper and Lower Romania' from custom duties, and inviting the Levantine Jewish merchants to reside in Venice, 2 June, 1541

È ridotta la mercantia di questa nostra città a tal termine per haver preso il corso in altri loci per causa delli datii, eccessive spese et angarie imposteli, essendo massime molto più alleviata in alcuni loci, come ad ognuno è benissimo noto, che quasi si pol esser certi, che quella si habbi del tutto a deviare, a gravissimo danno si del publico, come delli privati habitanti in essa. Et essendo essa mercantia uno delli principal fondamenti di questa città, et havendo li progentitori nostri con summo studio invigilato sempre di mantenerla, et con diverse provision et ordeni di augumentarla, così al presente non è da differir più una presta et gagliarda provision, per dar modo a quelli che la conduceno in altri loci, la conduchino de qui, et a quelli la conduceno che la possino con maggior loro satisfattione condure per utile et beneficio che ne è, per conseguir si il publico come il particular interesse di ciascuno.

Però, l'anderà parte, che per auttorità di questo consiglio sii preso che tutte le robbe che de cetero serano condutte in questa città tratte della Romania alta et bassa, et che in quelle provintie nascono, non debbano pagar datio de sorte alcuna, cio è intrada, tre per cento, do per cento, messe in loco de decime, et mezi noli, ne alcuna altra gravezza, sichè tutte le sopraditte robbe siano tratte dalle doanne nostre senza pagamento alcuno, eccettuata però la giusta mercede delli ministri di esse doanne, secondo che per li Cinque savii nostri sopra la mercantia serà redutto et regulato, juxta la libertà a loro attributa dal conseglio nostro di X sotto dì XVI fevrer prossime passato. Et la presente provision habbi a durar per anni do prossimi, principiando dal giorno del prender di essa, eccettuando però grassa, vini et frumenti, et etiam tutte sorte di mercantie, che si traze della Soria, Azimia, Egitto et altri lochi, videlicet sede, specie, et altre mercantie che capitasseno de quì per via di quelle Romanie, le qual habbino a pagar secondo che al presente pagano.

Sia medesimamente preso, che tutte sorte de carisee et panni oltra fini et armentini di ponente non debbano pagar datio di sorte alcuna, ma siano alla medesima et istessa conditione che sono le robbe delle Romanie nominate, et assolte di datio, ut supra, et questo perchè ditta sorte pannina è molto deviata da questa città, lequal sono l'insconto de tutte mercantie che capitano della Romania alta et bassa sopraditta.

Siano obligati li conduttori di tutte le robbe, si extentate come non extentate, et così da mar come da terra, far le bollete et contralettere sue solite et ordinarie, si come fanno al presente. Et non le facendo, se intendino esser contrabando. Et siano mandati li quadri bollati alli loci soliti, si come al presente sono mandati. Et quelli delle doanne nostre a chi spetta tenir conto et nota particular di tutte le robbe sopraditte, siano obligati continuar come fanno al presente che pagano, et questo per information della Signoria nostra, acciò per l'avenir si possa veder il frutto della presente deliberation. Et sia obligato il Collegio nostro et li Cinque savii sopra la mercantia venir a questo conseglio uno mese inanti il finir delli anni do contenuti in la presente parte per far quelle deliberation circa ciò che parerà espediente per beneficio di questa cità.

Et perchè la vallonia è potissima causa di far condur tutte altre sorte de mercantie delle Romanie in Ancona et altri loci, respetto alli partidi che hanno li navilii per causa di esse vallonie, è ben conveniente accomodarle di tal sorte, che più volentieri li conduttori et patroni di esse le possino condur in questa città più presto che in loci alieni. Però, sia preso, che l'obligatione della piezaria, che al presente dano all'officio di Governatori nostri dell'intrate li conduttori et patroni di essa, li sia levata, et restino libere, sicome sono tutte altre sorte mercantie che sono condutte in questa città, restando però obligati li conduttori over patroni di quelle far le sue contralettere solite a Corfù, Zante et altri loci, juxta la parte sopra ciò disponente, sotto tutte quelle pene in essa parte contenute, delle qual pene non se li possi per alcun rettor o altro magistrato nostro far gratia, don, over remission alcuna, ma integramente exequir la parte prefata, sotto pena a essi rettori, o altri magistrati, de ducati trecento, da esserli tolta per cadaun patron del Arsenal, un terzo della qual sia di quel, o quelli patroni che farano la esecutione, un terzo dell'accusator, et l'altro terzo del Arsenal prefato. Et ogni gratia che fusse fatta se intendi de nium valor. Et siano obligati li datiari di tutte le terre nostre tenir particular et distinto conto del iusto peso di tutte le vallonie che entrerano in essa città, el qual conto debbino mostrar ad ogni rechiesta del datier nostro dell'insida, occiò che si possa veder quelli che defraudasseno ditto datio. Et trovando inganno, el datier habbi libertà di poterli far condannar, secondo che disponeno le lezze nostre, et ducato uno de più per mozo.

Et per liberar la mercantia da tante strussie et impedimenti che continuamente è gravata, si per far bolletini a molti et diversi officii, come per sequestri et intromissioni, però sii preso, che tutte sorte di mercantie che de cetero serano condutte in questa città, sia de che conditione esser si voglia, non possino esser sequestrate, ne intromesse per debito alcun, si publico come particular, inanti entrerano nelle doanne nostre, ne in esse doanne, ma siano libere et sicure dalli sopraditti impedimenti, et se intendano alla medema conditione che sono i danari di banco. Et li mercanti non siano astretti a far bolletini ad alcuno officio di Extraodinarii et Cantinelle.

Et perchè la maggior parte delle mercantie che vengono della Romania alta et bassa, per quanto si vede, è condutta et è in mano di hebrei mercadanti levantini viandanti, li quali, havendo supplicato alli Cinque savii nostri sopra la mercantia, che non havendo loco da poter stantiar in ghetto, per la strettezza sua, sicome per li prefati Cinque savii nostri sopa la mercantia è sta veduto, li sia provisto di stantia per l'allozar suo. Però sia preso, acciò che habbino maggior causa di venir con le mercantie sue in questa città a beneficio di quella, et haver loco dove allozar possino, chel sia per il collegio dato libertà a qual magistrato li parerà, che debbano veder di accommodar ditti hebrei mercadanti levantini viandanti in ghetto, et non li potendo allozar per la stretezza di quello, habbiano auttorità di allozarli in ghetto vecchio, come meglio li parerà, con quelli modi et ordeni che per il Collegio serano dati al predetto magistrato, restando però sempre ditti hebrei serrati et custoditi, si come sono al presente quelli del ghetto nuovo, non possendo etiam ditti mercadanti hebrei levantini viandanti far banco, strazarie, ne exercitio alcuno, salvo la sua simplice mercantia tantum. Et tutto quello che per quel magistrato a chi tal carrico serà commesso serà fatto, sia fermo et valido, come se fatto fusse per questo conseglio.

Et perchè della presente deliberation li datiari delli prediti datii et altri poleno pretender de esser interessati, però sia statuito che il Collegio, con intervento delli Cinque savii sopra la mercantia predetti, debba aldir li prediti datiari et altri, che havesseno interesse per poter poi venir a questo conseglio et deliberar quanto parerà convenirsi alla justitia et honestà.

[for]	+	80
[against]		1
[abstentions]		11

ASV, Senato, Mar, reg. 26, ff. 44v-46.

III: Agreement for the constitution of a partnership between Ḥayyim Saruq and Joseph di Segura, Venice, 18 Tishri 5325 (24 Sept. 1564)[15]

בה

להיות אשר הוצרך להעתיק שטר זה הכתוב למטה מעם השטר הראשון ב"ה לשלח העתק
הזה למקום אחר ולהניח פה גוף השטר העתקנו זה השטר אות באות תיבה בתיבה מעם
השטר הראשון וזהו העתקו.

בפנינו עדים חתומי[ם] מטה בא הנשא ונעלה כה"ר חיים ן סרוק יצ"ו ואמר לנו
הוו עלי עדים נאמנים וקנו ממני בקנין גמור במנא דכשר למקנייא ביה וכתבו בכל לשון
של זכות ויפוי כח וחתמו כדי להנתן ביד המעולה הה"ר יוסף די סיגורה בן האלוף והטפסר
כמה"ר אהרן יצ"ו להיות בידו לראיה ולזכות מחמת שאני מודה בפניכם הודאה גמורה

---

[15] *Calendar for 6,000 Years*, Founded by the Late A.A. Akavia. Tables and Introduction prepared by N. Fried, edited by D. Zakai, Jerusalem, 1976, p. 486.

כמודה לפני ב"ד חשוב ומקום המשפט בלב שלם ובנפש חפצה בלתי שום זכר אונס
כלל. איך מחברה אחת [א' מעל לכתוב] שיש לי עם ה"ר יוסף הנז[כר] שהיא לתשלום
ארבעה שנים רצופים נמנים מי"ח לתשרי שנת השב"ה הנני מתחייב שכל זמן משך החברה
הנז[כרת] לא יהיה לי רשות ולא אוכל לעשות חברה ולהשתתף עם שום אדם שבעולם
בעסק ובמשא ובמתן בליואנטי כל זמן משך חברתי עמו.

וכן הנני מתחייב עוד שלא לשלוח לשום מקום בתוגרמה לשום אדם בעולם שום
מין סחורה שימכרנה לי לשמי ולשלוח לי התמורה. באחריותי אמנם יהיה לי רשות לשלוח
לאחי כה"ר יצחק יצ"ו עד סכום ת"ק פרחים לחשבונו חולת אחי הנז[כר] מהכמות הנז[כרת]
לשום אדם אחר לא אוכל לשלוח כלל ועיקר ולא יהיה לי שום מין משא ומתן כי אם
מחשבון החברה הנז[כרת] אשר לי עם כה"ר יוסף הנז[כר] אם לא שיהיה ברשות ורצון
וסדר כה"ר יוסף הנזכר.

עוד אני מתחייב שלא להוציא שום מין סחורה בלתי פרעון המכס ר"ל שלא לעשות
קונטראבאנדו בשום אופן בעולם כל זמן משך החברה הזאת לא על ידי ולא על יד זולתי
כל הימים שנהיה בחברה אחת יחד לא אוכל לעשות הדבר הזה אם לא שיהיה ברשותו
ורצונו.

זאת ועוד הנני מתחייב של[א] להכנס ערב לשום אדם ושלא לעשות ערבות ממאה
פרחים ולמעלה לשום אדם בעולם לא ליהודי ולא לגוי ולא לשום אדם אם לא שאהיה
בטוח ומוחזק ומשכון בידי שאז אוכל לעשות ערבות כפי הבטחון שיש בידי, אכן בלתי
משכון והבטחה לא אוכל לעשות ערבות מק' פרחים ולמעלה.

ועוד הנני מתחייב שלא לקחת בעד שום אדם אחר בעולם שיש מין סחורה בהמתנה
אם לא שיהיה לחשבון אחי עד הסך הנז[כר].

ואת כל אלה ידי עשתה ופי ולבי שוים והנני מתחייב בשבועה חמורה על דעת המקום
ב"ה ועל דעת הנשבעים באמת בלי ערמה ותחבולה כלל לשמור ולעשות ככל הכתוב
לעיל ולהסתחר בכל מין סחורה שיזמין השי"ת לפני בכל עוז ותעצומות בלי התרשלות
כלל הכל לתועלת החברה הנז[כרת]. וכמו כן יהיה רשות לה"ר יוסף להסתחר בכל מין
סחורה שיראה לו ויוכל לשלוח איש או אנשים בכל מקום שיחפוץ להסתחר לתועלת
החברה וכל מה שיעשה יהיה עשוי ומאושר ומקובל עלי וכמובן מה שאעשה אני.

וכל זמן משך החברה הנז[כרת] כל אשר נסתחר וכל אשר נשלח הכל הוא לחצאין
איש כאחיו וכל ריוח והנאה שיזמין השי"ת בכל זמן הנז[כר] הוא לחצאין וכן כל אחריות
הוא לחצאין.

וחומר וחוזק שטר זה כחומר וחוזק כל שטרי מעליי דנהיגי בישראל מן יומא דנן
ולעלם כהוגן וכתיקון חז"ל דלא כאסמכתא ודלא כטופסי דשטרי בביטול כל מודעי
ומודעי דמודעי עד סוף כל המודעות. ושטר זה לא יפסל מחמת מחק וגרר ולא מחמת
אות או תיבה יתיר או חסיר ולא מלשנא דמשתמע לתרי אנפי.

היה כל זה ועבר לפנינו היום יום א' י"ח לחדש תשרי השב"ה ליצירה.

וקנינן אנן סהדי ח"מ מכה"ר חיים הנז[כר] קנין גמור ושלם כמנא דכשר למקנייא
ביה לקיים ולגמור כל מאי דכתוב ומפורש לעיל פה העיר ויניצייא הבירה א' ביני שיטי
כל ביני שיטי וקיים.

והעדים החתומים בו הם אלו. שמואל בכ"ר יעקב בוינו ז"ל. ניסים אבוראבי סופר

ועד.

וכמותם תלתא כחדא הויגא אנחנא כי הגא דחתימין לתתא כד [?] הועתק שטרא דגא
ואתקיימו חתימות העדים הנז[כרים] דחתומים בו ראינון שמואל בכ"ר יעקב בוינו ז"ל.
וניסים אבוראבי סופר ועד ואשרנוהי וקיימנוהי כראוי וקים.

<table>
<tr><td>משה [?] ...</td><td>דוד נאבארו</td><td>יצחק הלוי</td></tr>
<tr><td>דין</td><td>דין</td><td>דין</td></tr>
</table>

ASV, Senato, Lettere e scritture turchesche, filza 2, No [blue] 199v

IV: Copy of a letter sent by Giovanni Miches, *alias* Don Joseph Nassí,
to the Jewish merchants detained in Venice during the Cyprus war
[April-June 1571, or slightly later]

Copia di una lettera scritta da Giovanni Miches, Duca di Nixia, in
risposta agl'Hebrei Levantini ritenuti in Venezia

Se bene non ho fin a quest'hora risposto alle lettere vostre, non ho
per questo mancato mai di operare appresso questo altissimo Signore
et fortissimo, tutto quello che l'obligo mio ricercava ch'io facessi a
beneficio vostro, si come il Ragazzoni, venuto qua particolarmente
per la liberatione di questi mercatanti Christiani et delle robbe loro
ritenute qua per l'occasione della guerra, vi potria notificare; dil che
son sicuro che mai havete dubitato, sapendo bene che l'oggetto mio
fu, è, et sarà sempre di preservare et aumentare la nostra natione con
la nostra benedetta legge. Ma perchè le cose di questa aventurata Porta
vanno consideratissime, et caminano per la vera via della giustitia,
non si è potuto ancora accappare cosa di rilevamento in favor vostro.
   Con tutto questo non vi havete da sgomentare, percioche quando
bene per via ordinaria non si potesse haver la liberatione vostra et delle
vostre merci, si haverà qui a suo tempo non solamente l'equivalente,
ma la duplicatione di esse. Vi essorto dunque tutti a soffrire
patientemente finchè in effetto si veda che quell'illustrissimo Dominio
vi puo bene impedire il viaggio di ritornare a Costantinopoli, ma non

la strada di andare in Paradiso, la quale si fa alle anime nostre, come sapete, tanto più facile quanto che li corpi nostri hanno patito et sopportato diverse persecutioni et angustie, per liquali tutti noi habbiamo da passare, chi per un verso et chi per un altro, secondo il voler di Dio.

In quanto poi a quelle che mi havete scritte, che quelli Signori Illustrissimi si dogliono di me, non possi per hora darvi altra risposta se non che vi faccio sapere che io non ho mai sfavorito le cose loro, ma se ho fatto et faccio qualche servitio a questo Felicissimo Signore ne ho havuto et ho molto ben ragione, perciò che se vorrò riguardare ad una minema parte del favore et gratie che mi ha fatto et fa nell'utile et honore, sarò astretto di confessare, che quanto haverò posto la propria vita in servitio suo non haverò fatta cosa veruna. Sichè non hanno ragione di biasimarmi, ne di rinfacciarmi, come dicete, sicome non havevano restringere voi ne ritenersi le vostre robbe con dire che questo fortunatissimo Signore habbi voluto et voglia alcuna cosa da loro. Et per haver me alli suoi commandi, pretendono in conseguentia contra di voi, percioche se tenessero loro al servitio di quella repubblica suddito di Francia o altro dal quale ricevessero alcun servitio contra questa serenissima Porta, come potrebbono havere, non sarebbe però honesto che qua fossero ristretti tutti li francesi o altri della natione del servitore, come non si restringerebbe mai. Ma sia come si voglia, che spero in breve che noi poveri perseguitati racquisteremo la nostra di promissione terra, con favore et gratia di chi fin a quest'hora meritamente l'ha posseduta et possiede. Et io non mancarò mai, né col pensiero né con l'opera, d'aiutare la nostra prosapia, sicome voi, dall'altra banda dovrete attendere a fare il medesimo in quello che vi sarà concesso dagl'huomini et permesso da Dio eterno, il quale sopra tutte le cose dovemo havere nella mente e nel cuore.

Giovanni Miches

Biblioteca Ambrosiana, Milan, Ms. G 121 inf. (4).

V: Documents pertaining to the compensation awarded to Joshua Davizzolo and Joseph Marzan, Jewish Levantine merchants detained in Venice during the Cyprus war, 1570-74.

A: The renewed request of Joshua Davizzolo and Joseph Marzan, 1574

Serenissimo Principe Illustrissima Signoria
Sono più di qattro mesi che noi Josue Davizolo et Josef Marzan hebrei mercanti levantini supplicammo avanti Vostra Serenità con pregarla ad esser contenta per giustitia provedere che rihabbiamo la nostra robba ritenuta per ordine di Vostra Serenità nel tempo della guerra, secondo che per la parte presa è stato restituita alli altri mercanti di Levante, et perchè la nostra mercantia tutta, per quanto si dice, è stata rubbata nella volta sotto chiave delli ministri delli Clarissimi Signori Governatori dell'entrate mentre eravamo ritenuti nelle priggioni insieme con gli altri levantini, et quando demmo la supplicatione parse alla Serenità Vostra rimettere questa nostra causa alli Signori Savii, gli quali hanno tanto prolungato il darne risposta, che anco come il primo giorno ne ritrovamo senza alcuna risolutione. Et per nostra disgratia la determinatione fatta dalla Serenità Vostra che sia rimessa la causa alli Signori Savii non può apparire, essendo abbrusciata la supplica nel cancello del Magnifico Secretario Saetta, fra molte altre scritture, in quel giorno che s'accese il fuoco nel palazzo.

Però noi, Josue Davizzolo e Josef Marzan sopradetti di nuovo riverentemente ne gittamo alli piedi di Vostra Serenità pregandola che per giustitia, per gratia et pietà voglia provedere quanto prima alla indennità di noi meschini, che hormai non potemo più trattenersi in questa magnifica città, per la gran spesa, né il ritornar in Levante è a noi siguro, per esser debitori di turchi, né habbiamo altro nel mondo per sostentamento della nostra famiglia che l'utile quale ne può opportare di detta robba ritenuta da Vostra Serenità, la quale pregamo iddio la conservi perpetuamente felice.

B: An official report including the inventory of goods kept in the Rialto warehouse of Josue Davizolo and Joseph Marzan, and a description of the effects of the burglary committed there during the Cyprus war.

Serenissimo Principe Illustrissima Signoria,
Essendo sta comesso da vostra Sublimità a me Agostin Spinelli, humilissimo suo servitore, ch'io mettessi in scrittura quello che le dissi in voce intorno il successo del furto seguito delle robbe che si trovavano nella volta tenuta ad affitto per Josua Davizzol, hebreo levantino, riverentemente le dico che nel principio della guerra, che fu il mese di marzo 1570, per l'officio delli Clarissimi Signori Governatori delle intrade furono bollate tutte le volte quali si trovavano in Rialto, et quelli che si trovorono esser tenuti per levantini furono per detto officio diligentemente inventariate, come nel sudetto officio appar. Tra le quali ne fu bollata et inventariata una alle Fabriche nove No 34, della Magnifica Madonna Laura Baseglio, tenuta ad affitto per Josua Davizzol, hebreo levantino, con la presentia di esso Josuà, et furono in detta volta trovate le infrascritte robbe, videlicet:

Carisea incarnada disse pezza una	duc.
Colli doi disse esser seda	duc.
Caldiere colletti quattro	duc.
Sachetto uno disse esser grana	duc.
Morteretto uno di bronzo	duc.
Involto uno in carta disse esser Damasco T^a 78	duc.
Cavezzetto uno di Damasco verde con un'altro cavezetto disse di Damasco	duc.
Lana disse da Patrasso grossa sacco uno, qual robba disse esser del detto Josuà.	

Nella detta volta disse esser di ragion di Josef Marcian hebreo levantin ut infra:

Panni, disse balle quattro, disse esser panni otto	duc.
Involto uno in griso, disse esser panno uno turchin	duc.
Sachetto uno, disse esser polvere	duc.
Sachetin uno di sachi di lana Rodi	duc.

Panno uno in bandinella verde, disse esser scarlatin   duc.
Berette zucotti rossi in casse tre bianche, disse esser
dozene 200   duc.
In una delle tre casse oltrascritte ligata et serrata
disse esser panni di seda pezze due, et tabi [?]
car^{zo} [?] uno   duc.
Razzetto uno a fogliazze, disse esser di ragion di
Samuel Cimicà hebreo   duc.
Bacil uno di Petre   duc.
Cassetta una, nella qual si trovò sachetto uno con
lire 9 soldi 2 di moneda, disse esser di ragion di
Josua Davizzol, portati al officio et fatta la partita.
In detta cassetta alquante masse di seda   duc.
Cassa una di Noghera.

Dapoi fatto il soprascritto inventario, fu serrata detta volta et bollata, et portate le chiavi nell'officio delli Clarissimi Signori Governatori delle intrade. All'officio delli quali, alli 6 novembre 1570 fu dinontiato per il capitano della guardia di Rialto esser sta rotta detta volta et rubbata la robba. Onde li Clarissimi Signori governtori immediate riccorsero alli Clarissimi Signori Avogadori di comun, richiedendo che fusse formato processo per l'officio suo sopra questo furto. Et così fu da sue Clarissime Signorie mandato uno de suoi nodari alla detta volta per questo effetto. Et fu trovato esser sta segato il bolzon del cadenazzo della prima porta fra la serradura et il cadenazzo, et così aperta la prima porta era stata poi rotta la seconda porta, nella quale era sta fatto come un fenestrino, per il quale era sta rotta la serradura della seconda porta et portate via quasi tutte le robbe et rotte tutte le casse, quali erano sta lassate vode dalli ladri nella detta volta. Et così formato il processo, li Clarissimi Signori Avogadori andorono all'Exellentissimo Consiglio di Quarantia Criminal, per il quale fu dato taglio conveniente al delitto. Il che fu publicato sopra le scalle, secondo il costume della città. Non di meno, mai si è potuto intender cosa alcuna. Fu ancho inventariata la robba la qual si trovò esser rimasta nella volta sopradetta, ut infra:
Una cassa di Noghera con la serradura et fiorio rotto
Casse tre di Talpon con le serradure et fiorii rotti
La serradura della seconda porta desfitta [?] et rotta
Sachetto uno mezo di granna

Scrignetto uno negro rotto, col fiorio serrato, qual fiorio fu rotto per il capitano per veder ciò che vi era dentro, et non vi trovò cosa alcuna.
Lavezo uno di Bronzo rotto
Sacco uno con lina succida
Sachi di griso et imboggi
Bariletto uno vodo

Le qual robbe sono sta consignate a Josuà Davizzol hebreo sopradetto alli 16 marzo 1574.
Questo è quanto io posso dir a vostra sublimità intorno questo fatto et in sua buona gratia humilissimamente mi raccommando.

C: Valuation of the merchandise stolen from the Rialto warehouse [in a different handwriting]

Carisea incarnada pezza una bastarda	duc. 14
Seda colli doi a modo suo, L[ibra] 630	duc.450
Caldiere balle 4 L[ibre] 800, a modo suo	duc.120
Damasco cremesin b[razz]a 78	duc. 80
Damasco verde b[razz]a 46 et	
alatado b[razz]a 24	duc. 70
Panni diese de diversi colori	duc.700
Polvere di grana s[achett]o uno,	
a modo suo L[ibra] 100	duc. 80
Grana s[achett]o uno L[ibra] 200 a modo suo	duc.100
Barette zucotte dozzene 200	duc.600
Tabi paonazzo b[razz]a 36	duc. 20
Raso paonazzo pezze doi a modo suo	
b[razz]a 205	duc.260
Razzato uno a fogliazze e baril uno	
di peltre	duc. 16
Summa:	duc.2510

D: Decision of the Council of Ten to compensate the two Jewish merchants, 27 August 1574

In additione

Fra le altre robbe che furno retenude nel principio della guerra turchesca se ne ritrovorno alcune di Giosef Merchan et Jusua Danizzuol hebrei levantini, lequali furno posti in una volta di Rialto di dove forono rubbate. Et ricercando essi la refattione, si è trattata compositione col mezzo del dilettissimo nobile nostro Marc Antonio Barbaro procurator, il qual doppo diverse difficultà ha operato che si contentino di ducati mille per resto e saldo di ogni loro pretensione, obligandosi a fare quelle ricepute di esse che serano necessarie.

Et perchè è conveniente esborsargli li sopradetti mille ducati, l'anderà parte, ch delli denari della Signoria Nostra siano dati ducati mille alli Gevernatori nostri dell'intrade con ordine che debbano contarli alli predetti Giosef et Josua per resto et saldo de ogni loro pretensione, sicome di sopra è dechiarito. Et siano fatte le debite chiarezze alla presentia di testimonii turchi con sottoscrittione di quelli. Et questo sia et s'intenda senza pregiudizio delle ragion della Signoria nostra contra quoscumque

[The above *parte* was not approved, not having obtained the necessary three quarters of the votes]

Die 30 dicti, in additione

Capita rursus posuerunt partem suprascriptam cum hac additione videlicet:
Che sia datta autorità al Collegio nostro di poter accomodar la difficultà con un altro hebreo con spender da ducati cento in giù per certi veri che gli sono stati robbati.

[This time the motion obtained the necessary three quarters of the votes and was thus approved]

E: A Document signed by Joseph Marcian (Marzan), Joshua da Vizziol (Davizzolo) and Solomon Ashkenazi, acknowledging receipt of 1,000 ducats as indemnity for merchandise stolen at Rialto during the war, 3 September 1574

Havendo noi, Iosef Marcian et Josue da Viciol da Patrasso supplicato la Serenità vostra li giorni passati che Lei volesse con la bontà sua compassionar la miseria nostra per il danno che habbiamo patito di quelle nostre robbe che furono tratenute nel tempo del romper della guerra, si de quelle ch'erano in una nostra volta, come dell'altre che furono scaricate dalla nave Moceniga et Leze, et poste nella stessa volta, le qual tutte robbe furono dipoi robbate. Et essendosi la Serenità vostra per dicta nostra suplicatione mossassi a pietà, ha voluto, per benignità sua, et in gratificatione del Signor Domino rabbi Salamone, solevarne de tanto danno nostro, facendosi esbursar ducati mille, quali noi sopraditti Iosef Marcian et Iosue da Viciol habbiamo riceputi dal Clarissimo meser Zuambattista Quirini, Governator de l'intrate, chiamandosi contenti et satisfatti a ogni qualunque nostra pretensione che sopra tutte le predite robbe potesemo haver, ringratiandone anco la Serenità Vostra che per sua bontà si sia degnata de farci detta gratia, della quale, acciò che in ogni tempo ne appari vera probatione de tal nostra satisfattione, ne habbiamo fatta la presente scrittura alla presentia del predetto Signor Domino rabbi Salamon, et delli altri testimonii qui sotto nottati, la quale serà ancho sottoscritta di nostra propria mano. In Venetia, alli 3 di settembre 1574, alla Iudeca nell'allogiamento del predetto Signor rabbi Salamon.

מודה אני יוסף מירצאן כל מה שכתוב לעיל שקבלתי במעות כנזכר ואני מפויס
מכל דכתוב לעיל
מודה אני יהושע וויציולו כל מה שכתוב לעיל שקבלתי במעות כנזכר ואני
מפויס מכל דכתוב לעיל

Io docttor Salamon Natan Ascanasi fo presente quando fo contadi li sopra ditti ducati 1000 per mano del Clarissimo meser Piero Alberto, rasonato ducalle.
Io Marco dalla Fratina fui presente et visti contare li sopra scritti dinari.
Io Domenego de Bagliano [?] fui presente a quanto si contiene di sopra et visto contare li sopra detti ducati mille ali sopraditti.

Confesso io Iosef Mirzan tutto quello se scritto de sopra che ho receputo
il danaro sopra ditto et io me contento de tutto il sopra scritto, come
contento ancora Iesua Damizzola dice il medesimo.

ASV, Cons. X, Secreti, filza 18 [1574]

VI: The Code-Book of Ḥayyim Saruq, 1571.

Acmat bassa	Rabi Abram
Andrinopoli	Pera
Armata cristiana	Rabi Mose Abuduaram
Arsenal in Costantinopoli	Galata
Artegliaria	Specchi da Muram
Armisi	Carte da Giocar
Armata turca	Caravana d'Angori
Archibusieri	Mocagiari ganzanti
Aga di ghianizari	Rabi Aron Coem
Assedio	Amalado
Assalti	Febre
Alessandria	Rabi Abram Basseloni
Assamoglanj[o?]	Mocagiari greci
Asapi	Cordovani
Alger	Rabi Abram Levi
Alepo	Rabi Isac Cabib
Arabi	Pevere assi
Asdragan	Fiera di Moscolari
Aprile	Jiar
Agosto	Elul
Belerbei di Natolia	Rabi Samuel Matalon
Belerbei di Grecia	Rabi David Abudara
Bassa di Egitto	Rabi David Navara
Bassa di Damasco	Rabi Abram [Co?]luin
Bassa di Aleppo	Rabi Elia Levi
Bassa di frontiere di Persia	Rabi Salamon Coem [sic]
Bassa di Buda	Rabi Naftalin Coem [sic]
Barbaria	Zaffet

Bursia
Borsina
Biscotti
Bassa del mar
Bassa da Terra in armada
Buda
Bateria
Bassa di essercito
Bando
Moldavia overo Bogdania
Cipri
Castel nuovo
Cerigo
Candia
Cefalonia
Cataro
Corfù
Cavallaria turchesca
Comandamento
Cristiani sudditi turcheschi
Caramania
Caramusoli
Costantinopoli
Cavalla
Dardanelli del stretto
Dardanelli di Lepanto
Divam
Divam a cavallo
Damasco
Danni
Dalmatia
Decembre
Essercito
Ebrei
Famagosta
Fanteria
Fuste de turchi
Fregata
Friul

Salonichi
Comerchina
Ochiali
Rabi Maier Coem (Maier Coen)
Rabi Josef Caro
Rabi Jacob Eitasam
Soleatar
Rabi Beniamin Mascona
Ascama
Filipopoli
Rabi Samuel Barocas
Rabi David Lindo
Rabi Abram Codara
Rabi David Brudo
Rabi Mose Gierchi
Scopia
Rabi Salamon di Medina
Campanelle
Ho scritto overo, ho scritto
Panina de Saloniche
Rabi Josef Sadoch
Carisee da Salonichi
Casa mia
Rabi Asser Coem [sic]
Rabi Isaac Saruch
Mi cugna'
Esnoga
Alla guerta a comer
Rabi Jacob Alfanderi
Garbelar
Rabi Mordacai
Tevet
Caravana
Rabi Mose
Rabi Chia Baroches
Spetie
Sacchi di goton
Lettera di aviso
Soffia

Feriti	Carta da strazzo
Francia	Don Abram Benvenisti
Febraro	Adar
Gente di Egitto	Spetiarie di Mitsraim
Gente di Soria	Spetiarie di Aleppo
General del mar	Rabi Jocanam Alcadef
General di terra	Rabi Matagia
Governatori di galie	Carta da scriver
Governator d'Alger	Il compagno di Rabi Abram Levi
Governator di Tripoli di Barberia	Il compagno di Rabi Natan Sori
Governator di Alessandria	Il cugna' di Rabi Abram Barselona
Governator di Galipoli	Il cugna' di Rabi Baruch Crespe
Galipoli	Rabi Baruc Crespin
Governator della Cavalla	Il compagno di Rabi Asser Coen
Governator di Salonichi	Il compagno di Rabi Mose Sulam
Governador di Morea	Il compagno di Rabi Mose Rosso
Governador di Negroponte	Il figliuol di Rabi Absalon
Governador di Lepanto	Il fratello di Rabi Sachiel Sacchi
Governador della Prevesa	Il fratello di Rabi Daniel Zafram
Governador d'Albania	Il nevodo di Rabi Avram Sarfati
Governador della Valona	Il compagno di Rabi Reuben Soriano
Genti di Natolia	Filadi di Natolia
Genti di Romania alta et bassa	Panine da Salonichi bassa
Gente della Bossina	Cordovani di Bossina
Gente della Morea	Seda della Morea
Governador di Castel Nuovo	Il compagno di David Lindo
Governador della Bossina	Il compagno di Rabi Necamie
Governador di Ziget	Il figliuolo di Rabi Besalel
Governador di Metelin	Il fratel di Rabi Jacob Salom
Governador di Scio	Il fratel di Rabi Manuel Namies
Governador di Rodi	Il cugna' di Rabi Isach Erisa
Governador di Cipro	L'ermano di Samuel Barocas
Governador di Famagosta	Il nevodo di Chia Barucas
Governdoe delle Smire	Il fratello di Rabi Jona Zabocas
Governador di Setelia	Il fratel di Mair Lombroso

Galie sotil	Seda lisin
Galiotte de Leventi	Seda Mamodea
Guastatori	Cori secchi
Gemen	Mitsraim
Gente	Danari
Guerra	Negotio
Galiotti turchi	Turchese
Galiotti cristiani	Rubinetti
Giugno	Tamus
Genaro	Sevat
Gente d'Ongaria	Stagno
Gente di Moldavia	Lana di Filipopoli
Gente di Valacchia	Cori di Valacchia
Hicomini di comando	Zambelotti cinque fili
Ha preso	Ha fatto basar
Ha mandato	Ha comprato, overo ho comprato
Istria	Rabi Alvener Alfarin
Imbasciatori	Fatori
Imperador	D. Samuel Abravanel
Impresa	Ha guadagnato
Jo	Sultam Selim
Luglio	Af
Leventi	Zambelotti gresi
Morat figliuolo dl Signor	Il figliuolo di Rabi Elieser Calef
Memet Bassa	Rabi Esaia
Mamut Bassa	Rabi Gabriel
Mustafa Bassa	Rabi Israel
Mar Maggior	Bursia
Moscovia	Rabi Josef Amigo
Morea	Rabi Mose Rosso
Modon	Rabi Mose Saruch
Maone	Seda paesana
Malta	Rabi Jacob Abentestel
Maistranza	Sbiacca
Murlacca	Monesterio
Monition	Merce
Mori	Pevere gavro
Mancamento	Rechiesta
Morti	Bagnado

Morbo	Spedition
Marani	Marsey
Marzo	Nissam
Maggio	Sivam
Millesimo 1571	5332 principiando da settembre
Nave grosse	Filadi sotil
Nave piccole	Filadi grossi
Negroponte	Rabi Absalon
Napoli di Romania	Rabi Isaac Alfanderi
Natolia	Rabi Natam Franco
Novembre	Chislef
Ongari	Contadori, overo rasonati
Ongaria	Rabi Daniel Menachin
Ottobre	Chesvam
Pertau Bassa	Rabi Mose Alfanderi
Piali Bassa	Rabi Josef Crespim
Proveditor dell'arsenal	Rabi Esdra Mamias
Persia	Rabi Josef Iacar
Polonia	Rabi Isac Daiula
Patras	Rabi Mose Sori
Palanderia	Seda cremesina di Bursia
Polvere ogni cantara	Una pezza di cumazzi
Primo tempo	Al primo del mese
Puglia	Rabi Aaron Mazza
Paese del Turco vicin alla Dalmatia	I parenti di Rabi Mordacai
Papa	Il raf, o rab
Pace	Compagnia
Prigioni	Resentiti
Persiani	Cutni
Ragusi	Rabi Mose Abenini
Rodi	Rabi Samuel Erisa
Re di Franza	Rabi Mair Cases
Re di Polonia	Rabi Salamon Cuti
Re di Persia	Rabi Jacob Tabon
Re di Moscovia	Rabi Abram Tapiero
Re Filippo	Don Isach Abravanello
Re diTartari	Rabi Sabatai di Boton
Re di Tansilvania	Rabi Samuel di Boton
Remi di galia	Veri da finestre

Robamenti	Robe
Settembre	Tiseri
Solevamento di gente	Falimenti
Sicilia	Rabi Abram Aboaf
Scio	Rabi Mair Eschenisi
Soltan Silin	Rabi Eliaser Calef
Sanzachi	Tavole di robe d'Angori
Sebenico	Larso
Salonichi	Rabi David Jachia
Signoria di Ragusi	Il fradello di Rabi Mose Abenini
Schiavi	Cremese
Spachi	Zambelotti zachirini
Turchi	Droghe
Tripoli di Barbaria	Rabi Natan Sori
Tripoli di Soria	Rabi Abram Aberini
Tartaria	Toscia
Tartari	Mocagiari di Toscia
Transilvania	Il cugna' di Samuel Boton
Tradimento	Ingano
Tutti li luoghi	Tutte le boteghe
Tregua	Matrimonio
Tributo	Limosina per poveretti
Tine	Rabi Aaron Mossodo
Valona	Rabi Reuben Sonano
Valachia	Rabi Isac Aborove
Venturieri	Garofali
Vittovaglie	Spetiarie
Zara	Ragusi
Zante	Rabi Natan Sab[?]lom
Zighet	Rabi Efraim Pinto

Como vorrò far che un numero piccolo summi assai gli porrò una a dinanzi che significarà ogni dieci esser cento.
Et quando vi porò inanzi on o, ogni dieci vorà dir mille.
Le mansioni delle mie lettere farò in tre modi, una a Letitia mia consorte, o a Caliman de Grassia, o ad Isac Naso.

ASV, Cons. X, Secreti, filza 15 [1571].

SOURCES AND BIBLIOGRAPHY

I. UNPUBLISHED SOURCES

A. Archivio di Stato, Venice [ASV]

Archivio notarile, Atti [AN], buste 8244-8274 (not. G.B. Monte).
Capi del Consiglio dei Dieci, Lettere da Costantinopoli [Capi X, Lett. CP], buste
    3, 4, 5, 6
Capi del Consiglio dei Dieci, Lettere da Candia [Capi X, Lett. Candia], busta 285
Capi del Consiglio dei Dieci, Lettere da Cipro [Capi X, Lett. Cipro], busta 290
Cinque savi alla mercanzia, reg. 137
Collegio, Notatorio, reg. 38
Collegio, Relazioni, busta, 4 (*Diario di Maestro di Casa di Marcantonio Barbaro*);
    busta 61.
Commemoriali, reg. 22
Consiglio dei Dieci [Cons. X], Comuni, filza 101, filza 112
Consiglio dei Dieci, Secreti, reg. 8, 9, 10, 11; filze 12, 15, 18
Dieci, poi venti savi del corpo del senato, busta 178
Documenti turchi, 87, 476, 537-38 (490-91), and Indice Bombaci [IB]
iscellanea codici, No 894 (M. Barbaro, *Arbori de' patritii veneti*).
Senato, Deliberazioni Costantinopoli [Sen. Delib. CP], reg. 3, 4, 5, 6; filze 2, 3
Senato, Deliberazioni secrete, reg. 61, 63
Senato, Dispacci da Cipro [Sen. Disp. Cipro], filza 4 blue
Senato, Dispacci da Costantinopoli [Sen. Disp. CP], filze 1, 2, 5
Senato, Lettere e scritture turchesche [LST], filza 2
Senato, Mar, reg. 23, 26, 27, 36, 39, 43; filza 36
Senato, Secreti, reg. 11
Senato, Terra, reg. 48, 49; filza 117

B. Biblioteca Nazionale Marciana, Venice [BNM]

Ms. It. VII 390-91 (8872-73), [Barbaro's Letter-book]
Ms. It. VII 213 (8836) [Cronaca Lippomano]

C. Biblioteca del Civico Museo Correr, Venice [MCC]

Ms. P.D. 396, c/45

D. Biblioteca Ambrosiana, Milan

Ms. G 121 inf. (4)

E. Biblioteca Apostolica Vaticana

Ms. Vat. Lat. 3933

II. PUBLISHED SOURCES

Almosnino, Moses, *Sefer Meamez Koah (Reinforcing Strength)*, Venice, 1588 (reprint: Westmead, 1969) [Hebrew].

Andreas, W., "Eine unbekannte venetianische Relation über die Türkei (1567)", *Sitzungsberichte der Heidelberger Akademie der Wissenschaften. Philosophisch-historische Klasse*, 5 (1914), pp. 1-13.

A stampa dell'università degli Ebrei di Corfù [place and date unspecified].

Belon, P., *Les observations de plusieures singularités et choses memorables trovés en Grèce, Asie, Iudée, Egypte, Arabie et autres pays étrangers* etc., Paris, 1588.

Benjamin of Tudela, *The Itinerary*, ed. and tr. M.N. Adler, London, 1907.

Blessi, Manoli [pseudonym of Antonio Molin, called "Il Burchiella"], *Dialogo de Selin con Giosuf ebreo* etc., Venice, n.a.

Brulez, W., *Marchands flamands à Venise (1568-1605)*, Bruxelles and Rome, 1965.

Calepio, A., "Vera et fidelissima narratione del successo dell'espugnatione et defensione del Regno di Cipro", in E. de Lusignan, *Chorografia et breve historia universale dell'isola di Cipro*, Bologna, 1573, pp. 92v-123v.

Capsali, Rabbi Elijah, *Beauty and Bands*, ed. M. Benayahu, Tel Aviv, 1990 [Hebrew].

Cavalli, Marino, *Informatione dell'ofitio dell'ambasciatore di Marino Cavalli il vecchio, MDL*, ed. T. Bertelè, Florence-Rome, 1935.

Correspondance politique de Guillaume Pellicier, Ambassadeur de France à Venise, 1540-42, ed. A. Tausserat-Radel, Paris, 1899.

Corrispondenza da Madrid di Leonardo Donà, eds. E. Vitale and M. Brunetti, Venice-Rome, 1963.

Dernschwann, H., *Hans Dernschwann's Tagebuch einer Reise nach Konstantinopel und Kleinasien (1553-55)*, ed. F. Babinger, Munich, 1923.

D.F.N.A.E. [Filippo Nani], *Prattica civile delle corti del palazzo*, Venice, 1694.

Documenti finanziari ser. II, vol. 1/1: Bilanci Generali, ed. F. Besta and F. Visentini, R. Commissione per la pubblicazione dei documenti finanziari della Repubblica di Venezia, Venice, 1912.

Filiarchi, Cosimo, *Trattato della guerra e dell'unione de' principi Cristiani contra i Turchi e gli altri infedeli*, Venice, 1572.

Hacohen, Joseph, *Emek Habacha [The Vale of Tears]*, tr. M. Wiener, Leipzig, 1858.

Heyd, U., *Ottoman Documents on Palestine 1552-1615. A Study of the Firman according to the Mühime Defteri*, Oxford, 1960.

Istanbul Vakıfları tahrîr defteri 953 (1546), eds., O.L. Barkan and E.H. Averdi, Istanbul, 1970.

The Jews in the Medieval World, ed. J.R. Marcus, Cleveland, New York and Philadelphia, 1961.

Le Carlier, Jean, Sr de Pinon, *Voyage en Orient*, ed. E. Blochet, Paris, 1920.

I libri commemoriali della Repubblica di Venezia, Regesti, ed. R. Predelli, 8 vols. [*Monumenti storici pubblicati dalla Deputazione Veneta di Storia Patria*, ser. I, vols. 1, 3, 8-9, 11-13, 17] Venice, 1876-1914.

Life in Istanbul, 1588. Scenes from a traveller's picture book, Bodleian Library Picture Books, Oxford, 1977.

Lopez, R.S., and Raymond, I.W., *Medieval Trade in the Mediterranean World*, New York, n.d.

Luzzatto, S., *Discorso circa il stato de gl'hebrei et in particular dimoranti nell'inclita città di Venezia*, Venice, 1638,

Marlowe, Christopher, "The Jew of Malta", in *The Complete Works of Christopher Marlow*, ed. F. Bowers, vol. 1, Cambridge, 1973, pp. 253-340.

Medina, Rabbi Samuel de, *Responsa, Tur hoshen Hamishpat*, New York, 1959

Minute Book of the Council of the Jewish Community of Padua 1577-1603, ed. D. Carpi, 2 vols., Jerusalem, 1973-1979 [Hebrew].

Monumenta Germaniae Historica. Epistolae, vol. 2, ed. C. Hatmann, 2nd edition, Berlin, 1957.

Nazari, Giovanni Battista, *Discorso della futura e sperata vittoria contra il turco etc*, Venice, 1570.

Negociations de la France dans le Levant, ed. E. Charrière, 4 vols. Paris, 1848-1860.

Nicolay, Nicolas de, *Discours et histoire véritable des navigations, pérégrinations et voyages faites en la Turquie etc.*, Antwerp, 1586.

Nunziature di Venezia, vols 1-6 (1533-1554) ed. F. Gaetà, Rome, 1558-1567; vols 8-10 (1566-1573), ed. A. Stella, Rome, 1963-1977; vol.11 (1573-1576), ed. A. Buffardi, Rome, 1972.

Pivetta, P.G., *L'arte di ben apprendere la pratica civile e mista del foro veneto*, vol. 2, Venice, 1791.

Poma, C., "Il consolato Veneto in Egitto con le relazioni dei consoli Daniele Barbarigo (1554) e Marco Zen (1664)", *Bollettino del Ministerio degli Affari Esteri*, ser. I, 109 (1897), pp. 463-502.

Processi del S. Uffizio di Venezia contro ebrei e giudaizzanti, ed. P.C. Ioly Zorattini, 11 vols. published thus far, Florence, 1980-

Regesta pontificum romanorum ab condita ecclesia ad annum post Christum natum MCXCVIII, ed. P. Jaffé, 2nd edition revised by G. Wattenbach, 2 vols. Leipzig, 1885-1888.

Regnaud, Antoine, Discours du voyage d'Outre-mer au Sainct-Sépulcre de Ierusalem et autres lieux de la Terre Saincte en 1548, Lyons, 1573.

Relazioni degli ambasciatori veneti al Senato durante il secolo decimosesto, ed. E. Albèri, ser. III, Relazioni dell'Impero Ottomano, 3 vols. and Appendix, Florence, 1840-1863.

Sanderson, John S., *The Travels in the Levant (1584-1602)*, ed. W. Foster, London,

1931.

Sanuto, Marino, *I Diarii*, 58 volumes, Venezia, 1879-1903.

Stampa delli signori priori o siano presidenti del Collegio degl'Intervenienti di Corfù al taglio contro li capi dell'università degl'Ebrei di Corfù [place and date unspecified].

Statuta iudaeorum Candiae eorumque memorabilia, eds. E.S. Artom and H.M.D. Cassuto, Jerusalem, 1943.

Tiepolo, Lorenzo, *Relazioni dei Consolati di Alessandria e di Siria per la Repubblica Veneta negli anni 1552-1560*, ed. E. Cicogna, Venezia, 1857.

Valerio, Agostino, *Dell'utilità che si può tirare delle cose operate dai veneziani*, Padua, 1787.

Viola, A.A., *Compilazione delle leggi [...] in materia di offici e banchi in Ghetto*, Venice, 1786.

III. BIBLIOGRAPHY

Anselmi, S., "Motivazioni economiche della neutralità di Ragusa nel Cinquecento", in *Il Mediterraneo nella seconda metà del '500 alla luce di Lepanto*, ed. G. Benzoni, Florence, 1974, pp. 33-70.

Aodeh, S., *Eleventh-Century Arabic Letters of Jewish Merchants from the Cairo Geniza*, unpublished Ph.D. Dissertation, Tel Aviv University, 1992 [Hebrew].

Arbel, B., "The Jews in Cyprus: New Evidence from the Venetian Period", *Jewish Social Studies*, 41 (1979), pp. 23-40.

----, "Venezia, gli ebrei e l'attività di Salomone Ashkenazi nella guerra di Cipro", in *Gli ebrei e Venezia*, ed. G. Cozzi, Milan, 1987, pp. 163-197.

----, "Venice and the Jewish Merchants of Istanbul in the Sixteenth Century", in A. Toaff and S. Schwarzfuchs eds., *The Mediterranean and the Jews: Banking, Finance and International Trade (XVI-XVIII Centuries)*, Ramat Gan, 1989, pp. 92-109.

----, "Salomone Ashkenazi, mercante e armatore", in *Il mondo ebraico. Gli ebrei tra Italia nord-orientale e Impero asburgico dal Medioevo all'Età contemporanea*, Pordenone, 1991, pp. 109-128.

----, "Nūr Bānū (c. 1530-1583): a Venetian Sultana?", *Turcica*, 24 (1992), pp. 241-59.

----, "The Mystery of Abraham Castro, and its Solution", in *Chapters in the History of the Jews in the Ottoman Empire*, forthcoming [Hebrew].

----, "A List of Able-Bodied Jews at Canea, Crete (1536)", in *Studies in Honour of D. Carpi*, forthcoming.

Arce, A., "Espionaje y ultima aventura de Jose Nasi (1569-1574)", *Sefarad*, 13 (1953), pp. 257-286.

Aschkenasi, A., "L'etonnante carrière d'un médecin juif au XVI⁰ siècle: Solomon Aschkenasi", *Revue d'Histoire de la Medicine Hébraïque*, 32 (1979), pp. 5-10, 27-32.

Ashtor, E., "Venetian Supremacy in the Levantine Trade: Monopoly or Pre-Colonialism?" *Journal of European Economic History*, 3 (1974), pp. 5-53.

----, "New data for the History of Levantine Jewries in the Fifteenth Century", *Bulletin of the Institute of Jewish Studies*, 3 (1975), pp. 67-102.

----, "The Jews in Mediterranean Trade in the Fifteenth Century", in *Wirtschaftskräfte und Wirtschaftswege, I: Mittelmeer und Kontinent* (Festschrift fur Hermann Kellenbenz), ed. J. Schneider, Nuremberg, 1978, pp. 441-454.

----, "Gli inizi della comunità ebraica a Venezia", in *Venezia ebraica*, ed. U. Fortis, Rome, 1982, pp. 17-39.

----, "The Jews of Trapani in the Later Middle Ages", *Studi Medievali*, 3rd ser., 25 (1984), pp. 1-32.

Aymard, M., *Venise, Raguse et le commerce du blé pendant la seconde moitié du seizième siècle*, Paris, 1966.

Babinger, F., "Zum turkisch-venedigischen Friedensvertrag vom Jahre 1540", *Rivista Degli Studi Orientali*, 8 (1919-20), pp. 651-652.

----, "Ja'qûb Pascha, ein Leibarzt Mehmed's II. Leben und Schiksale des Maestro Iacopo aus Gaetà", *Rivista degli studi orientali*, 26 (1951), pp. 87-113.

Baratier, E. and Reynaud, F., *Histoire du commerce de Marseilles, t. 2: de 1291 à 1480,*, Paris 1951.

Barkan, O.L., "Research on the Ottoman Fiscal Surveys", in *Studies in the Economic History of the Middle East from the Rise of Islam to the Present Day*, ed. M.A. Cook, London, 1970, pp. 163-171.

Baron, S.W., *A Social and Religious History of the Jews*, vol. 4, New York-London, 1965; vol. 18, Philadelphia, 1983.

Bashan, E., "The Freedom of Trade and the Imposition of Taxes and Customs Duties on Foreign Jewish Traders in the Ottoman Empire", in *East and Maghreb*, eds. H.Z. Hirshberg and E. Bashan, Ramat Gan, 1974, pp. 105-166 [Hebrew].

----, "Economic Life from the 16th to the 18th Century", in J.M. Landau, ed., *The Jews in Ottoman Egypt (1515-1917)*, Jerusalem, 1988, pp. 63-112 [Hebrew].

Benayahu, M., "Further Evidence on Hayyim ben Saruk in Venice", *Otsar Yehudei Sefarad*, 8 (1965), pp. 135-137 [Hebrew].

----, *Relations between Greek and Italian Jewry*, Tel Aviv, 1980 [Hebrew].

----, "The Sermons of R. Yosef b. Meir Garson as a Source for the History of the Expulsion from Spain and the Sephardi Diaspora", *Michael*, 7 (1981), pp. 42-205.

Bertelè, T., *Il palazzo degli ambasciatori di Venezia a Costantinopoli e le sue antiche memorie*, Bologna, 1932.

Blumenkranz, B., "Les Juifs dans le commerce maritime de Venise (1592-1609), à propos d'un livre recent", *Revue des Etudes Juives*, 3rd ser., 2 (1961), pp. 143-151.

Boerio, G., *Dizionario del dialetto veneziano*, Venice, 1856.

Bonfil, R., "New evidence on the life of Rabbi Menahem Azaria of Fano and his Times", in *Chapters in the History of Jewish Society in the Middle Ages and the Modern Era dedicated to Prof. Jacob Katz*, Jerusalem, 1980, pp. 98-135 [Hebrew].

Bonelli, L., "Il trattato turco-veneto del 1540", *Centenario della nascita Michele Amari*, Vol. 2, Palermo, 1910, pp. 332-363.

Borgherini, M., *L'arte della lana in Padova durante il governo della Repubblica di Venezia, 1405-1797*, Venice, 1964.

Bornstein-Makovetsky, L., "Jewish Brokers in Constantinople during the 18th Century According to Hebrew Documents", in *The Mediterranean and the Jews. Banking,*

Finance and International Trade, XVIth-XVIIIth Centuries, eds. S. Swarzfuchs and A. Toaff, Ramat Gan, 1989, pp. 75-104.

Boškov, A., "Die hüccet-Urkunde - Diplomatische Analyse", in *Studia turcologica memoriae Alexii Bombaci dicata*, Naples, 1982, pp. 81-87

Braslavsky, J., *Studies in our Country, its Past and Remains*, Tel Aviv, 1954 [Hebrew].

Braudel, F., *The Mediterranean and the Mediterranean World in the Age of Philip II*, London, 2 vols, London, 1973.

Braudel, F., and Romano, R., *Navires et cargaisons à l'entrée du port de Livourne, 1547-1611*, Paris, 1951.

Brown, H., "Venetian Diplomacy at the Sublime Porte during the Sixteenth Century", in his *Studies in the History of Venice*, vol. 2, London, 1907, pp. 1-38.

----, "The Venetians and the Venetian Quarter in Constantinople to the Close of the Twelfth Century", *Journal of Hellenic Studies*, 40 (1920), pp. 68-88.

Byrne, E.H., *Genoese Shipping in the Twelfth and Thirteenth Centuries*, Cambridge, Mass., 1930.

Cahen, C., "Y a-t-il eu des Rahdānites?", *Revue des Etudes Juives*, 3 (1964), pp. 499-505.

Calendar for 6,000 years, Founded by the Late A.A. Akavia. Tables and Introduction prepared by N. Fried, edited by D. Zakai, Jerusalem, 1976.

Carpi, D., "The Expulsion of Jews from the Papal State under Paul V and the Trials against the Jews of Bologna (1566-1569), in *Scritti in memoria di Enzo Sereni*, eds. D. Carpi, A. Milano and U. Nahon, Jerusalem, 1970, pp. 145-64 [Hebrew].

Cassandro, G.I., *Le rappresaglie e il fallimento a Venezia nei secoli XIII-XVI*, Turin, 1938.

Cohen, A., "Were the Walls of Jerusalem Built by Abraham Castro?", *Zion*, Vol. 47, 1982, pp. 407-418 [Hebrew].

----, *Jewish Life Under Islam. Jerusalem in the Sixteenth Century*, Cambridge Mass. and London, 1984.

----, "The Walls of Jerusalem", in C.E.Bosworth *et alii*, eds., *The Islamic World from Classical to Modern Times: Essays in Honour of Bernard Lewis*, Princeton, 1989, pp. 467-477.

Collegio dei X poi XX savi del corpo del senato, ed. G. Tamba, Rome, 1977.

Collier, R. and Billioud, J., *Histoire du commerce de Marseille, Tome III: de 1480 à 1599*, Paris, 1951.

Cooperman, B.D., "Venetian Policy Towards Levantine Jews and Its Broader Italian Context", in *Gli ebrei e Venezia*, ed. G. Cozzi, Milan, 1987, pp. 65-84.

Corazzol, G., "Varietà notarile: scorci di vita economica e sociale", in *Storia di Venezia, vol 6: Dal Rinascimento al Barocco*, eds. G. Cozzi and P. Prodi, Rome, 1994, pp. 775-791.

Cozzi, G., "Politica, società, istituzioni", in *La Repubblica di Venezia nell'età moderna, vol. 1: Dalla guerra di Chioggia al 1517*, eds. G. Cozzi and M. Knapton, Turin, 1986, pp. 3-274.

Crisis and Change in the Venetian Economy in the Sixteenth and Seventeenth Centuries, ed. B. Pullan, London, 1968.

Da Mosto, A., *L'archivio di stato di Venezia, indice generale*, 2 vols, Rome, 1937-1940.

David, A., "The Termination of the Office of *Nagid* in Egypt and Biographical Data

Concerning the Life of Abraham Castro," *Tarbiz* 41/3 (1972), pp. 325-337 [Hebrew].

----, "The Economic Status of Egyptian Jewry in the Sixteenth Century According to the Responsa of RADBAZ", in *Miqqedem Umiyyam. Studies in the Jewry of Islamic Countries*, Haifa, 1981, pp. 85-99 [Hebrew].

----, "New Data about Abraham Castro in Some Cairo Geniza Documents," *Michael*, 9 (1985), pp. 147-162 [Hebrew].

Delumeau, Jean., *L'alun de Rome, XVᵉ-XIXᵉ siècle*, Paris, 1962.

----, "Ancône, trait d'union entre l'Órient et l'Occident à l'époque de la Renaissance", *Sociétés et compagnies de commerce en Orient* (Huitième colloque international d'histoire maritime, Beyrouth, 1966), Paris, 1970, pp. 419-433.

Demetriades, V., "Some Observations on the Ottoman-Turkish Judicial Documents (*Hüccets*)", *Balkan Studies*, vol. 26 (1985), pp. 25-39.

Diehl, C., "La colonie vénitienne à Constantinople à la fin du XIVe siècle", in his *Etudes Byzantines*, Paris, 1905, pp. 241-275.

Diena, M., "Rabbi Scelomò Askenazi e la Repubblica di Venezia", *Atti del Regio Istituto veneto di Scienze, lettere ed arti*, ser. 7, vol. 9 (1897-98), pp. 616-37.

I documenti turchi dell'Archivio di Stato di Venezia. Invenatrio ... con l'edizione dei regesti di Alessio Bombaci, ed. M.P. Pedani Fabris, Venice, 1994.

Earle, P., "The Commercial Development of Ancona, 1479-1551", *The Economic History Review*, ser. 2, 22 (1969), pp. 28-44.

Epstein, M.A., *The Ottoman Jewish Communities and their Role in the Fifteenth and Sixteenth Centuries*, Freiburg, 1980.

Faroqhi, S. "Ein Günstling des osmanischen Sultan Murad III: David Passi", *Der Islam* 47 (1971), pp. 290-297.

----, "Textile production in Rumeli and the Arab Provinces. Geographical Distribution and Internal Trade (1560-1650)", *The Journal of Ottoman Studies*, 1 (1980), pp. 61-83.

Ferro, M., *Dizionario del diritto comune e veneto etc.*, 2nd ed., 2 vols, Venice, 1845-1847.

Finlay, R., "The Venetian Republic as a Gerontocracy: Age and Politics in the Renaissance", *Journal of Medieval and Renaissance Studies*, 8 (1978), pp. 157-178.

Fortune, S.A., *Merchants and Jews. The Struggle for British West India Commerce, 1650-1750*, Gainesville, FA, 1984.

Freehof, S., "A Brief History", in *Encyclopedia of Jews in Sport*, eds., B. Postal, J. Silver and R. Silver, New York, 1965.

Galanté, A. *Médecins juifs au service de la Turquie*, Istanbul, 1938.

----, *Histoire des Juifs d'Istanbul depuis la prise de cette ville en 1453 par Fatih Mehmed II jusqu'à nos jours*, 2 vols. Istabul, 1941-1942.

Gerber, H. "Enterprise and International Commerce in the Economic Activity of the Jews of the Ottoman Empire in the 16th-17th Centuries", *Zion*, 43 (1978), pp. 38-67 [Hebrew].

----, "An Unknown Turkish Document on Abraham Castro," *Zion*, Vol. 45, 1980, pp. 158-163 [Hebrew].

----, *Economic and Social Life of the Jews in the Ottoman Empire in the 16th and 17th Centuries*, Jerusalem, 1982 [Hebrew].

----, "Jewish Tax-Farmers in the Ottoman Empire in the 16th and 17th Centuries",

Journal of Turkish Studies, 10 (1986), pp. 143-154.

Gibb, H. and Bowen, H., *Islamic Society and the West. A Study of the Impact of Western Civilization on Moslem Culture in the Near East*, 1 vol. in 2 parts, London-New York-Toronto, 1963-1965.

Gil, M., "The Rādhānite Merchants and the Land of Rādhān", *Journal of the Economic and Social History of the Orient*, 17 (1974), pp. 299-328.

Goffman, D., *Izmir and the Levantine World, 1550-1650*, Seattle and London, 1990.

Goitein, S.D., *Jews and Arabs. Their Contacts Through the Ages*, New York, 1955.

----, *A Mediterranean Society*, vol. 1: Economic Foundations, Berkeley-Los Angeles, 1967.

Gökbilgin, T. "Venedik Devlet Arsivindeki vesikalar kulliyatinda Kanuni Sultan Süleyman devri belgeleri", *Belgeler*, 1/2 (1964), pp. 119-220.

Goodblatt, M., *Jewish Life in Turkey in the Sixteenth Century as Reflected in the Legal Writings of Samuel de Medina*, New York, 1952.

Graetz, H.H., *Geschichte der Juden*, 11 vols., Leipzig 1853-1876.

Grendler, P.F., *The Roman Inquisition and the Venetian Printing Press, 1504-1605*, Princeton, 1977.

----, "The Destruction of Hebrew Books in Venice, 1568", *Proceedings of the American Academy for Jewish Research*, 45 (1978), pp. 103-130.

Grunebaum-Ballin, P., *Joseph Naci, duc de Naxos*, Paris, 1968.

Haddey, M.J.M., *Le livre d'or des Israélites algériens*, Algiers, 1872.

Hammer-Purgstall, J. von, *Geschichte des Osmanischen Reiches*, 2nd ed., 4 vols., Pest, 1835-1840.

Hanak, A., *Physical Education of Jews in the Middle Ages and Early Modern Times*, Tel Aviv, 1987.

Heers, M.L., "Les Génois et le commerce de l'alun à la fin du Moyen Age", *Revue d'Histoire Economique et Sociale*, 32 (1954), pp. 30-53.

Heyd, U., "Moses Hamon, Chief Jewish Physician to Sultan Süleymān the Magnificent", *Oriens*, 16 (1963), pp. 152-170.

----, "Turkish Documents on the Rebuilding of Tiberias in the Sixteenth Century", *Sefunot*, 10 (1966), pp. 193-210 [Hebrew].

Heyd, W., *Histoire du commerce du Levant au Moyen Age*, 2 vols., Leipzig, 1885-86.

Hill, G., *A History of Cyprus*, 4 vols., Cambridge, 1948-1952.

Hocquet, J.C., *Le sel et la fortune de Venise, vol. 2: Voiliers et commerce en Méditerranée, 1200-1650*, Lille, 1979.

Holt, P.M., *Egypt and the Fertile Crescent, 1516-1922*, London, 1966.

Inalcik, H., "Capital Formation in the Ottoman Empire", *The Journal of Economic History*, 29 (1969), pp. 97-140.

----, "The Ottoman Economic Mind and Aspects of the Ottoman Economy", in *Studies in the Economic History of the Middle East from the Rise of Islam to the Present Day*, ed. M.A. Cook, London, 1970, pp. 207-218.

----, *The Ottoman Empire: The Classical Age, 1300-1600*, London, 1973.

----, "An Outline of Ottoman-Venetian Relations", in *Venezia, centro di mediazione tra Oriente e Occidente (secoli XV-XVI), aspetti e problemi*, Atti del II Convegno internazionale di storia della civiltà veneziana (Venezia, 1973), Florence, 1977, I, pp. 83-90.

----, "Introduction to Ottoman Metrology", *Turcica*, 15 (1983), pp. 311-348.

----, "Jews in the Ottoman Economy and Finances, 1450-1500", in *The Islamic World from Classical to Modern Times: Essays in Honor of B. Lewis*, eds. C.E. Bosworth, C. Issawi, R. Savory and A.L. Udovitch, Princeton, 1989, pp. 513-550.

Ioly Zorattini, P.C., "Per la storia dell'ebraismo in Italia. Note e documenti per la storia degli Ebrei a Udine nel Cinquecento", *Officina dello storico. Ricerche di storia sociale e culturale*, Rassegna dell'Istituto di Storia della Facoltà di Lingue dell'Università degli Studi di Udine, 1 (1979), pp. 155-166.

----, "Gli Ebrei a Udine dal Trecento ai giorni nostri", *Atti dell'Accademia di Scienze, ed Arti di Udine*, 74 (1981), pp. 45-58.

Israel, J., *European Jewry in the Age of Mercantilism 1550-1750*, Oxford, 1985.

----, "The Contribution of Spanish Jewry to the Economic Life and Colonization in Europe and the New World", in *The Heritage of Sepharad*, ed. H. Beinart, Jerusalem, 1992, pp. 664-693 [Hebrew].

Jacoby, D., "Un aspect de la fiscalité vénitienne dans le Péloponnèse aux XIVᵉ et XVᵉ siècles: le zovaticum", *Travaux et Mémoires du Centre de Recherche d'Histoire et Civilisation Byzantines*, 1(1965), pp. 405-419, reprinted in his *Société et démographie à Byzance et en Romanie latine*, London, 1975, art. IV.

----, "Les Juifs à Venise du XIVᵉ au milieu du XVIᵉ siècle", in *Venezia, centro di mediazione tra Oriente e Occidente (secoli XV-XVI), aspetti e problemi*, Atti del II Convegno internazionale di storia della civiltà veneziana (Venezia, 1973), Florence, 1977, I, pp. 163-216.

Jones, T.F., *Venice and the Porte, 1520-1542*, unpublished Ph.D. thesis, Harvard University, 1910.

Kamen, H., *European Society 1500-1700*, London, 1986.

Kaplan, Y., "The Portuguese Community of Amsterdam in the Seventeeth Century", in *Proceedings of the Israel Academy of Sciences*, vol. 6/7 (1986), pp. 161-181 [Hebrew].

----, "The Path of Western Sephardi Jewry to Modernity", *Pe'amim*, 48 (1991), pp. 85-103 [Hebrew].

Kaufman, D.,"Die Vertreibung der Marranen aus Venedig im Jahre 1550", *Jewish Quarterly Review*, 13 (1900), pp. 520-532.

Kellenbenz, H. "Venedig als internationales Zentrum und die Expansions [sic] des Handels im 15. und 16. Jahrhundert", in *Venezia, centro di mediazione tra Oriente e Occidente (secoli XV-XVI), aspetti e problemi*, Atti del II Convegno internazionale di storia della civiltà veneziana (Venezia, 1973), Florence, 1977, vol. 1, pp. 281-305.

Lane, F.C., "Venetian Shipping during the Commercial Revolution", *American Historical Review*, 38 (1933), pp. 219-239, reprinted in his *Venice and History*, Baltimore, 1966, pp. 3-24, and in *Crisis and Change in the Venetian Economy in the Sixteenth and Seventeenth Centuries*, ed., B. Pullan, London, 1968, pp. 22-46.

----, "The Mediterranean Spice Trade: Its Revival in the Sixteenth Century", *American Historical Review*, 45 (1940), p. 581-590, reprinted in *Venice and History. The Collected Papers of F.C. Lane*, Baltimore, 1966, pp. 25-55, and in *Crisis and Change*, pp. 47-58.

----, *Venice, A Maritime Republic*, Baltimore and London, 1973.

Lehmann, W., *Der Friedensvertrag zwischen Venedig und der Türkei vom 2. Oktober 1540*, Bonner Orientalistischen Studien, 16, Bonn, 1936.

Levy, A., *The Sephardim in the Ottoman Empire*, Princeton, 1992.

Lewis, B., "A Privilege granted by Mehmed II to his Physician", *Bulletin of the School of Oriental and African Studies*, 14 (1952), pp. 550-563.

----, *Istanbul and the Civilization of the Ottoman Empire*, Norman, Okl., 1963.

----, *The Jews of Islam*, Princeton, 1984.

Litta, P., *Famiglie celebri italiane*, 11 vols, Milan and Turin, 1813-1899.

Luzzatto, G. *Storia economica di Venezia,* Venice 1961.

----, "Armatori ebrei a Venezia negli ultimi 250 anni della Repubblica", *La Rassegna Mensile di Israel. Scritti in Memoria di Federico Luzzatto*, Rome, 1962, pp. 160-168.

Luzzatto, L., "Un ambasciatore ebreo nel 1574", *Il Vessillo Israelitico*, 41 (1893), pp. 245-246.

Maestro, R., *L'attività economica degli ebrei levantini e ponentini a Venezia dal 1550 al 1700*, unpublished doctoral dissertation, University of Venice, 1935.

Μαλτέζου, Χ.Α., Ο Θεσμόσ του εν Κοσταντινουπόλει Βενετού Βαΐλου (1268-1453), Athens, 1970.

Mantran, R., *Istanbul dans la seconde moitié du XVIIᵉ siècle*, Paris, 1962.

Messadaglia, L., "Schienale e morona: storia di due vocaboli e contributo allo studio degli usi alimentari e dei traffici veneti con il Levante", in *Atti del R. Istituto Veneto di Scienze, Lettere e Arti, Classe di Scienze Morali e Letterarie*, vol. 101/II (1941), pp. 1-57.

Milano, A., *Storia degli ebrei italiani nel Levante*, Forence, 1949.

----, *Storia degli Ebrei in Italia*, Turin, 1963, pp. 267-268.

Mirkovich, N., "Ragusa and the Portuguese Spice Trade", *The Slavonic and East European Review*, 21 (1943), pp. 174-187.

Morpurgo, L., "Daniel Rodriguez i osnivanje splitske skele u XVI stoljeću", *Starine*, 52-53 (1962), pp. 185-248, 363-415.

Mueller, R.C. "Charitable Institutions, The Jewish Community and Venetian Society. A Discussion of the Recent Volume by Brian Pullan", *Studi Veneziani*, 14 (1972), pp. 37-81.

----, "Les prêteurs juifs de Venise au Moyen Age", *Annales ESC*, 30 (1975), pp. 1277-1302.

Olivieri, A., "Cavalli, Marino", *Dizionario biografico degli italiani*, vol. 22, Rome, 1979, pp. 749-754.

Paci, R. *La 'scala' di Spalato e il commercio veneziano nei Balcani fra Cinque e Seicento*, Venice, 1971.

Patai, R., *Jewish Seafaring in Ancient Times. A Contribution to the History of Palestinian Culture*, Jerusalem, 1938 [Hebrew].

----, "Jewish Seafaring in Ancient Times", *Jewish Quarterly Review*, 32 (1941-42), pp. 1-26.

Pedani, M.P. *In nome del Gran Signore. Inviati ottomani a Venezia dalla caduta di Costantinopoli alla guerra di Candia*, Venice, 1994.

Pernoud, R., *Histoire du commerce de Marseille, T. 1: Le Moyen Age jusqu'en 1291*, Paris, 1949.

Pirenne, H., *Mohammed and Charlemagne*, London, 1968

Poliakov, L., *History of Anti-Semitism*, 4 vols., London, 1974.

Pollack, A.N., "The Jews and the Egyptian Mint in the Times of the Mamluks and the beginning of the Turkish Rule," *Zion*, 1 (1935), pp. 24-36 [Hebrew].

Preto, P. *Venezia e i Turchi*, Florence, 1975.

----, *I servizi segreti di Venezia*, Milan, 1994.

Pullan, B. *Rich and Poor in Renaissance Venice*, Oxford and Cambridge, Mass., 1971.

----, "A Ship with Two Rudders: Righetto Marrano and the Inquisition in Venice", *The Historical Journal*, 20 (1977), pp. 25-58.

----, "The Inquisition and the Jews of Venice: The Case of Gaspare Ribeiro, 1580-1581", *Bulletin of the John Rylands University Library of Manchester*, 62 (1979), pp. 207-231.

----, *The Jews of Europe and the Inquisition of Venice, 1550-1670*, Oxford, 1983.

Queller, D., "The Civic Irresponsibility of the Venetian Patriciate", in *Economy, Society and Government in Medieval Italy: Essays in Memory of Robert L. Reynolds*, eds., D. Herlihy, R.S. Lopez S. Slessarev, Kent, Ohio, 1969 [also in *Explorations in Economic History*, 7 (1969-70), pp. 223-235].

----, *The Venetian Patriciate: Reality versus Myth*, Urbana and Chicago, 1986.

Rabinowitz, L., *Jewish Merchant Adventurers. A Study of the Radanites*, London, 1948.

Racine, P., "A propos d'une matière première de l'industrie textile placentine: La *Carzatura*", in *La lana come materia prima. I fenomeni della sua produzione e circolazione nei secoli XIII-XVII*, ed. M. Spallanzani, Florence, 1974, pp. 177-184.

----, "Les débuts des consulats italiens outre-mer", in M. Balard, ed., *Etat et colonisation au Moyen Age et à la Renaissance*, Lyons, 1989, pp. 267-276.

Ravid, B. "The Establishment of the Ghetto Vecchio of Venice, 1541: Background and Reappraisal", *Proceedings of the Sixth World Congress of Jewish Studies* (Jerusalem, 1973), Jerusalem, 1975, pp. 153-167.

----, "The First Charter of the Jewish Merchants of Venice, 1589", *Association of Jewish Studies Review*, I (1976), pp. 187-222.

----, "The Jewish Mercantile Settlement of Twelfth and Thirteenth-Century Venice: Reality or Conjecture?", *Association for Jewish Studies Review*, 2 (1977), pp. 210-25.

----, *Economics and Toleration in Seventeenth-Century Venice: the Background and Context of the "Discorso" of Simone Luzzatto*, Jerusalem, 1978.

----, "The Socioeconomic Background of the Expulsion and Readmission of the Venetian Jews, 1571-1573", in *Essays in Modern Jewish History. A Tribute to Ben Halpern*, London and Toronto, 1982, pp. 27-54.

----, "Money, Love and Power Politics in Sixteenth Century Venice: The Perpetual Banishment and Subsequent Pardon of Joseph Nasi", in *Italia Judaica. Atti del I Convegno internazionale (Bari, 1981)*, Rome, 1983, pp. 159-181.

----, "The Religious, Economic and Social Background and Context of the Establishment of the Ghetti of Venice" in *Gli ebrei e Venezia*, ed. G.Cozzi, Milan, 1987, pp. 211-260.

----, "An Autobiographical memorandum by Daniel Rodriga, *Inventore* of the *Scala* of Spalato", *The Mediterranean and the Jews. Banking, Finance and International Trade, XVI-XVIII*, ed. S. Swarzfuchs and A. Toaff, Ramat Gan, 1989.

----, "Daniel Rodriga and the First Decade of the Jewish Merchants of Venice", in

Exile and Diaspora. Studies in the History of the Jewish People Presented to Professor Haim Beinart, Jerusalem, 1991, pp. 203-223.

----, "A Tale of Three Cities and their *Raison d'Etat*: Ancona, Venice, Livorno, and the Competition for Jewish Merchants in the Sixteenth Century", *Mediterranean Historical Review*, 6/2 (1991), pp. 138-162.

----, "The Third Charter of the Jewish Merchants of Venice: a Case Study in Complex Multifaceted Negotiations", *Jewish Political Studies Review*, 6 (1994), pp. 83-134.

Redhouse, J., *New Redhouse Turkish - English Dictionary*, 12th ed., Istanbul, 1992.

Roberti, M., "Ricerche intorno alla colonia veneziana in Costantinopoli nel secolo XII", in *Scritti in onore di Camillo Manfroni nel XL˙ anno dell'insegnamento*, Padua, 1925, pp. 136-147.

Romanin, S., *Storia documentata di Venezia*, 10 vols., Venice, 1925.

Romano, R., "La marine marchande vénitienne au XVIᵉ siècle", in *Les sources de l'histoire maritime en Europe du Moyen Age au XVIIIᵉ siècle*, ed. M. Mollat, Paris, 1962, pp. 33-68.

Romanos, J.A., "Histoire de la communauté israélite de Corfou", *Revue des Etudes Juives*, 23 (1891), pp. 63-74.

Rosanes, S.A., *History of the Jews in Turkey and the Lands of the East*, 6 vols., Sophia, 1908-1945 [Hebrew].

Rose, C., "New Information on the Life of Joseph Nasi, Duke of Naxos: The Venetian Phase", Jewish Quarterly Review, 60 (1970), pp. 330-344.

Rothenberg, G.E., "Venice and the Uskoks of Senj, 1537-1618", *Journal of Modern History*, 33 (1961), pp. 148-156.

Roth, C., *Venice*, Jewish Communities series, Philadelphia, 1930.

----, *The House of Nasi: Doña Gracia*, Philadelphia, 1947.

----, *The House of Nasi: The Duke of Naxos*, Philadelphia, 1948.

----, "Dr. Samuel Ashkenazi and the Election to the Throne of Poland, 1574-75", *Oxford Slavonic Papers*, 9 (1959), pp. 8-20.

----, "Joseph Nasi, Duke of Naxos, and the Counts [sic] of Savoy", in *The Seventy-Fifth Anniversary Volume of the Jewish Quarterly Review*, eds. A.A. Neuman and S. Zeitlin, Philadelphia, 1967, pp. 460-72.

----, "Ashkenazi, Solomon", in *Encyclopaedia Judaica*, Jerusalem, 1971, vol. 3, pp. 731-33.

Rozen, M., "The *fattoria*: A Chapter in the History of Mediterranean Commerce in the 16th and 17th Centuries", in *Miqqedem Umiyyam. Studies in the Jewry of Islamic Countries*, Haifa, 1981, pp. 101-132 [Hebrew].

----, "Contest and Rivalry in Mediterranean Maritime Commerce in the First Half of the Eighteenth Century: The Jews of Salonika and the European Presence", *Revue des Etudes Juives*, 147 (1988), 309-352.

----, "Strangers in a Strange Land: The Extraterritorial Status of Jews in Italy and the Ottoman Empire in the Sixteenth to the Eighteenth Centuries", in *Ottoman and Turkish Jewry: Community and Leadership*, ed. A. Rodrigue, Bloomington, IN, 1992, pp. 123-166.

----, "La vie économique des Juifs du bassin méditerranéen de l'expulsion d'Espagne (1492) à la fin du XVIIIᵉ siècle", in *La société juive à travers l'histoire*, ed. S. Trigano, Paris, 1993, pp. 296-570.

Saperstein, M., "Martyrs, Merchants and Rabbis: Jewish Communal Conflict as

Reflected in the *Responsa* on the Boycott of Ancona", *Jewish Social Studies*, 43 (1981), pp. 215-228.

Sardella, P., "L'épanouissement industriel de Venise au XVIᵉ siècle", *Annales E.S.C.*, 2 (1947), pp. 195-196.

Schiavi, L.A., "Gli Ebrei in Venezia e nelle sue colonie", *Nuova Antologia*, ser. III, 47 (1893) [vol. 132 of the collection], fasc. 18, pp. 309-333, fasc. 19, pp. 485-519.

Schwarzfuchs, S., "La 'Nazione Ebrea' livournaise au Levant", *La Rassegna Mensile di Israel*, ser. III, 50 (1984), pp. 707-724.

Segre, R., "Nuovi documenti sui Marrani d'Ancona (1555-1559)", *Michael*, 9 (1985), pp. 130-232.

----, "Sephardic Settlements in Sixteenth-Century Italy: A Historical and Geographical Survey", *Mediterranean Historical Review*, 6 (1991), pp. 112-137.

Sella, D. "The Rise and Fall of the Venetian Woollen Industry", in *Crisis and Change in the Venetian Economy in the Sixteenth and Seventeenth Centuries*, ed. B. Pullan, London, 1968, pp. 106-126.

Shaw, S. *The Jews of the Ottoman Empire and the Turkish Republic*, New York, 1991.

Shmuelevitz, A., *The Jews of the Ottoman Empire in the Late Fifteenth and Sixteenth Centuries. Administrative, Economic, Legal and Social Relations as Reflected in the Responsa*, Leiden, 1984.

Shochetman, E. "Additional Information on the Life of Abraham Castro", *Zion*, 48 (1983), pp. 387-405 [Hebrew].

Shtober, S., "On the Issue of Customs Collectors in Egypt", *Pe'amim*, 38 (1989), pp. 68-94 [Hebrew].

Simon, B., "Contribution à l'étude du commerce vénitien dans l'Empire Ottoman au milieu du seizième siècle (1558-1560)", *Mélanges de l'Ecole Française de Rome, Moyen Age - Temps Modernes*, 96/2 (1984), pp. 973-1020.

----, "Venise et les corsaires (1558-1560)", *Byzantinische Forschungen*, 12 (1987) [Mélanges Freddy Thiriet], pp. 693-715.

Simonsohn, S., "Marranos in Ancona under Papal Protection", *Michael*, 9 (1985), pp. 234-267.

Singer, C., *The Earliest Chemical Industry*, London, 1948.

Soave, M., "Un ambasciatore ebreo nel 1574", *Il Corriere israelitico*, 17 (1878-79), pp. 6-7.

Soloveitchik, H., *The Use of Responsa as Historical Source*, Jerusalem, 1990 [Hebrew].

Sperber, D., *Nautica talmudica*, Ramat Gan, 1986.

Spretti, V., *Enciclopedia storico-nobiliare italiana*, 8 vols, Milan, 1928-1935.

Stoianovich, T., "The Conquering Balkan Orthodox Merchants", *The Journal of Economic History*, 20 (1960), pp. 234-313.

Svoronos, N. *Le commerce de Salonique au XVIIIᵉ siècle*, Paris, 1956.

Tamar, D. "Three Comments to the Article 'The Termination of the Office of Nagid in Egypt and Biographical Data Concerning the Life of Abraham Castro'", *Tarbiz*, 43, 1974, pp. 325-337 [Hebrew].

Tenenti, A. *Naufrages, corsaires et assurance maritime à Venise, 1592-1609*, Paris, 1959.

----, *Piracy and the Decline of Venice*, London, 1967.

----, "La Francia, Venezia e la Sacra Lega", in *Il Mediterraneo nella seconda metà del Cinquecento alla luce di Lepanto*, ed. G. Benzoni, Florence, 1974, pp. 400-407.

Tenenti, A. and Tenenti, B., *Il prezzo del rischio. L'assicurazione mediterranea vista da Ragusa (1563-1591)*, Rome, 1985.

Tiepolo, M.F., "Archivio di Stato di Venezia", in Ministero per i Beni Culturali e Ambientali. Ufficio Centrale per i Beni Archivistici, *Guida generale degli archivi di stato italiani*, Rome, 1994, pp. 869-1148.

Toaff, A., "Nuova luce sui marrani di Ancona (1556)", in *Studi sull'ebraismo italiano in memoria di Cecil Roth*, Rome, 1974, pp. 261-280.

Toaff, R., *La nazione ebrea a Livorno e a Pisa (1591-1700)*, Florence, 1990.

Tolkovsky, S., *Jewish Seamen*, Tel Aviv, 1970 [Hebrew].

Trachtenberg, J., *The Devil and the Jews. The Medieval Conception of the Jew and its Relation to Modern anti-Semitism*, Cleveland, New York and Philadelphia, 1961.

Tucci, U., "The Psychology of the Venetian Merchant in the Sixteenth Century", in *Renaissance Venice*, ed. J.R. Hale, Lonodon, 1973, pp. 346-378.

----, "Un ciclo di affari commerciali in Siria (1579-1581)", in his *Mercanti, navi monete nel Cinquecento veneziano*, Bologna, 1981, pp. 95-144.

Vanzan Marchini, N.E., "Medici ebrei a Venezia nel Cinquecento", in *Venezia ebraica*, ed. U. Fortis, Rome, 1979, pp. 55-84.

Veinstein, G., "Une communautée ottomane: les Juifs d'Avlonya (Valona) dans la deuxième moitié du XVIe siècle", in *Gli Ebrei e Venezia, secoli XIV-XVIII*, ed. G. Cozzi, Milan, 1987, pp. 781-828.

Weinrib, D., "Problems in the Research of the History of the Jews in Palestine", *Zion*, new series, 2 (1937), pp. 181-215; 3 (1938), pp. 58-83 [Hebrew].

Winter, M. "The Jews of Egypt in the Ottoman Period According to Turkish and Arabic Sources", *Pe'amim*, 16 (1983), pp. 5-21 [Hebrew].

----, *Egyptian Society under Ottoman Rule, 1517-1798*, London, 1992.

W.S.S., "Anglo-Jewish Ships' Names", *The Jewish Historical Society of England. Miscellanies*, Part III (1937), pp. 103-105.

Ya'ari, A., *On the Burning of the Talmud in Italy*, Tel Aviv, 1954 [Hebrew].

Yehuda, Y.Y., "The Egyptian Scroll", *Reshumot*, Vol. 5 (1927), pp. 385-403 [Hebrew].

Yriartre, C., *La vie d'un patricien de Venise au XVIe siècle*, Paris, 1884.

INDEX

The index includes names of persons, places and ships (in italics)

BRILL'S SERIES
IN JEWISH STUDIES

The following books have been published in the series:

1. COHEN, R. *Jews in Another Environment.* Surinam in the Second Half of the Eighteenth Century. 1991.
ISBN 90 04 09373 7

2. PRAWER, S.S. *Israel at Vanity Fair.* Jews and Judaism in the Writings of W.M. Thackery. 1992.
ISBN 90 04 09403 2

3. PRICE, J.J. *Jerusalem under Siege.* The Collapse of the Jewish State 66-70 C.E. 1992.
ISBN 90 04 09471 7

4. ZINGUER, I. *L'hébreu au temps de la Renaissance.* 1992.
ISBN 90 04 09557 8

5. GUTWEIN, D. *The Divided Elite.* Economics, Politics and Anglo-Jewry, 1882-1917. 1992.
ISBN 90 04 09447 4

6. ERAQI KLORMAN, B.-Z. *The Jews of Yemen in the Nineteenth Century.* A Portrait of a Messianic Community. 1993.
ISBN 90 04 09684 1

7. BEN-DOV, N. *Agnon's Art of Indirection.* Uncovering Latent Content in the Fiction of S.Y. Agnon. 1993.
ISBN 90 04 09863 1

8. GERA, D. *Judea and Mediterranean Politics* (219-162 B.C.).
ISBN 90 04 09441 5. *In preparation*

9. COUDERT, A.P. *The Impact of the Kabbalah in the 17th Century.*
ISBN 90 04 09844 5. *In preparation*

10. GROSS, A. *Iberian Jewry from Twilight to Dawn.* The World of Rabbi Abraham Saba. 1995.
ISBN 90 04 10053 9

11. FLESCHER, P.V.M. and D. URMAN. *New Perspectives on Ancient Synagogues.*
ISBN 90 04 09904 2. *In preparation*

12. AHRONI, R. *The Jews of the British Crown Colony of Aden.* History, Culture, and Ethnic Relations. 1994.
ISBN 90 04 10110 1

13. DEUTSCH, N. *The Gnostic Imagination.* Gnosticism, Mandaeism and Merkabah Mysticism. 1995.
ISBN 90 04 10264 7

14. ARBEL, B. *Trading Nations.* Jews and Venetians in the Early Modern Eastern Mediterranean. 1995.
ISBN 90 04 10057 1